D0085131

EX LIBRIS

Pace
University
New York · Westchester

PLEASANTVILLE/BRIARCLIFF
NEW YORK

A PROFESSIONAL AND LEGAL ANALYSIS
OF THE
UNIFORM GUIDELINES ON
EMPLOYEE SELECTION PROCEDURES

A Professional and Legal Analysis
of the
Uniform Guidelines on
Employee Selection Procedures

(Adopted on August 25, 1978; effective September 25, 1978 by the Equal
Employment Opportunity Commission, the United States Department of
Labor, the Department of Justice and the Office of Personnel Management;
adopted by the Department of the Treasury on September 11, 1978.)

The Ad Hoc Group on
Uniform Selection Guidelines
Virgil B. Day, Frank Erwin and Alan M. Koral, Editors

THE AMERICAN SOCIETY FOR PERSONNEL ADMINISTRATION
Berea, Ohio 44017

© 1981 American Society for Personnel Administration, 30 Park Drive, Berea, Ohio 44017

All rights reserved. No part of this publication may be reproduced, stored in a retrieval system, or transmitted in any form or by any means, electronic, mechanical, photo copying, recording or otherwise, without the prior written permission of the copyright holder.

All legal citations reflect applicable cases through January 1981.

First printing July, 1981
Second printing February, 1982
ISBN 0-939900-02-5

Printed in the United States of America

HF
5549.5
.S38
A6

Contents

PART I

What the Guidelines
Are All About

PART I: What The Guidelines Are All About

Introduction

Why This Analysis

The Uniform Guidelines on Employee Selection Procedures (the "Uniform Guidelines" or "Guidelines") represent a significant attempt by the federal equal employment opportunity ("EEO") agencies to achieve consistency in interpreting the requirements of equal employment opportunity laws as such laws impact on employer personnel practices. Some provisions are pragmatic and helpful and, if properly interpreted, should discourage unwarranted litigation while encouraging employers to use selection procedures that are job-related and consistent with sound equal employment opportunity objectives. The Guidelines leave many questions unanswered, however, and some crucial terms are professionally or legally unsound, or both. Employers will not only find that attainment of EEO objectives will be enhanced by an understanding of what the Guidelines require, but also that guidance as to the more doubtful, as well as the most positive points in the Guidelines will enable them to deal in a practical way with the realities of compliance.

The legal importance of the Guidelines to employers lies both in their scope and the use to which they will be put by the Equal Employment Opportunity Commission (EEOC) and the other federal EEO agencies.[1] The Uniform Guidelines cover not merely paper-and-pencil tests but virtually all employee selection procedures other than recruitment. They mark the likely parameters of enforcement efforts by the federal agencies having EEO enforcement powers, especially in determining whether to prosecute pattern and practice or systemic discrimination cases. Even though they are not "regulations" in the strict sense of the word—EEOC lacks the authority to issue regulations and the Justice Department did not use its rule-making authority in adopting the Guidelines—the Guidelines will have a very important effect on employers' ability to defend against Title VII charges of discrimination. (See the discussion of the prefatory material in Part II of the Analysis.)

Employers and the government have a common interest in ensuring that selection devices are predictive of job performance. As a matter of law and social policy, the government legitimately tries to protect individuals from discrimination. As a matter of economics, employers must endeavor to select the most qualified and productive employees available. These interests are not incompatible. Many employers develop their tests scientifically, adhering to the *Standards for Educational and Psychological Tests* of the American Psychological Association, the American Educational Research Association and the National Council on Measurement in Education (hereafter, *Standards*) and to the *Principles for the Validation and Use of Personnel Selection Procedures* (hereafter, *Principles*) of Division 14 (Division of Industrial and Organizational Psychology) of the American Psychological Association (APA). A similar concern for accuracy, job-relatedness and non-discrimination marks the use of other selection instruments by sophisticated employers.

There is no reasonable alternative to selection of employees based on job-related qualifications if an employer is to have an effective workforce. If the selection processes used to achieve that purpose adversely affect

---

[1] The Guidelines were promulgated simultaneously by the Equal Employment Opportunity Commission for enforcement of Title VII of the 1964 Civil Rights Act, as amended by the Equal Employment Opportunity Act of 1972, the Department of Labor for enforcement of Executive Order 11246 through the Office of Federal Contract Compliance Programs (OFCCP), the Department of Justice for enforcement of a variety of equal employment laws, including Title VII, and the U. S. Civil Service Commission (renamed the Office of Personnel Management under the Civil Service Reform Act of 1978) for enforcement of equal employment opportunity requirements for federal government employees (now the responsibility of EEOC) and for state and local governments receiving grant-in-aid funds under various federal statutes. The adoption of the Uniform Guidelines was followed by the official release of 90 explanatory questions and answers (Qs and As) in March of 1979. Three additional Qs and As were issued in the spring of 1980 and it is likely additional sets of Qs and As will appear periodically. These "Qs" and "As" are sometimes more than "interpretative"—in several instances they appear to expand the Guidelines' substantive scope. The "Qs" and "As" were not submitted to the same review and comment procedure which preceded the publication of most sections of the Guidelines text.

5

the job opportunities of minorities or women substantially, their job-relatedness must be demonstrated. The Guidelines set forth the enforcement agencies' criteria for determining *when* such a demonstration of job-relatedness is required and *how* it is to be done.

Why this analysis? An analysis is necessary not only because the Guidelines are important to employers, but because some provisions are ambiguous, some are too restrictive and some are clearly legally or professionally incorrect. Employers must be able to respond effectively to the requirements of enforcement personnel. To do so adequately, they must be aware of the legal justification—or possible lack thereof—for particular requirements. They also should know which provisions reflect the standards generally accepted by practicing industrial psychologists and which do not. Indeed, such information is probably essential not only for assuring a confident and knowledgeable posture *vis a vis* the government EEO enforcement agencies, but also for enhancing the employer's ability to maintain voluntary compliance with federal EEO requirements without agency prodding.

It should be stated at the outset that this Analysis is intended primarily to be an objective review of the Guidelines rather than a manual showing the steps an employer should follow to achieve compliance with them. Where particular provisions are criticized, it is by no means the contributors' intention to encourage employers or industrial psychologists to ignore the provisions involved or to engage in controversy with any enforcement agency. Any decision to deviate from the Guidelines requirements could lead to costly litigation. However, in making decisions regarding existing or proposed employment practices—and such decisions should only be made after careful legal and professional consultation—employers and industrial psychologists can judge best what course to follow if they also know not only what is required but which requirements are sound in the view of many experienced practitioners and which are subject to legal or professional dispute. Thus this Analysis may occasionally criticize matters which are not necessarily of great importance, but the correctness of which cannot be casually assumed.

THE GUIDELINES IN BRIEF

The fundamental legal concepts set forth in the Guidelines can be summarized as follows:

1. If the overall selection rate for any racial, ethnic or sex group is less than 80 percent of that of the most successful group (typically whites or males), this will generally be deemed to constitute "prima facie" (i.e., initial) evidence of discrimination because the selection process has "adverse impact" on that group. Each component procedure of the overall selection process must then be examined for adverse impact on the group in question, using the same 80 percent rule. Components need not generally be examined if the overall process does not have adverse impact.

2. The employer then has four choices to forestall liability for components having adverse impact:

    a. Demonstrate the job-relatedness of the selection procedure;

    b. Modify the procedure so that the adverse impact is eliminated, or modify the method of use of the selection procedure to eliminate adverse impact;

    c. Abandon the procedure and adopt a different procedure without adverse impact;

    d. Otherwise justify the procedure in accord with federal law, such as through showing "business necessity".

3. If the employer chooses to demonstrate the job-relatedness of the selection procedure, the Guidelines require:

    a. Validation studies conforming to highly detailed requirements or validity evidence from other users that conform to the Guidelines' rules governing transportability of validity data;

    b. Detailed recordkeeping;

    c. Investigation of alternative valid selection devices that have less adverse impact.

The Practical and Legal Significance
of the Uniform Guidelines

The requirements of the Uniform Guidelines supersede the 1976 Federal Executive Agency Guidelines on testing and selection procedures promulgated by the Departments of Justice and Labor and the Civil Service Commission, as well as EEOC's own 1970 Guidelines. The 1976 Guidelines were regarded by many employers as reasonably workable, positive rules designed to permit employers to pursue principles of merit selection by showing the job-relatedness (e.g., through validity studies) of their selection procedures where such procedures had an adverse impact on particular groups of employees or applicants. The EEOC's 1970 Guidelines, on the other hand, were widely criticized as imposing validation requirements which were inconsistent with professional practice. EEOC refused to accept the 1976 Guidelines agreed to by the other agencies, however, and in the following year led the other agencies into renewed discussion to achieve a uniform approach to monitoring employee selection procedures for compliance with EEO requirements.

The Guidelines' Legal Significance

The importance of the Guidelines is best approached by clarifying their role in defining critical aspects of federal equal employment opportunity law. Except for certain merit system requirements placed on public sector employers, the government does not require employers to justify the job-relatedness, fairness or reasonableness of most employment decisions. Only when employment practices have an apparently discriminatory effect (shown through statistics demonstrating adverse impact) on particular groups of employees or applicants do federal EEO laws require such a showing. This principle—that any statistically demonstrated "adverse impact" of employment procedures must be justified by a showing of "job-relatedness" or "business necessity"—was first discussed at length by the Supreme Court in *Griggs v. Duke Power Co.,* 401 U.S. 424 (1971), and has remained the bedrock of Title VII legal analysis to date.

The Guidelines present the standards by which the federal EEO enforcement agencies will evaluate most discrimination cases involving employee selection procedures. They address such critical issues as:

what kinds of numbers will be considered by the federal agencies to demonstrate "adverse impact";

what kinds of records an employer must keep to show whether selection procedures have "adverse impact";

what an employer should do when "adverse impact" is indicated;

how an employer can show the job-relatedness of selection procedures having "adverse impact".

It cannot be stressed too often that the Guidelines are exclusively concerned with *defining a certain kind of evidence of apparent employment discrimination and the appropriate defenses to such evidence.* Where employment procedures do not have statistically demonstrable "adverse impact" on one group or another, the requirements in the Uniform Guidelines do not apply.

Affirmative Action and the Guidelines

The Guidelines are only obliquely related to the fullfillment of affirmative action obligations by federal contractors and subcontractors, state and local governments and recipients of federal funds.[2] Compliance with the Guidelines is merely a defense to a charge of discrimination based on adverse impact statistical analysis. Thus federal contractors will likely find that OFCCP will use the Guidelines as a test of only one kind of compliance, i.e., of the prohibition against discrimination. If the Guidelines are not complied with, OFCCP may decide that the contractor is discriminating and an "affected class" determination may result.

But compliance with the Guidelines does not assure that an employer will be found to be in compliance with affirmative action obligations incurred through federal contracting or receipt of federal funds. It may not be enough merely to use employment procedures that do not have adverse impact or, if they have, that can be shown to be related to job performance. OFCCP—or the Office of Personnel Management (OPM) for public merit system employers—may use affirmative action requirements to encourage "good faith" efforts to meet goals by abandoning even demonstrably job-related procedures in favor of others that enhance the opportunities of minorities and women. Indeed, OFCCP's Compliance Manual interprets the Guidelines themselves in such a way as to suggest that affirmative efforts to maximize employment opportunities for minorities and women are required. This is incorrect as a matter of

---

[2]The federal government itself, because of the Garcia Amendment to the 1978 Civil Service Reform Act, is subject to special recruitment requirements. EEOC has issued guidelines for federal agencies subject to these requirements.

Title VII compliance or "affected class" analysis, at least in the absence of identified prior discrimination—see, for example, *Furnco Construction Co. v. Waters,* 438 U.S. 567 (1978)—and it is an inaccurate reflection of the contents of the Guidelines. However, it can hardly be denied that an employer's non-compliance with the Guidelines might legitimately suggest to OFCCP or to a federal granting agency not only that the employer is vulnerable to discrimination charges, but also that the employer is neglecting affirmative action commitments. Thus compliance with the Guidelines might be looked on as a first step in fulfilling affirmative action commitments.

Scope of the Guidelines

An additional point about the Guidelines' significance is worth making. While they may appear narrow in that they are addressed only to a particular kind of discrimination, they are actually very broad, because they apply to so many aspects of employment. Not merely tests, but all "selection procedures" are within the scope of the Guidelines (see Definition Q, Section 16). Thus all steps in the processes leading up to decisions on hiring, job placement, firing, demotion and layoff are potentially covered by the Guidelines (see Section 2B, Employment Decisions). So, too, are decisions regarding selection for training, transfer, apprenticeship or educational assistance when these decisions lead to other employment actions. Decisions based on "merit" or experience considerations rather than on strict seniority may also be open to scrutiny. Thus, virtually every aspect of the employment relationship is potentially affected by the Guidelines, provided only that its effects are statistically measurable so that "adverse impact" can be determined.

The Guidelines' Practical Significance

A final look at the Guidelines' significance requires a practical view of the way they will be used. The Guidelines are not definitive statements of the law. See, *Guardians Association v. Civil Service Commission of the City of New York,* 23 FEP Cases 909 (2d Cir., 1980). Only the courts can produce definitive interpretations and the Guidelines are merely administrative interpretations of what the law requires. The courts may reject a particular Guideline requirement, as a number of courts, including the Supreme Court, did with some provisions of the 1970 EEOC Guidelines (see, e. g., the cases cited in the discussion of Section VII of the

Overview to the Guidelines in Part II, below.). But the Uniform Guidelines are likely to be accorded great weight by the courts, especially since they constitute a unanimous and recent expression of agency interpretation. It remains to be seen whether the fact that some major Guideline provisions are inconsistent with professional opinion or are legally dubious will be taken into account by the courts.

Of greater practical importance is the use to which the Guidelines will be put. While it is true that the courts may tend to defer to the agencies' presumed expertise in interpreting the law, few employers wish to go to the expense, exposure and extreme trouble of seeking a court opinion. Unless Guidelines provisions are overturned by the courts, however, they will constitute the standards under which agency enforcement efforts will be pursued. Compliance with the Guidelines thus should avert active agency enforcement regarding matters within the Guidelines' scope. It also will assure "no probable cause" findings on Guidelines-related issues when EEOC investigates a charge. It is well to keep in mind, however, that even EEOC is without authority to prevent an individual plaintiff or class of plaintiffs from bringing suit under Title VII. However, the assurance of a "no probable cause" finding and of EEOC's abstention from bringing suit itself is of great practical value.

As stated above, the Guidelines apply to "adverse impact" types of discrimination under Title VII and Executive Order 11246. Technically, they do not apply to employment decisions subject to scrutiny under the Age Discrimination in Employment Act of 1967, as amended, the Rehabilitation Act of 1973, the Vietnam Era Veterans Readjustment Act or various state laws. As a practical matter, however, both the legal concepts and the technical standards in the Guidelines will be potentially influential in the administration of all of these statutes. The prestige of the agencies involved would prompt such deference, which is also mandated by common sense; job-relatedness for the purposes of one statute cannot be very different from job-relatedness for the purposes of another statute. However, it is worth noting that job-relatedness itself will not necessarily be enough to meet Rehabilitation Act and Vietnam Veterans Act standards, as "reasonable accommodation" and affirmative action are factors in those statutes in addition to non-discrimination. Such accommodation is not required under Title VII except with respect to applicants' and employees' religious beliefs and observances, matters that, properly, are not covered by the Guidelines.

The Enforcement Agencies and Relevant Legislation

Title VII:

The structure of equal employment opportunity requirements enforced by the Federal agencies through the Uniform Guidelines on Employee Selection Procedures is primarily based upon Title VII of the Civil Rights Act of 1964, as amended,[3] which applies to almost all employers having 15 or more employees.

Section 703(a) sets forth the basic rule:

> It shall be an unlawful employment practice for an employer—
>
> (1) to fail or refuse to hire or to discharge an individual, or otherwise to discriminate against any individual with respect to his compensation, terms, conditions, or privileges of employment, because of such individual's race, color, religion, sex, or national origin; or
>
> (2) to limit, segregate, or classify his employees in any way which would deprive or tend to deprive any individual of employment opportunities or otherwise adversely affect his status as an employee, because of such individual's race, color, religion, sex, or national origin.

The most important general exceptions to the Act's sweeping prohibitions against conduct by employers that would otherwise be unlawful are set forth in Section 703(h), which provides (in full):

> Notwithstanding any other provision of this title, *it shall not be an unlawful employment practice* for an employer to apply different standards of compensation, or different terms, conditions, or privileges of employment pursuant to a *bona fide seniority or merit system,* or a system which measures earnings by quantity or quality of production or to employees who work in different locations, provided that such differences are not the result of an intention to discriminate because of race, color, religion, sex, or national origin; *nor shall it be an unlawful employment practice for an employer to give and to act upon the results of any professionally developed ability test provided that such test, its administration or action upon the results is not designed, intended, or used to discriminate because of race, color, religion, sex, or national origin.* It shall not be an unlawful employment practice under this title for any employer to differentiate upon the basis of sex in determining the amount of the wages or compensation paid to employees of such employer if such differentiation is authorized by the provisions of Section 6 (d) of the Fair Labor Standards Act of 1938 as amended (29 USC 206 (d)) [the Equal Pay Act]. (Emphasis added.)

In the keystone *Griggs* case, striking down the use of tests and other selection criteria which had significant adverse impact on blacks and were not shown to be job-related, the Supreme Court stated the requirements of Title VII as follows:

> Nothing in the Act precludes the use of testing or measuring procedures; obviously they are useful. What Congress has forbidden is giving these devices and mechanisms controlling force unless they are demonstrably a reasonable measure of job performance. Congress has not commanded that the less qualified be preferred over the better qualified simply because of minority origins. Far from disparaging job qualifications as such, Congress has made such qualifications the controlling factor, so that race, religion, nationality and sex become irrelevant. What Congress has commanded is that any tests used must measure the person for the job and not the person in the abstract.
>
> . . . good intent or absence of discriminatory intent does not redeem employment procedures or testing mechanisms that operate as 'built-in head winds' for minority groups and are unrelated to measuring job capability. . . .
>
> Congress directed the thrust of the Act to the *consequences* of employment practices, not simply the motivation. More than that, Congress has placed on the employer the burden of showing that any given requirement must have a manifest relationship to the employment in question.[4] (Emphasis added.)

It is worth noting that *Griggs* does not impose a duty

---

[3]The Civil Rights Act of 1964 was amended in 1972 by the Equal Employment Opportunity Act to bring under its coverage federal, state and local government employers, among other changes.

[4]*Griggs v. Duke Power Co.,* 401 U. S. 424, 3 FEP Cases 175 (1971).

of affirmative action upon employers. It reinforces the Title VII command that employment practices be neutral in their effects and provides that employers must justify practices which are not neutral by showing their job-relatedness.

Title VII is enforced by EEOC which has the authority to investigate and conciliate charges of employment discrimination and to bring suit against private employers to enforce the provisions of Title VII on the basis of its investigations. The Department of Justice is authorized to sue state and local governments to enforce Title VII, either at EEOC's behest or as a result of its own investigations.

Executive Order 11246:

In addition to Title VII obligations, employers who are contractors and subcontractors engaged in government contracts or subcontracts having an aggregate value of $10,000 or more must agree to fulfill the requirements of Executive Order 11246, as amended. E. O. 11246 forbids employment discrimination based upon race, color, religion, sex or national origin and, in addition, mandates "affirmative action" to assure equal employment opportunity. Enforcement action has been delegated to the Department of Labor's Office of Federal Contract Compliance Programs (OFCCP).

The key element of the equal opportunity requirement in E.O. 11246 is contained in an "equal opportunity clause" that is deemed to be included in federal contracts and subcontracts. This clause provides (in part) as follows:

> (1) The contractor *will not discriminate* against any employee or applicant for employment because of race, color, religion, sex, or national origin. The contractor *will take affirmative action* to ensure that applicants are employed, and that employees are treated during employment without regard to their race, color, religion, sex or national origin. Such action shall include, but not be limited to the following: employment, upgrading, demotion or transfer, recruitment or recruitment advertising; layoff or termination; rates of pay or other forms of compensation; and selection for training, including apprenticeship. The contractor agrees to post in conspicuous places, available to employees and applicants for employment, notices to be provided by the contracting officer setting forth the provisions of this non-discrimination clause. (Emphasis added)

Thus, federal contractors are under dual obligations to avoid discrimination and to take "affirmative action". As explained above, the Uniform Guidelines are relevant to OFCCP findings of "affected class" discrimination, but not directly pertinent to monitoring of a contractor's fulfillment of its affirmative action obligations.

OFCCP may penalize contractors who are found to have violated their promises in the EEO clause through a number of administrative sanctions imposed after administrative hearings. These include contract suspension or cancellation and debarment from future federal contracting or subcontracting. Alternatively, the agency may ask the Justice Department to sue in federal court for breach of contract. OFCCP also claims the right to order remedies for alleged victims of discrimination. These remedies include back pay, front pay and seniority overrides. OFCCP's authority to order such remedies has been contested by a number of contractors, but the issue has not yet had significant court review.

Public Sector Employer EEO Obligations

For public sector state and local government employers, the following chart suggests the scope of EEO requirements to which the Guidelines may apply beyond Title VII and E.O. 11246:

Source of Funds	Statute	Enforcement Agency
Office of Revenue Sharing Funds	State and Local Fiscal Assistance Act of 1972	Department of Treasury
Law Enforcement Assistance Act Funds	Omnibus Crime and Safe Streets Act	Department of Justice
Grant-in-Aid Funds (derived under various federal laws)(may be covered by Merit System Standards)	Intergovernmental Personnel Act of 1970 (Administration of Merit System Standards)	Office of Personnel Management[5]
Other federal funds for health and education	Miscellaneous appropriations statutes, Title VI, Title IX	Office of Civil Rights (HEW), now OCR, Department of Education and OCR, Department of Health and Human Services

---

[5]OPM's *Standards for A Merit System of Personnel Administration*, designed to provide guidance for public sector employers who are recipients of Federal grant-in-aid funds, are not altogether consistent with the Uniform Guidelines. It has been pointed out, for example, that the OPM Standards oppose use of whole list certification, while the Uniform Guidelines appear to encourage such certification through such provisions as the required justification for rank ordering in Section 5G.

11

Evolution of Uniform Guidelines on Employee Selection Procedures

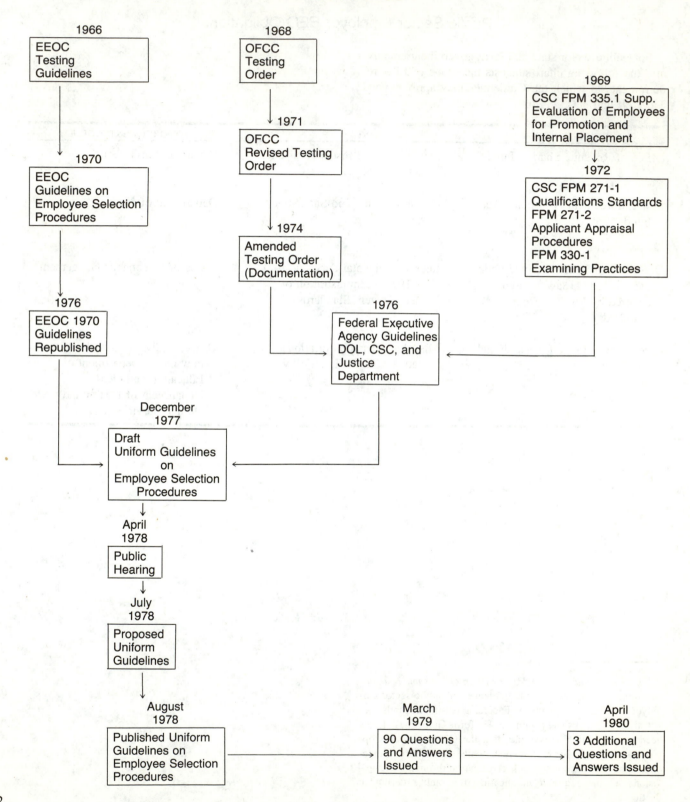

1966
EEOC
Testing
Guidelines

1968
OFCC
Testing
Order

1969
CSC FPM 335.1 Supp.
Evaluation of Employees
for Promotion and
Internal Placement

1970
EEOC
Guidelines on
Employee Selection
Procedures

1971
OFCC
Revised Testing
Order

1972
CSC FPM 271-1
Qualifications Standards
FPM 271-2
Applicant Appraisal
Procedures
FPM 330-1
Examining Practices

1974
Amended
Testing Order
(Documentation)

1976
EEOC 1970
Guidelines
Republished

1976
Federal Executive
Agency Guidelines
DOL, CSC, and
Justice
Department

December 1977
Draft
Uniform Guidelines
on
Employee Selection
Procedures

April 1978
Public
Hearing

July 1978
Proposed
Uniform
Guidelines

August 1978
Published Uniform
Guidelines on
Employee Selection
Procedures

March 1979
90 Questions
and Answers
Issued

April 1980
3 Additional
Questions and
Answers Issued

12

Format of the Legal and Professional Analysis

As officially published, the Guidelines included three kinds of text: first, prefatory language stating the names of the agencies and the authority under which they acted; second, an essay-like "Overview" and "Analysis of Comments" in which the agencies give their views on a number of important legal and professional issues raised by the Guidelines text; and finally, the official text of the Guidelines themselves. In addition, as already noted, the Guidelines were followed by 90 official Questions and Answers published in 1979. Several additional Qs and As were published in 1980 and more are anticipated.

Because of the different legal significance of the three kinds of text published by the agencies, the Ad Hoc Group's Analysis of the Uniform Guidelines will address each aspect of the official publication separately, despite the frequent overlap among them. Only the official text of the Uniform Guidelines should have actual legal significance,[6] but the other material contains statements commenting on either legal or professional matters and these comments include some matters upon which there are important differences of opinion. In order to avoid repetition, however, discussion of similar issues will be cross-referenced rather than repeated.

The left-hand page of Parts II and III of the Analysis reprints the language of the prefatory material and the Guidelines' text. Where the agencies' official Questions and Answers are pertinent to this material, the Question and Answer are reproduced as well.

The right-hand page is devoted to the "Professional and Legal Analysis." In Part II and portions of Part III the issues raised are either legal or professional and the commentary is accordingly either legal or professional in nature. However, portions of Part III raise legal and professional issues that must be addressed separately and the commentary is therefore divided into two sections:

Legal analysis—discussion of the legal principles underlying the provision and the justification for such a provision under current case law.

Professional analysis—discussion of the principles of industrial psychology that are applicable to the issues raised by the provision.

---

[6]The court in *Allen V. City of Mobile,* 464 F. Supp. 433 (S.D. Ala. 1978), quoted one of the two prefaces, not the Guidelines' text. Once cited by a court, it would seem the prefaces could gain "legal significance".

The Ad Hoc Group

The Ad Hoc Group was formed to contribute an employer and professional view to the development of uniform Federal guidelines on employee selection procedures. The Group includes leaders of personnel management and industrial psychologists from the private sector, as well as public sector representatives and representatives from the legal profession. All share a deep concern about Federal guidelines on tests and other employee selection practices.

Because employers found it virtually impossible to meet the requirements of the 1970 EEOC Guidelines, the Group was organized in 1974 to develop sound positions and the best professional thinking as to how equal employment opportunity could be implemented without denigrating the concept of merit employment.

Prior to 1976, the Group successfully developed a series of proposals supported by many practicing professional psychologists for consideration by the Equal Employment Opportunity Coordinating Council (EEOCC) and the various EEO agencies.[7] Many of these proposals were ultimately included by the EEOCC in guidelines proposed for general adoption by the EEO agencies. In late 1976, they were formally adopted by the Departments of Justice and Labor and the Civil Service Commission as the 1976 Federal Executive Agency Guidelines.

The Ad Hoc Group was also an active commentator during the development of the present Uniform Guidelines on Employee Selection Procedures.

Contributors to the Analysis

Contributors to the Analysis include professional industrial psychologists and personnel professionals involved in implementing the Guidelines for major American companies and public and private employer groups:

V. Jon Bentz (Sears), Virginia R. Boehm (Standard Oil of Ohio), Leonard R. Brice (American Society for Personnel Administration), Patricia Dyer (International Business Machines), Jack W. English (Mobil Oil), Frank Erwin (Richardson, Bellows, Henry & Co.), James Herring (Exxon), John Holmes (General Motors Corp.), Earl Ingram (West Point Pepperell), Joyce Lawson (General Electric), William V. Machaver (Sun Chemical Co.), Lloyd Marquardt (Travelers Insurance), Kenneth Pederson (Dow Chemical), Elliott Pursell (Weyerhaeuser), Marilyn Quaintance (International Personnel Management Association), John Rauschenberger (Armco, Inc.), Julius Scheffers (Inland Steel), James Sharf (Richardson, Bellows, Henry & Co.), C. Paul Sparks (Exxon), Paul Stuber (Reynolds Metals), Mary L. Tenopyr (American Telephone and Telegraph), William Ulmer, Jr. (DuPont), John Turner (Ford), Lawrence Vickery (General Motors Corp.), Richard H. Webb, Jr. (Reynolds Metals), Stephen Wunder (Exxon).

Legal analysis in general has been the responsibility of Alan M. Koral and Virgil B. Day (Vedder, Price, Kaufman, Kammholz & Day). Contributions also have come from other practicing EEO attorneys: R. Lawrence Ashe, Jr. (Paul, Hastings, Janofsky & Walker), Carl F. Goodman (Surrey & Morse), Thomas F. Hilbert (Vedder, Price, Kaufman, Kammholz & Day), Lawrence Lorber (Breed, Abbott & Morgan) and Thompson Powers (Steptoe & Johnson).

Frank Erwin (Richardson, Bellows, Henry & Co.) served as editor of the professional analysis. Alan M. Koral and Virgil B. Day (Vedder, Price, Kaufman, Kammholz & Day) served as editors of the legal analysis.

---

[7]The EEOCC had been established by the 1972 amendments to Title VII to eliminate duplications and inconsistencies among the federal agencies' EEO enforcement activity. The first project of the Coordinating Council was to achieve uniform selection guidelines.

PART II

The Federal Agencies'
Prefatory Material,
"Overview"
And "Analysis of Comments"
On The
UNIFORM GUIDELINES

PART II: The Federal Agencies' Prefatory Material, "Overview" And "Analysis of Comments" on The Uniform Guidelines

Executive Summary

Although the prefatory material, the government's "Explanatory Overview" and "Analysis of Comments" are introductory and summary in nature, it is possible that they may be referred to by agencies or courts for clarification of the Guidelines themselves. This justifies commenting on the legal and professional issues raised by statements in these sections.

Outline of the Prefatory Materials

PREFATORY PARAGRAPH
OVERVIEW OF THE GUIDELINES
  I. Background
  II. Adverse Impact
  III. Is Adverse Impact To Be Measured By The Overall Process?
  IV. Where Adverse Impact Exists: The Basic Options
  V. Validation: Consideration of Alternatives
  VI. Testing For Higher Level Jobs
  VII. How Is Validation To Be Conducted?
  VIII. Simplification Of Reporting and Record-keeping Requirements
ANALYSIS OF COMMENTS ON THE GUIDELINES

Prefatory Paragraph

This is a formal statement describing the action of adoption of the Guidelines. Although basically non-controversial, it creates an impression that the Guidelines carry greater weight for purposes of Title VII and the Executive Order than they actually do. It should be kept in mind that the Guidelines are interpretations of Title VII and not binding regulations.

Overview Of The Guidelines

The "Overview" is a series of essay-like arguments seeking to justify some of the more important or controversial features of the Guidelines. It does not have the legal significance of the Guidelines themselves, but it does suggest the agencies' rationale and may influence courts. The Overview is not consistently accurate about legal precedent and is not altogether complete in its account of historical matters.

I. BACKGROUND.—The "background" section correctly acknowledges Congress' interest in protecting employers' right to use professionally developed tests when it enacted Title VII in 1964. However, the dis-cussion sets out an idealized version of the development of government guidelines on employee selection procedures and overlooks areas of deep controversy. It also is inaccurate with respect to several important principles of law and industrial psychology.

II. ADVERSE IMPACT.—This discussion describes the adoption of the four-fifths or 80 percent rule for determining adverse impact, which is a desirable and legally sound development. However, the commentary implies that adoption of the 80 percent rule (as a "rule of thumb") was completely voluntary on the part of government and does not acknowledge that the Supreme Court has always required substantial statistical disparities to constitute evidence of discrimination. The discussion attempts to justify the Guidelines' various exceptions to the four-fifths rule (such as an employer's "bad" reputation) and seeks to defend the controversial failure to include a test of statistical significance as a companion to the four-fifths rule.

III. Is ADVERSE IMPACT TO BE MEASURED BY THE OVERALL PROCESS?—This discussion describes the adoption of the "bottom line" concept, a concept favored by most employers. Under this concept, the government will not challenge the components of a selection process if the overall process (hiring, promotion, etc.) produces statistics that meet the four-fifths rule for determining adverse impact. The discussion attempts to justify the Guidelines' controversial exceptions to the "bottom line" concept by contending that the matter "has not been definitively answered by the courts" and that it is merely an exercise of "prosecutorial discretion" rather than a legal principle. In fact, several courts have endorsed the "bottom line" concept. Limiting the "bottom line" to total applicant data without some allowance for qualifications limits the practical benefits of the "bottom line".

IV. WHERE ADVERSE IMPACT EXISTS: THE BASIC OPTIONS.—This discussion summarizes the Guidelines' three basic options where adverse impact is shown. The employer can: 1) modify the selection procedure or its method of use; 2) validate it; or 3) abandon it. But the discussion uncritically assumes that modification is professionally feasible and would be lawful despite possible "reverse discrimination" liability. It also fails to note that some selection procedures lend themselves to proof that they are job-related through means other than formal validation.

V. VALIDATION: CONSIDERATION OF ALTERNATIVES.—There are legal as well as professional questions raised by the Guidelines' recommendation that an employer seek unvalidated alternatives to a selection procedure which has adverse impact and the requirement that employers always separately justify the manner in which validated selection procedures are used (i.e., cutoff scores, grouping by scores, or rank ordering).

VI. TESTING FOR HIGHER LEVEL JOBS.—This discussion notes that entry level candidates may properly be tested for qualifications related to higher than entry jobs in situations where the entry level job is only temporary or transient. There are professional concerns, however, about the specific provisions regarding this matter. (See comments on Section 5I of the Guidelines in Part III.)

VII. HOW IS VALIDATION TO BE CONDUCTED?—This discussion describes in general terms the three basic aspects of validity: 1) criterion-related, 2) content and 3) construct. The discussion seems to recognize the need for flexibility and adaptability to change in approaching the subject of validation, but this contrasts with the more rigid and inflexible approach to validation in the text of the Guidelines.

VIII. SIMPLICATION OF REPORTING AND RECORDKEEPING REQUIREMENTS.—The assertion that reporting and recordkeeping requirements have been simplified seeks to meet current concerns about excessive governmental regulations. As shown in the discussion of Section 15 in Part III, however, the Guidelines impose burdensome, costly and unnecessary recordkeeping and reporting requirements on employers.

Analysis of Comments

This part of the preliminary material is represented as being a review of the comments received by the agencies before and during the "comment period" beginning December 30, 1977. The review describes with particularity the concerns of civil rights groups, but does not recount the specifics of the many objections of professional groups, notably those of Division 14 of the American Psychological Association. The discussion also ignores the radical alterations in the documentation requirements in Section 15 of the Guidelines between the December, 1977 draft and final form of the Guidelines, alterations upon which there was no opportunity for formal comment.

The "Analysis of Comments" then turns to a discussion of specific parts of the Guidelines, including six "General Principles" and five "Technical Standards", in terms of comments and the government's reactions to them. Although much of this subject matter is covered in Part III under the headings of the specific Guideline sections, some aspects of the government's "Analysis of Comments" are appropriate for discussion here.

GENERAL PRINCIPLES

1. *Relationship between validation and elimination of adverse impact and affirmative action*

Two subjects of concern are treated under this principle:
(a) the rule that there are two options available to an employer where a selection procedure is shown to have adverse impact:
   —validation (or other showing of job-relatedness) of the procedure, or
   —elimination of the adverse impact;
(b) inclusion in the Guidelines of language encouraging affirmative action.

As to (a), the government analysis does not take into account the dangers of illegality inherent in the concept of "elimination of adverse impact" and ignores alternative approaches to showing job-relatedness: a selection procedure may be shown to be obviously job-related; and validity evidence may be transported (i.e., if the selection procedure has been validated elsewhere, that evidence of validity may be used in certain circumstances).

As to (b), the agencies transferred the language recommending affirmative action to an "Appendix" to the Guidelines.[8] This is not a proper response to the argument that affirmative action, though a very desirable concept, has no place in these Guidelines, which historically have had the discrete purpose of setting forth minimum criteria for compliance with federal laws regarding discrimination.

2. *The bottom line (Section 4C)*

The discussion again defends the concept that the "bottom line" is a "general enforcement policy" instead of a binding legal principle. (See the discussion of Point II of the Overview and discussion of Section 4C in Part III.)

3. *Investigation of alternative selection procedures and alternative methods of use (Section 3B)*

This discussion defends the agencies' requirement that alternative selection procedures and methods of use be investigated, despite the lack of persuasive legal precedent for such a requirement. (See discussion of Point V of the Overview and discussion of Section 3B in Part III.)

4. *Establishment of cutoff scores and rank ordering*

This discussion treats the requirement for separate justification for the *method* in which a selection procedure is used (i.e., cutoff scores, grouping by scores or rank ordering) if the method chosen has adverse impact. This requirement exceeds professional testing standards in some cases and restricts an employer's ability to select employees on the basis of their relative qualifications.

5. *Scope: Requests for exemptions for certain classes of users*

The agencies rejected the requests of a number of types of organizations for exemption from the Guidelines, including "licensing and certification boards". The refusal to exempt such boards is inconsistent with the weight of judicial authority.

6. *The four-fifths rule of thumb (Section 4D)*

The discussion defends the "80 percent rule of thumb" against various criticisms from both employer groups and civil rights activists. (See comments on Point II of the Overview and Section 4D in Part III.)

TECHNICAL STANDARDS

7.[9] *Criterion-related validity*

The discussion defends the retention of the "fairness" doctrine in Section 14B (8), despite the impressive body of professional opinion refuting the fairness concept and its companion, differential validity. (See comments on Point III of the Overview and Section 14B (8) in Part III.)

8. *Content validity*

The discussion refers to the agencies' decision to incorporate a language compromise in Section 14C on the sensitive issue of the "representative" nature of a test in terms of the duties of the job being tested. Despite the language changes, the section remains inconsistent with prevailing professional opinion in its insistence on too restrictive a level of fidelity between test content and job content. Moreover, the required separate justification for rank ordering on the results of content valid procedures seriously limits the usefulness of content validity for many users. (See comments on Sections 5G and 14C in Part III.)

9. *Construct validity (Section 14D)*

The discussion addresses the claim of employers and professional groups that the language of the Guidelines "virtually eliminates" the use of construct validity. Although some minor language changes are noted in Sec-

---

[8]The "Appendix" is also listed, however, as Section 17 of the Guidelines.

[9]The "Analysis of Comments" numbers the Technical Standards consecutively following the six General Principles.

tion 14D, the final language, in a practical sense, excludes construct validity because each construct measure must be linked to the job by a criterion-related study. (See comments on Section 14D in Part III.)

10. *Documentation (Section 15)*

The discussion claims that the agencies sought to meet complaints by "clarifying and minimizing" the recordkeeping burden. This is disputed by many employers. Moreover, the documentation sections include new substantive requirements that never were subjected to public comment because they were included in the radical revisions made to Section 15 after the public comment period on the original draft unveiled in December, 1977 had passed. (See comments on Point VIII of the Overview and Section 15 in Part III.)

11. *Definitions (Section 16)*

The agencies indicate that they made "significant" definitional changes, particularly as to "work behavior" and "adverse impact". The specifics of the definitions in Section 16 are covered in Part III of this Analysis.

Prefatory Paragraph

Title 29—Labor

CHAPTER XIV—EQUAL EMPLOYMENT OPPORTUNITY COMMISSION

PART 1607—UNIFORM GUIDELINES ON EMPLOYEE SELECTION PROCEDURES (1978)

Title 5—Administrative Personnel

CHAPTER I—CIVIL SERVICE COMMISSION

PART 300—EMPLOYMENT (GENERAL)

Title 28—Judicial Administration

CHAPTER I—DEPARTMENT OF JUSTICE

PART 50—STATEMENTS OF POLICY

Title 41—Public Contracts and Property Management

CHAPTER 60—OFFICE OF FEDERAL CONTRACT COMPLIANCE PROGRAMS, DEPARTMENT OF LABOR

PART 60-3—UNIFORM GUIDELINES ON EMPLOYEE SELECTION PROCEDURES (1978)

Adoption of Employee Selection Procedures

AGENCIES: Equal Employment Opportunity Commission, Civil Service Commission, Department of Justice and Department of Labor.

ACTION: Adoption of uniform guidelines on employee selection procedures as final rules by four agencies.

SUMMARY: This document sets forth the uniform guidelines on employee selection procedures adopted by the Equal Employment Opportunity Commission, Civil Service Commission, Department of Justice, and the Department of Labor. At present two different sets of guidelines exist. The guidelines are intended to establish a uniform Federal position in the area of prohibiting discrimination in employment practices on grounds of race, color, religion, sex, or national origin. Cross reference documents are published at 5 CFR 300.103(c) (Civil Service Commission), 28 CFR 50.14 (Department of Justice), 29 CFR Part 1607 (Equal Employment Opportunity Commission), and 41 CFR Part 60-3 (Department of Labor) elsewhere in this issue.

EFFECTIVE DATE: September 25. 1978.

Prefatory Paragraph:

"ADOPTION OF EMPLOYEE SELECTION PROCEDURES"

The Guidelines' official publication begins with a formal statement setting forth the technical action of adoption of the Guidelines by the several agencies. Despite its brevity and the relatively uncontroversial nature of this material, it may be misleading in some respects.

ACTION.—This section states that the "action" is "[a]doption of uniform guidelines on employee selection procedures as final rules by four agencies." This is not completely accurate, as only the Civil Service Commission (now called the Office of Personnel Management) and the Department of Labor have used formal rule-making authority. EEOC lacks such authority altogether and cannot regard the Uniform Guidelines as anything other than guidelines, while the Justice Department has adopted the Guidelines under the rubric of a "statement of policy", 28 C.F.R. Part 50. Without denigrating the Guidelines' significance as being entitled to great weight in the courts, *Griggs v. Duke Power Co.*, 401 U.S. 424, 3 FEP Cases 175 (1971), their characterization as "final rules" adopted by "four agencies" may give an exaggerated impression of their legal significance. As a practical matter, of course, the EEO enforcement agencies are themselves bound to operate according to the Guidelines, whether they have the force of "rules", "policy statements" or guidelines. (See Introduction, The Practical and Legal Significance of the Guidelines, in Part I.)

SUMMARY.—The goal announced in this small section, i.e., establishing "a uniform Federal position in the area of prohibiting discrimination in employment practices" is somewhat exaggerated, perhaps inadvertently. The Guidelines do not cover all employment practices; they are confined to employee selection procedures (broadly defined) used to make certain employment decisions and are probably irrelevent to such matters as discipline, compensation, benefits or working conditions. Indeed, the kind of "discrimination" addressed by the Guidelines is exclusively of the "*Griggs*" variety, in which an ostensibly neutral employee selection procedure has a statistically demonstrable "adverse impact" on a particular group and must therefore be justified as being job-related. Even with respect to employee selection procedures, the Uniform Guidelines do not "establish a uniform Federal position" regarding discrimination of the *McDonnell Douglas Corp. v. Green*, 411 U.S. 792 (1973) variety, in which an employer engages in disparate treatment of employees or applicants according to their race, sex, color, national origin or religion. An example of disparate treatment would be an employer's requiring black applicants to take a pre-employment test but not requiring white applicants to do so. (See the discussion of Section 11 of the Guidelines in Part III.)

Not only does the Summary appear to imply application to all "employment practices" and to both types of employment discrimination, it suggests that the Guidelines have some relationship to religious discrimination issues. No court has ever approached religious discrimination from a *Griggs* point of view and it is unlikely that any such approach could be viable given the unlikelihood of obtaining data.

Finally, the Summary speaks of "employment discrimination" without specifying which statutes are addressed. Only Title VII, however, and Executive Order 11246 lend themselves to *Griggs*-type analysis, depending entirely upon statistical disparities to establish an initial inference of discrimination. This is not to say that various principles set forth in the Guidelines will be without strong influence in construing employers' duties under other statutes. But the limited *Griggs*-type range of the discrimination addressed by the Guidelines must be underscored. It is clear, for example, that discrimination violative of the Constitution is outside the scope of the Guidelines, as the Supreme Court, in *Washington v. Davis*, 426 U.S. 229 (1976), expressly held that intentional discrimination must be proved to make out a constitutional violation. Most courts have recognized that proof of intention is required under the 1866 Civil Rights Act (42 U.S.C. § 1981) as well. Intentional discrimination is not addressed by the Guidelines, as the Guidelines deal only with inferences of discrimination derived from numerical evidence of the "adverse impact" of facially neutral practices. Accordingly, the Guidelines cannot "establish a uniform Federal position in the area of prohibiting discrimination" except where a statistical implication of discrimination through a showing of adverse impact is appropriate. Title VII and the Executive Order permit this kind of proof. The Summary would be clearer in stating that federal policy regarding discrimination under other statutes and the Constitution is not affected by the adoption of the Uniform Guidelines.

A possible exception to the statement above may affect state and local public sector employers. Such employers may find that EEO regulatory activity under federal funding statutes monitored by one or another of the adopting agencies—e.g., Office of Personnel Management (Intergovernmental Personnel Act), Department of the Treasury (Revenue Sharing)—may include applications of Uniform Guidelines standards in determining compliance.

25

SUPPLEMENTARY INFORMATION:

An Overview of the 1978 Uniform Guidelines on Employee Selection Procedures

Supplementary Information:

AN OVERVIEW OF THE 1978 UNIFORM GUIDELINES ON EMPLOYEE SELECTION PROCEDURES

This heading introduces the second major division of the Guidelines. The essay-like "Overview" attempts to support the agencies' more controversial legal and professional positions in the Guidelines and the "Analysis of Comments" seeks to meet specific objections raised during the public comment period by employers, civil rights advocates, labor unions, professional psychologists and other interested persons or organizations.

It would be inadvisable to rely upon the Guidelines' Overview as an accurate statement of Guideline require-ments, professional standards or legal criteria. The Overview has obvious surface appeal, but it includes discussions and explanations of legal and technical points which are sometimes incomplete or misleading. Those reading the Overview might conclude that the Guidelines contain only what has been uniformly required by the courts and endorsed by the professional community, but in a number of areas the Guidelines depart from judicial precedent, or professional standards, or both.

BACKGROUND:
PARAGRAPH 1
PARAGRAPH 2

I. BACKGROUND

One problem that confronted the Congress which adopted the Civil Rights Act of 1964 involved the effect of written preemployment tests on equal employment opportunity. The use of these test scores frequently denied employment to minorities in many cases without evidence that the tests were related to success on the job. Yet employers wished to continue to use such tests as practical tools to assist in the selection of qualified employees. Congress sought to strike a balance which would proscribe discrimination, but otherwise permit the use of tests in the selection of employees. Thus, in title VII, Congress authorized the use of "any professionally developed ability test provided that such test, its administration or action upon the results is not designed, intended or used to discriminate * * *".[1]

At first, some employers contended that, under this section, they could use any test which had been developed by a professional so long as they did not intend to exclude minorities, even if such exclusion was the consequence of the use of the test. In 1966, the Equal Employment Opportunity Commission (EEOC) adopted guidelines to advise employers and other users what the law and good industrial psychology practice required.[2] The Department of Labor adopted the same approach in 1968 with respect to tests used by Federal contractors under Executive Order 11246 in a more detailed regulation. The Government's view was that the employer's intent was irrelevant. If tests or other practices had an adverse impact on protected groups, they were unlawful unless they could be justified. To justify a test which screened out a higher proportion of minorities, the employer would have to show that it fairly measured or predicted performance on the job. Otherwise, it would not be considered to be "professionally developed."

---

[1] Section 703(h), 42 U.S.C. 2000e(2)(h).

[2] See 35 U.S.L.W. 2137 (1966).

28

The Overview

I. Background

Paragraph 1:

The Background section's apparent purpose is to explain the need for Uniform Guidelines on Employee Selection Procedures by describing the significance of testing under Title VII and tracing the history of prior guidelines on the subject. The first paragraph, for example, acknowledges that the 1964 Congress, which enacted Title VII, focused primarily on written pre-employment tests, and that in §703 (h)[10] of the statute, it expressly acted to protect the interest of employers in using tests "as practical tools to assist in the selection of qualified employees." See the discussion of the legislative history set forth in connection with Sections 5G and 14B (8) in Part III. The paragraph also acknowledges that Congress' primary concern was with the effects of testing on minorities. Unfortunately, the remaining paragraphs of the Background section do not accurately recount the history of the prior guidelines and are not wholly accurate in stating the legal principles upon which the present Uniform Guidelines rest.

Paragraph 2:

The claim that EEOC's 1966 Guidelines could "advise employers and other users what the law and good industrial psychology practice required" is inaccurate. At the time, there was no case law, so EEOC's version of the law's "requirements" was no better than an educated guess. The panel that drafted the 1966 Guidelines included only one industrial psychologist and one individual could hardly undertake single-handedly to define "good" professional practice. The reference to "tests or other practices" later in the paragraph is too broad, as the 1966 Guidelines addressed little more than paper and pencil tests.

The statement that the 1966 Guidelines (or any legal standard developed since 1964, for that matter) required that employers "justify a test which screened out a *higher proportion* of minorities" (emphasis added) is incomplete. In *Griggs v. Duke Power Co.,* 401 U.S. 424 (1971), *Albemarle Paper Co. v. Moody,* 422 U.S. 405, 425 (1975), and virtually every other decision regarding establishment of a statistical prima facie case of discrimination, the Supreme Court has spoken of "substantial", "significant" or "gross" disproportions. *See also, Williams v. Tallahassee Motors, Inc.,* 607 F.2d 689 (5th Cir., 1979), *Guardians Association v. Civil Service Commission,* 23 FEP Cases 909 (2d Cir., 1980).

The implication that ultimate job performance is the only criterion that can be used in developing valid selection procedures is too narrow. For instance, success in training has been held to be an acceptable criterion or goal of selection. *Washington v. Davis,* 426 U.S. 229, 250–51 (1976). *See also, U.S. v. South Carolina,* 445 F. Supp 1094, *aff'd mem., sub nom National Education Association v. South Carolina,* 434 U.S. 1026 (1978).

Finally, any implication that the doctrine of "fairness" has been present in the Guidelines since the beginning is misleading, as there was no mention of fairness in the 1966 EEOC Guidelines and there were no fairness studies required in the 1968 DOL Testing Order.

---

[10]The Supreme Court has noted: "Section 703(h) applies only to tests. It has no applicability to the high school diploma requirement." *Griggs v. Duke Power Co.,* 401 U.S. 424 N. 7 (1971). See the discussion of *Griggs* in Part I, above.

BACKGROUND: PARAGRAPH 3

In succeeding years, the EEOC and the Department of Labor provided more extensive guidance which elaborated upon these principles and expanded the guidelines to emphasize all selection procedures. In 1971 in *Griggs* v. *Duke Power Co.*,[3] the Supreme Court announced the principle that employer practices which had an adverse impact on minorities and were not justified by business necessity constituted illegal discrimination under title VII. Congress confirmed this interpretation in the 1972 amendments to title VII. The elaboration of these principles by courts and agencies continued into the mid-1970's,[4] but differences between the EEOC and the other agencies (Justice, Labor, and Civil Service Commission) produced two different sets of guidelines by the end of 1976.

[3] 401 U.S. 424 (1971).
[4] See, *e.g.*, *Albermarle Paper Co.* v. *Moody*, 422 U.S. 405 (1975).

Paragraph 3:

The Background section covers the period from the 1968 DOL Testing Order to *Griggs* in 1971 by noting that EEOC and the DOL provided ''more extensive guidance'' and ''expanded'' the Guidelines to emphasize all selection procedures. A more accurate and complete description of the process would note that the effort at achieving uniform guidelines commenced in early 1969 when the then-OFCC Advisory Committee on Selection and Testing, consisting of a group of eminent psychologists, provided suggestions for a revised Testing Order and revised guidelines. In the spring of 1969, an inter-agency task force of the Departments of Labor and Justice and EEOC made a first attempt at drafting Uniform Guidelines. The agencies were close to completing their work when EEOC, without consultation with the other agencies, unilaterally and without provision for public comment, issued its 1970 Guidelines, stating that the Department of Labor soon would follow with its own version. The DOL thus found itself with a choice of confrontation with EEOC or issuance of a revised Order similar to the EEOC publication. It chose the latter course and issued its 1971 Order. However, such elements as the search for suitable alternatives contained in the 1970 EEOC Guidelines were not included in the 1971 OFCC Testing Order. By 1972, when the second effort at uniform guidelines development began, a broad consensus in the industrial psychology community was consistently attacking the EEOC's 1970 Guidelines as unworkable.

The reference to ''business necessity'' (as a defense to a showing of adverse impact) cited in connection with *Griggs* in the Background section is misleading. The Court clearly meant ''business necessity'' and ''job-related'' to be interchangeable (*Griggs*, fn. 11). EEOC, however, apparently has adhered to the view that ''business necessity'' always requires a showing that the employer would go out of business if it did not use the challenged procedure. (This is the so-called ''plant closing'' test.) To say that Congress confirmed this interpretation in 1972 is incorrect. Congress merely rejected an extremely broad proposed amendment that would have eliminated *Griggs*-type statistical proof altogether.

It may be added that *Griggs* does not address all employment practices. It is concerned with practices neutral on their face but which nevertheless disproportionately impede the advancement of minorities or women substantially.

The citation of *Albemarle Paper Co. v. Moody* in this connection is also misleading. *Albemarle* did not endorse a ''business necessity'' requirement that would go beyond a showing of job-relatedness. A more accurate view of ''business necessity'' versus ''job-relatedness'' is provided by *United States v. South Carolina, supra,* which permitted consideration of costs in looking to a business-necessity defense. Also relevant are the human and economic risks of failure. The greater the risk, the lower the standard of proof necessary to prove job-relatedness. *New York City Transit Authority v. Beazer,* 440 U.S. 568 (1979); *Spurlock v. United Air Lines, Inc.,* 475 F.2d 216, 219 (10th Cir., 1972); *Townsend v. Nassau County Medical Center,* 558 F.2d 117, 120 (2d Cir., 1977), *cert. denied,* 434 U.S. 1015 (1978).

The agencies do not explain the nature of the ''differences'' between EEOC and the other agencies about the 1976 Federal Executive Agency Guidelines. The fact that the other agencies in 1976 could not accept EEOC's 1970 Guidelines is noteworthy.

It also should be observed that the staff representatives of EEOC reached agreement with the other agencies regarding the content of the 1976 FEA Guidelines, but were subsequently overruled by EEOC. It is not accurate, in this context, to say that the agencies produced two sets of Guidelines by the end of 1976, as EEOC in fact had produced nothing new since 1970 and simply republished its 1970 Guidelines in the *Federal Register* verbatim, again without provision for public comment, the day after the other agencies published the 1976 FEA Guidelines. EEOC acted unilaterally and repudiated the agreement of its own staff representatives with the other agency representatives on the 1976 FEA Guidelines, despite widespread criticism of the 1970 Guidelines by the professional community.

BACKGROUND: PARAGRAPH 4

With the advent of the Carter administration in 1977, efforts were intensified to producé a unified government position. The following document represents the result of that effort. This introduction is intended to assist those not familiar with these matters to understand the basic approach of the uniform guidelines. While the guidelines are complex and technical, they are based upon the principles which have been consistently upheld by the courts, the Congress, and the agencies.

The following discussion will cite the sections of the Guidelines which embody these principles.

ADVERSE IMPACT: PARAGRAPH 1

II. ADVERSE IMPACT

The fundamental principle underlying the guidelines is that employer policies or practices which have an adverse impact on employment opportunities of any race, sex, or ethnic group are illegal under title VII and the Executive order unless justified by business necessity.[5] A selection procedure which has no adverse impact generally does not violate title VII or the Executive order.[6] This means that an employer may usually avoid the application of the guidelines by use of procedures which have no adverse impact.[7] If adverse impact exists, it must be justified on grounds of business necessity. Normally, this means by validation which demonstrates the relation between the selection procedure and performance on the job.

[5] *Griggs,* note 3, supra; uniform guidelines on employee selection procedures (1978), section 3A, (hereinafter cited by section number only).

[6] *Furnco* v. *Waters,* 98 S.Ct. 2943 (1978).

[7] Section 6.

ADVERSE IMPACT: PARAGRAPH 2

The guidelines adopt a "rule of thumb" as a practical means of determining adverse impact for use in enforcement proceedings. This rule is known as the "⅘ths" or "80 percent" rule.[8] It is not a legal definition of discrimination, rather it is a practical device to keep the attention of enforcement agencies on serious discrepancies in hire or promotion rates or other employment decisions. To determine whether a selection procedure violates the "⅘ths rule", an employer compares its hiring rates for different groups.[9] But this rule of thumb cannot be applied automatically. An employer who has conducted an extensive recruiting campaign may have a larger than normal pool of applicants, and the "⅘ths rule" might unfairly expose it to enforcement proceedings.[10] On the other hand, an employer's reputation may have discouraged or "chilled" applicants of particular groups from applying because they believed application would be futile. The application of the "⅘ths" rule in that situation would allow an employer to evade scrutiny because of its own discrimination.[11]

[8] Section 4D.

[9] Section 16R (definition of selection rate).

[10] Section 4D (special recruiting programs).

[11] *Ibid* (user's actions have discouraged applicants).

32

Paragraph 4:

The statement that the Guidelines "are based upon the principles which have been consistently upheld by the Courts, the Congress, and the agencies" is only partly true, as noted above. The claim that there has been "consistency" among the agencies in principle is inaccurate. The Uniform Guidelines contain principles that were rejected by EEOC in 1976 and also principles that were rejected by the other agencies at that time but which have reappeared in the 1978 document.

Equally unsupportable is the inference that the Congress has interested itself in the principles underlying the Guidelines, one way or the other. Beyond endorsing the fundamental concept of testing in 1964 and rejecting an amendment in 1972 that would have prevented the use of statistics to establish a case of discrimination, Congress has never addressed the specific principles in the Uniform Guidelines that have aroused controversy.

The courts have generally departed from federal guidelines where they have been shown to be inconsistent with sound professional practice or judicial precedent. See, e.g., *Washington v. Davis, U.S. v. South Carolina, Friend v. Leidinger, Commonwealth v. O'Neill, Guardians Association v. Civil Service Commission.* The inconsistency of many Guidelines sections with court precedent is noted at greater length and in more detail in connection with the particular sections in Part III.

II. Adverse Impact

Paragraph 1:

The principle that adverse impact requires justification by "business necessity" under Title VII and the Executive Order is unobjectionable, provided the agencies recognize that the standard for "business necessity" is that the selection procedure is job-related rather than that the plant will close unless the procedure is used. *See Griggs, supra,* fn. 11; *Furnco Construction Co. v. Waters,* 438 U.S. 567 (1978); *Keene State College v. Sweeney,* 439 U.S. 24 (1978). It should be noted, however, that the application of the "adverse impact" doctrine to all "employer policies or practices" is of dubious legality, as not all practices (or policies) lend themselves to statistical analysis. In any event, the statement is unnecessarily broad in this context, as the Guidelines deal only with employee selection procedures used to make certain employment decisions.

Paragraph 2:

The agencies state that the four-fifths rule is not "a legal definition of discrimination", see *Rich v. Martin Marietta Corp.,* 467 F.Supp. 587 (D.Colo. 1979), and that it is a "practical device to keep the attention of enforcement agencies on serious discrepancies in hire or promotion rates or other employment decisions." But it is also true that the Supreme Court has always been very careful to avoid any definition of discrimination that demands anything approaching actual statistical parity for every ethnic or sex group, an approach mandated by Section 703 (j) of Title VII which expressly disclaims any intention of requiring proportional representation in employers' workforces.

In *International Brotherhood of Teamsters v. United States,* 431 U.S. 324 (1977), for example, the Court noted the "glaring" absence of minority group members as line drivers, n. 23, and showed that precedent sanctioned "the use of statistical proof, where it reached proportions comparable to those in this case, to establish a prima facie case of racial discrimination." The Court was careful to recognize that Section 703(j) of Title VII by its express terms does not require racial balance in an employer's workforce and noted that imbalance is probative of discrimination because it is or-

33

ADVERSE IMPACT: PARAGRAPH 2

The guidelines adopt a "rule of thumb" as a practical means of determining adverse impact for use in enforcement proceedings. This rule is known as the "⅘ths" or "80 percent" rule.[8] It is not a legal definition of discrimination, rather it is a practical device to keep the attention of enforcement agencies on serious discrepancies in hire or promotion rates or other employment decisions. To determine whether a selection procedure violates the "⅘ths rule", an employer compares its hiring rates for different groups.[9] But this rule of thumb cannot be applied automatically. An employer who has conducted an extensive recruiting campaign may have a larger than normal pool of applicants, and the "⅘ths rule" might unfairly expose it to enforcement proceedings.[10] On the other hand, an employer's reputation may have discouraged or "chilled" applicants of particular groups from applying because they believed application would be futile. The application of the "⅘ths" rule in that situation would allow an employer to evade scrutiny because of its own discrimination.[11]

[8]Section 4D.
[9]Section 16R (definition of selection rate).
[10]Section 4D (special recruiting programs).
[11]*Ibid* (user's actions have discouraged applicants).

dinarily expected that nondiscriminatory practices "will in time result in a workforce more or less" balanced, subject to statistics showing the composition of the pool of qualified applicants. *Id.*, fn. 20. But the *kind* of imbalance the Court had in mind is by no means subtle: "Evidence of *longlasting* and *gross* disparity between the composition of the workforce and that of the general population thus *may be* significant," the Court declared. *Id.* (Emphasis added.) *See also, Williams v. Tallahassee Motors, Inc., supra.*[11]

It thus seems clear that the agencies had little choice but to adopt some "rule of thumb", as the Supreme Court (in *Teamsters, supra,* and also in *Hazelwood School District v. U.S.,* 433 U.S. 299 (1977) and *New York City Transit Authority v. Beazer, supra*) plainly disfavored drawing an inference of discrimination arising from subtle statistical imbalances. It also seems clear that a narrower range than that of the four-fifths rule would not have conformed to the Court's stress on the "grossness" of the statistics from which it had been willing to infer discrimination. Indeed, it is doubtful whether the agencies' rejection of a combined standard of four-fifths *and* a test of statistical significance applied to the differences in group selection rate for the group will withstand court scrutiny, as discussed below. (See comments on Section 3A in Part III.)

The principle recited in this paragraph to the effect that special circumstances may affect the application of the four-fifths rule is essentially sound. However, the agencies' citation of an example involving an employer whose reputation "may have discouraged or 'chilled'

applicants from particular groups" is misleading in that it implies a light evidentiary burden. The Supreme Court was presented with this argument in *Teamsters* and, while endorsing it in principle, the Court demanded very strict proof of such effects, even though the employer's past policy of racial discrimination was incontrovertible. The agencies thus would be ill-advised to base an adverse impact finding on little more than rumor and unsupported assertions by late-coming witnesses as to the "chilling" effect of an employer's reputation, especially where the employer's statistics meet the four-fifths rule. It also should be noted that an employer's good reputation, as well as a special recruitment campaign, may produce an "abnormal" pool justifying an even less stringent standard than the four-fifths rule; the discussion here acknowledges a "special recruitment" exception, but not the "good reputation" exception.

Finally, the agencies offer little assistance in defining "applicant", as discussed later in connection with Section 4C. The word is meaningless as applied to persons who are not at least apparently qualified for the job in question and the presence of persons who lack such apparent qualifications can seriously distort the representativeness of an applicant pool for purposes of determining the adverse impact of a selection procedure when selection rates are used as the only basis for determining adverse impact. Moreover, an applicant (as opposed to a "curious person") is one who continues in the employer's selection process until rejected or accepted.

---

[11]An important question about the focus of statistical scrutiny also is raised by this paragraph. The discussion refers to "serious discrepancies in hire or promotion *rates*" (emphasis added), and there is indeed strong precedent for considering comparative *rates* of promotion or hire in establishing a prima facie case of discrimination. However, a prima facie case may also be established through showing serious discrepancies between workforce composition and external availability. The Guidelines deal only with the former in considering "adverse impact", but they do not address the question whether adverse impact in selection rates is absolute evidence of adverse impact, if in fact there is no serious disparity between the resulting workforce and external availability. This issue is of critical importance in interpreting and applying the "bottom line" and is addressed in the discussion of the following section of the "Overview".

ADVERSE IMPACT/ OVERALL PROCESS: PARAGRAPH 1

III. IS ADVERSE IMPACT TO BE MEASURED BY THE OVERALL PROCESS?

In recent years some employers have eliminated the overall adverse impact of a selection procedure and employed sufficient numbers of minorities or women to meet this "⅘th's rule of thumb". However, they might continue use of a component which does have an adverse impact. For example, an employer might insist on a minimum passing score on a written test which is not job related and which has an adverse impact on minorities.[12] However, the employer might compensate for this adverse impact by hiring a sufficient proportion of minorities who do meet its standards, so that its overall hiring is on a par with or higher than the applicant flow. Employers have argued that as long as their "bottom line" shows no overall adverse impact, there is no violation at all, regardless of the operation of a particular component of the process.

[12]See, *e.g.*, *Griggs* v. *Duke Power Co.*, 401 U.S. 424 (1971).

ADVERSE IMPACT/ OVERALL PROCESS: PARAGRAPH 2

Employee representatives have argued that rights under equal employment opportunity laws are individual, and the fact that an employer has hired some minorities does not justify discrimination against other minorities. Therefore, they argue that adverse impact is to be determined by examination of each component of the selection procedure, regardless of the "bottom line." This question has not been answered definitively by the courts. There are decisions pointing in both directions.

III. Is Adverse Impact to be Measured by the Overall Process?

Paragraph 1:

This paragraph introduces the "bottom line" concept, whereby the agencies agree generally that if a selection process has no overall adverse impact, its components need not be examined. As an example, the agencies speak of a situation in which an employer uses a written test which has an adverse impact on minorities. However, this adverse impact is offset by hiring a sufficient proportion of minorities "so that the overall hiring is on a par with or higher than the applicant flow." First, the "bottom line" is subject to the "four-fifths" rule, so the statement "on a par with or higher than the applicant flow" may be misleading. Second, the agencies' emphasis on "applicant flow" is misplaced. It would be more accurate to refer to "flow of qualified applicants", as pure applicant flow may readily result in unrepresentativeness by the presence of an abnormal proportion of clearly non-qualified persons. As is indicated in *Teamsters,* fn. 20, the appropriate bottom line consideration may also be the makeup of the relevant labor market.[12] Thus there should properly be two "bottom lines", one comparing applicants to hires or offers, the other comparing external skilled availability to actual utilization. It may be added that stress on applicant flow in determining adverse impact has a potential unfortunate side effect: it may penalize employers for engaging in affirmative recruiting unless they can meet the burden of showing that special recruitment has distorted the makeup of the applicant pool. (See also discussion of Point 2 in the Analysis of Comments.)

The agencies' apparent approval of an employer's use of a non-job-related minimum passing score having no adverse impact to illustrate the "bottom line" is unfortunate, as such test use by an employer would be poor professional practice and ultimately would do little service to sound affirmative action progress. The point about the "bottom line" is that neither the adverse impact nor the questions of job-relatedness would be examined by the agencies if the "bottom line" for a particular job is satisfactory.

(See discussion of Section 4C in Part III.)

WARNING: As this volume went to press, the Second Circuit, in *Teal v. State of Connecticut,* 25 FEP Cases 529 (2d Cir. 1981), issued a ruling that, in effect, found the "bottom line" inconsistent with Title VII. See the discussion on page 97.

Paragraph 2:

Although it is true that there has been no "definitive" Supreme Court resolution of the "bottom line" debate, it is wrong to suggest an even split of authority. As illustrated in *EEOC v. Navajo Refining Co.,* 593 F. 2d 988 (10th Cir. 1979), the "bottom line" has been found so intrinsic to a *Griggs*-type of rationale that a showing of a "clean" bottom line forecloses all further inquiry into components of the selection process, even components that are frequently suspect, such as high school graduation requirements and nonvalidated tests.[13] See also, *Brown v. New Haven Civil Service Board,* 474 F.Supp. 1256 (D.Conn. 1979). This is as it must be: *Griggs* and its progeny deliberately look only at "bottom line" numbers to see whether through numbers alone an inference of discrimination may be raised. If those numbers fail to raise any inference of discrimination, no burden of explanation shifts to the employer regarding the employment practices involved.

The argument attributed by the agencies in this paragraph to "employee representatives"—in effect claiming that failure to examine component selection procedures paves the way for discrimination against

---

[12] As noted in the footnote in the preceding section, this is a critical issue. It cannot be said that *Teamsters* definitively decides the question, but it at least provides support for the argument that the Guidelines' apparent endorsement of applicant flow figures alone for establishing the "bottom line" may be mistaken. It is difficult to see why, especially as a matter of "prosecutorial discretion", the agencies would wish to scrutinize the employment procedures of an employer whose workforce reasonably reflects the relevant external availability.

---

[13] Note that this case uses a workforce utilization-external availability comparison to establish the "bottom line" defense.

ADVERSE IMPACT/ OVERALL PROCESS: PARAGRAPH 2

Employee representatives have argued that rights under equal employment opportunity laws are individual, and the fact that an employer has hired some minorities does not justify discrimination against other minorities. Therefore, they argue that adverse impact is to be determined by examination of each component of the selection procedure, regardless of the "bottom line." This question has not been answered definitively by the courts. There are decisions pointing in both directions.

ADVERSE IMPACT/ OVERALL PROCESS: PARAGRAPH 3

These guidelines do not address the underlying question of law. They discuss only the exercise of prosecutorial discretion by the Government agencies themselves.[13] The agencies have decided that, generally, their resources to combat discrimination should be used against those respondents whose practices have restricted or excluded the opportunities of minorities and women. If an employer is appropriately including all groups in the workforce, it is not sensible to spend Government time and effort on such a case, when there are so many employers whose practices do have adverse effects which should be challenged. For this reason, the guidelines provide that, in considering whether to take enforcement action, the Government will take into account the general posture of the employer concerning equal employment opportunity, including its affirmative action plan and results achieved under the plan.[14] There are some circumstances where the government may intervene even though the "bottom line" has been satisfied. They include the case where a component of a selection procedure restricts promotional opportunities of minorities or women who were discriminatorily assigned to jobs, and where a component, such as a height requirement, has been declared unlawful in other situations.[15]

[13] Section 4C.
[14] Section 4E.
[15] Section 4C.

ADVERSE IMPACT/ OVERALL PROCESS: PARAGRAPH 4

What of the individual who is denied the job because of a particular component in a procedure which otherwise meets the "bottom line" standard? The individual retains the right to proceed through the appropriate agencies, and into Federal court.[16]

[16] The processing of individual cases is excluded from the operation of the bottom line concept by the definition of "enforcement action," section 16I. Under section 4C, where adverse impact has existed, the employer must keep records of the effect of each component for 2 years after the adverse effect has dissipated.

Paragraph 2 (continued)

individuals—is based upon a misconception regarding the kinds of proof available under Title VII. Individuals who claim to be the victims of discrimination are properly foreclosed from using *Griggs*-type statistical evidence to support their individual claims in the absence of bottom line adverse impact, even if their own claims can be tied into a specific selection component having adverse impact. But they are not foreclosed from making a *McDonnell Douglas* case of discrimination by showing that they have been victimized by intentional disparate treatment. (See Section 11 in Part III.)

The relevant point about the "bottom line" is that it is an aspect of a *Griggs*-type proof—where the statistics are satisfactory, plaintiffs must produce something other than statistics to show that the employer has discriminated and that "something" must tend to show disparate treatment.

It is also important to stress once again that the "bottom line" concept is addressed only to discrimination issues. It is not a principle that provides a defense for an employer's failure to meet affirmative action commitments.

Paragraph 3:

As noted above, the "bottom line" legally constitutes something more than the mere exercise of prosecutorial discretion, not only under *Navajo Refining* but under other cases, such as *Griggs* and *New York City Transit Authority*. To say that the agencies have "decided" generally to pursue employers "whose practices have restricted or excluded the opportunities of minorities and women" implies that the agencies could pursue other employers if they chose. But the only other employers who could be pursued as discriminators under Title VII would be those who had engaged in intentional disparate treatment, a type of discrimination that is not covered by the Guidelines.[14] This explanation of "prosecutorial discretion" appears to leave the "bottom line" dependent upon the agencies' good will.

That an employer's general EEO posture may be rel-

evant to an agency's determination whether to exercise its enforcement authority in a close case is reasonable. Courts have certainly taken affirmative action efforts into account in determining Title VII liability, e.g., *Washington v. Davis*. But the relevance of this to the "bottom line" concept is questionable. If anything, EEO posture may be relevant to deciding whether to adhere to the four-fifths rule of thumb for determining the presence of adverse impact; but once the agencies determine that the bottom line shows no adverse impact, it is difficult to see what discretion remains to them. See further discussion under Section 4E in Part III.

Both examples of exceptions to the bottom line are unsatisfactory. See the discussion of Section 4C in Part III.

Paragraph 4:

It is important to note that the agencies have defined "enforcement action" to exclude the processing of individual cases, which still may be processed (and apparently investigated for a "cause" finding) by the agencies. (See Section 16I.) The exclusion of individual claims from the bottom line concept is illogical and weakens the practical protection of employer action afforded by the concept. Agency discretion to encourage individual cases through issuing individual "reasonable cause" determinations is unjustified. At the least, the

agencies should state that they believe that an individual who is denied an employment opportunity because of a particular component in a selection process that has no "bottom line" adverse impact cannot make out a *prima facie* case of discrimination merely by showing that the component itself has adverse impact. Such an individual should have to show evidence of disparate treatment. Otherwise, a "no reasonable cause" finding should be issued. See discussions of Sections 4C, 11 and 16I in Part III and the discussion of paragraph 2.

---

[14]Employers could be pursued under other, non-*Griggs*-related concepts as well as under statutes other than Title VII. Thus, the Merit System Standards adopted under the Intergovernmental Personnel Act could be used to challenge state and local government testing procedures if no discrimination is present.

39

ADVERSE IMPACT/ BASIC OPTIONS

IV. WHERE ADVERSE IMPACT EXISTS: THE BASIC OPTIONS

Once an employer has established that there is adverse impact, what steps are required by the guidelines? As previously noted, the employer can modify or eliminate the procedure which produces the adverse impact, thus taking the selection procedure from the coverage of these guidelines. If the employer does not do that, then it must justify the use of the procedure on grounds of "business necessity." [17] This normally means that it must show a clear relation between performance on the selection procedure and performance on the job. In the language of industrial psychology, the employer must validate the selection procedure. Thus the bulk of the guidelines consist of the Government's interpretation of standards for validation.

[17] A few practices may be used without validation even if they have adverse impact. See, e.g., *McDonnell Douglas v. Green*, 411 U.S. 792 (1973) and section 6B.

VALIDATION/ ALTERNATIVES

V. VALIDATION: CONSIDERATION OF ALTERNATIVES

The concept of validation as used in personnel psychology involves the establishment of the relationship between a test instrument or other selection procedure and performance on the job. Federal equal employment opportunity law has added a requirement to the process of validation. In conducting a validation study, the employer should consider available alternatives which will achieve its legitimate business purpose with lesser adverse impact. [18] The employer cannot concentrate solely on establishing the validity of the instrument or procedure which it has been using in the past.

This same principle of using the alternative with lesser adverse impact is applicable to the manner in which an employer uses a valid selection procedure. [19] The guidelines assume that there are at least three ways in which an employer can use scores on a selection procedure: (1) To screen out of consideration those who are not likely to be able to perform the job successfully; (2) to group applicants in accordance with the likelihood of their successful performance on the job, and (3) to rank applicants, selecting those with the highest scores for employment. [20]

The setting of a "cutoff score" to determine who will be screened out may have an adverse impact. If so, an employer is required to justify the initial cutoff score by reference to its need for a trustworthy and efficient work force. [21] Similarly, use of results for grouping or for rank ordering is likely to have a greater adverse effect than use of scores solely to screen out unqualified candidates. If the employer chooses to use a rank order method, the evidence of validity must be sufficient to justify that method of use. [22]

[18] *Albermarle Paper Co. v. Moody*, 422 U.S. 405 (1975); *Robinson v. Lorillard Corp.*, 444 F. 2d 791 (4th Cir. 1971).
[19] Sections 3B; 5G.
[20] *Ibid.*
[21] See sections 3B; 5H. See also sections 14B(6) (criterion-related validity); 14C(9) (content validity); 14D(1) (construct validity).
[22] Sections 5G, 14B(6); 14C(9); 14D(1).

IV. Where Adverse Impact Exists: The Basic Options

The agencies assume the lawfulness of an employer's deliberate "modification" of selection procedures in order to produce fewer successful candidates of one race, ethnic group or sex as a means of "taking [its practices] from the coverage" of the Guidelines. This assumption can be cause for concern as to legality under rules still being developed by the courts. See the discussion of Section 6A in Part III.

Additionally, although this section does use the word "normally" with respect to the duty to validate a procedure having adverse impact if it is to be retained, the "basic options" discussion downplays the frequent situation where there is evidence of job-relatedness that does not require formal validation. Sometimes this "evidence" is little more than common sense. Only *McDonnell Douglas v. Green* is cited, whereas numerous cases (such as *Furnco, New York City Transit Authority* and *Smith v. Olin Chemical*, 555 F.2d 1283 (5th Cir. 1977)), have accepted "business necessity" or job-relatedness defenses for a wide variety of job requirements having adverse impact without requiring anything resembling formal validation studies. "Validation" conforming to the Guidelines' requirements is therefore not the only way, or even the "normal" way, to show job-relatedness; it depends on what selection procedure is being questioned and in what job milieu. See the discussion of Section 6B in Part III.

V. Validation: Consideration of Alternatives

As previously noted, it is misleading to state that validation shows only the relationship between a selection procedure and job performance. See discussions of the different kinds of validation studies, Part III, Section 14. Beyond that, the remainder of the paragraph sets forth standards that few courts have found required by law. The "requirement" of a search for less adverse alternatives in validation studies has not been judicially endorsed[15], although such a search is a perfectly proper undertaking for purposes of meeting affirmative action commitments. *Furnco Construction Co. v. Waters, supra,* stands for precisely the contrary conclusion, as the Court declared that employers are not obliged to seek employment procedures that maximize the opportunities of minority group members.

The agencies' position apparently stems from a misreading of *Albemarle Paper Co. v. Moody,* a misreading that is increasingly difficult to reconcile with subsequent Supreme Court clarifications of an employer's duties under Title VII. *Albemarle* announced only a rule of evidence, not a rule of law: the use of a valid, adverse test is not an absolute defense to Title VII liability where an equally valid, less adverse test is available; if this is the case, the plaintiff may introduce the second test as rebuttal evidence to show that the employer's use of the first test is a "pretext" for discrimination. Not only is the *Albemarle* burden of presenting alternatives clearly on the plaintiff, but in practical terms, it is unlikely that a plaintiff will be able to come forward with a test the employer never knew about, and had no good reason to know about, in order to show that the use of the valid first test was a pretext. To the extent that any ambiguity remained as a result of *Albemarle,* however, *Furnco* and *Keene State College* have resolved it. The Court has unambiguously declared that affirmative efforts to maximize minority hiring are not a required element of any Title VII defense; an employer need do no more than show that a procedure is job-related, and it is improper to require a further showing that the use of the procedure is the use that maximizes the hiring of minorities. *Griggs,* the doctrinal source for virtually everything in the Guidelines, requires no more than validation to dispel the implication of discrimination arising from a statistical showing of adverse impact.

Another significant aspect of the search for less adverse alternatives is that it contains an element of self-incrimination, as it requires employers to determine not only whether their procedures have adverse impact, but whether less adverse procedures exist. There is no assurance that an employer's discovery of a second, less

---

[15]The apparent exceptions, *Allen V. City of Mobile* and *Dickerson v. U.S. Steel Corp.,* 582 F.2d 827 (3d Cir. 1978), are discussed in Part III in connection with Section 3B, and also in this Section in connection with Point VII, "How Is Validation to Be Conducted." See also *Guardians Association v. Civil Service Commission,* 23 FEP Cases 909 (2d Cir. 1980), rejecting a required search for alternatives.

V. VALIDATION: CONSIDERATION OF ALTERNATIVES

The concept of validation as used in personnel psychology involves the establishment of the relationship between a test instrument or other selection procedure and performance on the job. Federal equal employment opportunity law has added a requirement to the process of validation. In conducting a validation study, the employer should consider available alternatives which will achieve its legitimate business purpose with lesser adverse impact.[18] The employer cannot concentrate solely on establishing the validity of the instrument or procedure which it has been using in the past.

This same principle of using the alternative with lesser adverse impact is applicable to the manner in which an employer uses a valid selection procedure.[19] The guidelines assume that there are at least three ways in which an employer can use scores on a selection procedure: (1) To screen out of consideration those who are not likely to be able to perform the job successfully; (2) to group applicants in accordance with the likelihood of their successful performance on the job, and (3) to rank applicants, selecting those with the highest scores for employment.[20]

The setting of a "cutoff score" to determine who will be screened out may have an adverse impact. If so, an employer is required to justify the initial cutoff score by reference to its need for a trustworthy and efficient work force.[21] Similarly, use of results for grouping or for rank ordering is likely to have a greater adverse effect than use of scores solely to screen out unqualified candidates. If the employer chooses to use a rank order method, the evidence of validity must be sufficient to justify that method of use.[22]

[18] *Albermarle Paper Co.* v. *Moody*, 422 U.S. 405 (1975); *Robinson* v. *Lorillard Corp.*, 444 F. 2d 791 (4th Cir. 1971).

[19] Sections 3B; 5G.

[20] *Ibid.*

[21] See sections 3B; 5H. See also sections 14B(6) (criterion-related validity); 14C(9) (content validity); 14D(1) (construct validity).

[22] Sections 5G, 14B(6); 14C(9); 14D(1).

VI. TESTING FOR HIGHER LEVEL JOBS

Normally, employers test for the job for which people are hired. However, there are situations where the first job is temporary or transient, and the workers who remain are promoted to work which involves more complex activities. The guidelines restrict testing for higher level jobs to users who promote a majority of the employees who remain with them to the higher level job within a reasonable period of time.[23]

[23] Section 5I.

VALIDATION:

VII. HOW IS VALIDATION TO BE CONDUCTED

Validation has become highly technical and complex, and yet is constantly changing as a set of concepts in industrial psychology. What follows here is a simple introduction to a highly complex field. There are three concepts which can be used to validate a selection procedure. These concepts reflect different approaches to investigating the job relatedness of selection procedures and may be interrelated in practice. They are (1) criterion-related validity,[24] (2) content validity,[25] and (3) construct validity.[26] In criterion-related validity, a selection procedure is justified by a statistical relationship between scores on the test or other selection procedure and measures of job performance. In content validity, a selection procedure is justified by showing that it representatively samples significant parts of the job, such as a typing test for a typist. Construct validity involves identifying the psychological trait (the construct) which underlies successful performance on the job and then devising a selection procedure to measure the presence and degree of the construct. An example would be a test of "leadership ability."

The guidelines contain technical standards and documentation requirements for the application of each of the three approaches.[27] One of the problems which the guidelines attempt to meet is the "borderline" between "content validity" and "construct validity." The extreme cases are easy to understand. A secretary, for example, may have to type. Many jobs require the separation of important matters which must be handled immediately from those which can be handled routinely. For the typing function, a typing test is appropriate. It is justifiable on the basis of content validity because it is a sample of an important or critical part of the job. The second function can be viewed as involving a capability to exercise selective judgment in light of the surrounding circumstances, a mental process which is difficult to sample.

In addressing this situation, the guidelines attempt to make it practical to validate the typing test by a content strategy,[28] but do not allow the validation of a test measuring a construct such as "judgment" by a content validity strategy.

The bulk of the guidelines deals with questions such as those discussed in the above paragraphs. Not all such questions can be answered simply, nor can all problems be addressed in the single document. Once the guidelines are issued, they will have to be interpreted in light of changing factual, legal, and professional circumstances.

[24] Sections 5B, (General Standards); 14B (Technical Standards); 15B (Documentation); 16F (Definition).

[25] Sections 5B (General Standards); 14C (Technical Standards); 15C (Documentation); 16D (Definition).

[26] Sections 5B (General Standards); 14D (Technical Standards); 15D (Documentation); 16E (Definition).

[27] Technical standards are in section 14; documentation requirements are in section 15.

[28] Section 14C.

adverse procedure will not be considered by the agencies as evidence that the use of the first procedure was discriminatory. *See Senter v. General Motors,* 383 F. Supp. 222 (S.D. Ohio 1974), *aff'd.* 532 F. 2d 511 (6th Cir. 1976), *cert. denied,* 429 U.S. 870, (1976).

The requirement that separate justification is needed for the manner of use of a selection procedure is professionally questionable, although courts have accepted this requirement in a number of cases. See discussions of Sections 3B, 5C, 14B (6), 14C (9) and 14D (1) in Part III.

VI. Testing for Higher Level Jobs

The Guidelines permit testing for jobs at a higher level than the one for which candidates are being considered only when a majority of the employees who remain with the employer progress to the higher level job within a "reasonable" period of time. Legal and professional comment on this restriction will be found in the discussion of Section 5I, Part III.

VII. How is Validation to be Conducted?

As stated in this section, validation is often both "highly technical and complex".[16] It is also correct that the Guidelines "will have to be interpreted in light of changing factual, legal and professional circumstances." The seeming rigidity of the Guidelines' formulations of technical standards and documentation requirements in Sections 14 and 15 is therefore unfortunate. A mechanical "checklist" approach to enforcement is invited by the Guidelines' attempt to require rather than suggest bench marks of satisfactory validation. That this "mandate" approach is legally suspect is plainly foretold by the fate of past employee selection guidelines in the courts, from *Washington v. Davis* to *U.S. v. South Carolina* to *Friend v. Leidinger* to *Commonwealth v. O'Neill.* The efforts by plaintiffs and the government to persuade the Second Circuit to adopt such an approach to the Guidelines was flatly rejected in *Guardians Association v. Civil Service Commission,* 23 FEP Cases 909 (2d Cir. 1980), where the Court expressly declared, ". . . the Guidelines should

always be considered, but they should not be regarded as conclusive unless *reason* and *statutory interpretation* support their conclusions" (emphasis added). The Court adds that "the fact that an agency or group of agencies has announced the standards they will use does not convert those standards into mandatory legal rules." Throughout its decision the Circuit Court criticizes the Guidelines for excessive rigidity and narrowness. Indeed, Courts with near unanimity have rejected a rigid interpretation of agency testing guidelines, especially when presented with evidence that sound professional opinion differs in one material way or another from guideline provisions, as it does with sections of the Uniform Guidelines.

Typical of cases that appear to be contrary to this trend is *Allen v. City of Mobile,* 464 F. Supp. 433 (S.D. Ala. 1978), where the District Court faulted an employer's validation study for its failure to include a search for less adverse, equally valid alternatives as required by the Uniform Guidelines. However, this case is of dubious precedential value beyond its peculiar facts, notably the complete absence of blacks from the job in question. Furthermore, the judge by no means construed the government Guidelines as a formulation of law. For example, the judge stated that courts "have generally been unimpressed with [employers'] '11th hour' attempts to validate their employment procedures," but did not question the employer's right to present such studies as a defense. This contrasts with the Guidelines, which insist that employers have a pos-

---

[16]However, it must be repeated that formal validation is not the only legally acceptable means of demonstrating job-relatedness. Simple, common-sense evidence of job-relatedness has frequently been accepted by the courts. See, e.g., the discussion of Point IV, "Where Adverse Impact Exists", above, and Point I in the Analysis of Comments, "Relationship Between Validation and Elimination of Adverse Impact", below.

VALIDATION:

VII. HOW IS VALIDATION TO BE CONDUCTED

Validation has become highly technical and complex, and yet is constantly changing as a set of concepts in industrial psychology. What follows here is a simple introduction to a highly complex field. There are three concepts which can be used to validate a selection procedure. These concepts reflect different approaches to investigating the job relatedness of selection procedures and may be interrelated in practice. They are (1) criterion-related validity,[24] (2) content validity,[25] and (3) construct validity.[26] In criterion-related validity, a selection procedure is justified by a statistical relationship between scores on the test or other selection procedure and measures of job performance. In content validity, a selection procedure is justified by showing that it representatively samples significant parts of the job, such as a typing test for a typist. Construct validity involves identifying the psychological trait (the construct) which underlies successful performance on the job and then devising a selection procedure to measure the presence and degree of the construct. An example would be a test of "leadership ability."

The guidelines contain technical standards and documentation requirements for the application of each of the three approaches.[27] One of the problems which the guidelines attempt to meet is the "borderline" between "content validity" and "construct validity." The extreme cases are easy to understand. A secretary, for example, may have to type. Many jobs require the separation of important matters which must be handled immediately from those which can be handled routinely. For the typing function, a typing test is appropriate. It is justifiable on the basis of content validity because it is a sample of an important or critical part of the job. The second function can be viewed as involving a capability to exercise selective judgment in light of the surrounding circumstances, a mental process which is difficult to sample.

In addressing this situation, the guidelines attempt to make it practical to validate the typing test by a content strategy,[28] but do not allow the validation of a test measuring a construct such as "judgment" by a content validity strategy.

The bulk of the guidelines deals with questions such as those discussed in the above paragraphs. Not all such questions can be answered simply, nor can all problems be addressed in the single document. Once the guidelines are issued, they will have to be interpreted in light of changing factual, legal, and professional circumstances.

[24] Sections 5B, (General Standards); 14B (Technical Standards); 15B (Documentation); 16F (Definition).

[25] Sections 5B (General Standards); 14C (Technical Standards); 15C (Documentation); 16D (Definition).

[26] Sections 5B (General Standards); 14D (Technical Standards); 15D (Documentation); 16E (Definition).

[27] Technical standards are in section 14; documentation requirements are in section 15.

[28] Section 14C.

RECORDKEEPING:

VIII. SIMPLIFICATION OF REPORTING AND RECORDKEEPING REQUIREMENTS

The reporting and recordkeeping provisions which appeared in the December 30 draft which was published for comment have been carefully reviewed in light of comments received and President Carter's direction to limit paperwork burdens on those regulated by Government to the minimum necessary for effective regulation. As a result of this review, two major changes have been made in the documentation requirements of the guidelines:

(1) A new section 15A(1) provides a simplified recordkeeping option for employers with fewer than 100 employees;

(2) Determinations of the adverse impact of selection procedures need not be made for groups which constitute less than 2 percent of the relevant labor force.

Also, the draft has been changed to make clear that users can assess adverse impact on an annual basis rather than on a continuing basis.

itive duty to determine adverse impact and to validate on an ongoing basis. The Fifth Circuit observed as early as *Cooper v. Allen,* 467 F. 2d 836 (5th Cir. 1972), that the law does not require validation or other proof of job-relatedness prior to the implementation of a test as an employment standard, although it is usually good professional practice to do so. The court in *Allen v. City of Mobile, supra,* also noted the general acceptance of content validity studies by federal courts, even though EEOC's 1970 Guidelines required a showing of the infeasibility of conducting criterion studies before a content study could be performed. No court ever permitted that standard to serve as a statement of law.

It may also be noted that the defendant in *Allen v. City of Mobile* apparently did not have the opportunity to attack, either legally or professionally, the Guidelines' requirement that less adverse, equally valid alternatives be pursued. A court presented with a vigorous defense to this requirement would most likely not fault an otherwise sound validation study for failure to include evidence of such a search.

The rigid and often excessive technical and documentation standards of Sections 14 and 15 of the Uniform Guidelines contrast with the flexible interpretation suggested by the last paragraph of this section. As already indicated, the courts will almost certainly endorse the latter approach and reject rigidity except under special circumstances.

VIII. Simplification of Reporting and Recordkeeping Requirements

As demonstrated more fully in the discussion of Section 15 and other Guidelines sections in Part III of the Analysis, the Guidelines did not implement the President's directions to limit paperwork burdens on those regulated by the federal government and in many important respects do not "represent 'professionally accepted methods' of the psychological profession." The claim that the Guidelines are "consistent with the decisions of the Supreme Court and authoritative decisions of other Appellate Courts" is an overstatement. See, e.g., *Guardians Association v. Civil Service Commission, supra.*

ANALYSIS OF COMMENTS:

Analysis of comments. The uniform guidelines published today are based upon the proposition that the Federal Government should speak to the public and to those whom it regulates with one voice on this important subject; and that the Federal Government ought to impose upon itself obligations for equal employment opportunity which are at least as demanding as those it seeks to impose on others. These guidelines state a uniform Federal position on this subject, and are intended to protect the rights created by title VII of the Civil Rights Act of 1964, as amended, Executive Order 11246, as amended, and other provisions of Federal law. The uniform guidelines are also intended to represent "professionally acceptable methods" of the psychological profession for demonstrating whether a selection procedure validly predicts or measures performance for a particular job. *Albemarle Paper Co.* v. *Moody,* 442 U.S. 405, 425. They are also intended to be consistent with the decisions of the Supreme Court and authoritative decisions of other appellate courts.

Although the development of these guidelines preceded the issuance by President Jimmy Carter of Executive Order 12044 designed to improve the regulatory process, the spirit of his Executive order was followed in their development. Initial agreement among the Federal agencies was reached early in the fall of 1977, and the months from October 1977 until today have been spent in extensive consultation with civil rights groups whose clientele are protected by these guidelines; employers, labor unions, and State and local governments whose employment practices are affected by these guidelines; State and local government antidiscrimination agencies who share with the Federal Government enforcement responsibility for discriminatory practices; and appropriate members of the general public. For example, an earlier draft of these guidelines was circulated informally for comment on October 28, 1977, pursuant to OMB Circular A-85. Many comments were received from representatives of State and local govern-

ments, psychologists, private employers, and civil rights groups. Those comments were taken into account in the draft of these guidelines which was published for comment December 30, 1977, 42 FR 66542.

More than 200 organizations and individuals submitted written comments on the December 30, 1977, draft. These comments were from representatives of private industry, public employers, labor organizations, civil rights groups, the American Psychological Association and components thereof, and many individual employers, psychologists, and personnel specialists. On March 3, 1978, notice was given of a public hearing and meeting to be held on April 10, 1978, 43 FR 9131. After preliminary review of the comments, the agencies identified four issues of particular interest, and invited testimony particularly on those issues, 43 FR 11812 (March 21, 1978). In the same notice the agencies published questions and answers on four issues of concern to the commenters. The questions and answers were designed to clarify the intent of the December 30, 1977, draft, so as to provide a sharper focus for the testimony at the hearing.

At a full day of testimony on April 10, 1978, representatives of private industry, State and local governments, labor organizations, and civil rights groups, as well as psychologists, personnel specialists, and others testified at the public hearing and meeting. The written comments, testimony, and views expressed in subsequent informal consultations have been carefully considered by the four agencies. We set forth below a summary of the comments, and the major issues raised in the comments and testimony, and attempt to explain how we have resolved those issues.

The statement submitted by the American Psychological Association (A.P.A.) stated that "these guidelines represent a major step forward and with careful interpretation can provide a sound basis for concerned professional work." Most of the A.P.A. comments were directed to clarifica-

tion and interpretation of the present language of the proposal. However, the A.P.A. recommended substantive change in the construct validity section and in the definition of work behavior.

Similarly, the Division of Industrial and Organizational Psychology (division 14) of the A.P.A. described the technical standards of the guidelines as "superior" in terms of congruence with professional standards to "most previous orders and guidelines but numerous troublesome aspects remain." Division 14 had substantial concerns with a number of the provisions of the general principles of the draft.

Civil rights groups generally found the uniform guidelines far superior to the FEA guidelines, and many urged their adoption, with modifications concerning ranking and documentation. Others raised concerns about the "bottom line" concept and other provisions of the guidelines.

The Ad Hoc Group on Employee Selection Procedures representing many employers in private industry supported the concept of uniform guidelines, but had a number of problems with particular provisions, some of which are described below. The American Society for Personnel Administration (ASPA) and the International Personnel Management Association, which represents State and local governments, generally took the same position as the ad hoc group. Major industrial unions found that the draft guidelines were superior to the FEA guidelines, but they perceived them to be inferior to the EEOC guidelines. They challenged particularly the bottom line concept and the construct validity section.

The building trade unions urged an exclusion of apprenticeship programs from coverage of the guidelines. The American Council on Education found them inappropriate for employment decisions concerning faculty at institutions of higher education. Other particular concerns were articulated by organizations representing the handicapped, licensing and certifying agencies, and college placement offices.

The Analysis of Comments on the Guidelines

The agencies' account of their handling of comments omits important facts. No explanation is provided for the radical alterations in the documentation requirements between the December 30, 1977 draft and the version of June 1978. Furthermore, the account of the response of Division 14 (Industrial and Organizational Psychology) of the American Psychological Association understates the intensity of the criticisms leveled by that group and fails to mention any of the Division's numerous objections.[17] This is especially unbalanced when compared to the particularity with which the concerns of civil rights groups are detailed. The same lack of specificity is found in the agencies' account of the comments of the Ad Hoc Group, the American Society for Personnel Administration (ASPA) and the International Personnel Management Association (IPMA).

---

[17]The agencies' failure to repeat fully the concerns of professional psychologists persists. Asked to comment on three newly proposed Questions and Answers in the Spring of 1980, the prestigious Test Committee of the American Psychological Association produced a letter expressing reservations about various pertinent Guidelines' provisions but stating that overall the Guidelines appear to be consistent with professional standards. This "endorsement" was taken out of context and publicized widely by EEOC and other government officials, without mentioning that the Committee had expressed reservations about important Guidelines' provisions. The government's conduct so disturbed Committee members that a second letter, expressly disclaiming any endorsement, was speedily submitted to the agencies and the Committee sought various ways to publicize its disassociation from the "endorsement" claimed by the government.

GENERAL PRINCIPLES:
ITEM 1

1. *Relationship between validation and elimination of adverse impact, and affirmative action.* Federal equal employment opportunity law generally does not require evidence of validity for a selection procedure if there is no adverse impact; e.g., *Griggs* v. *Duke Power Co.*, 401 U.S. 424. Therefore, a user has the choice of complying either by providing evidence of validity (or otherwise justifying use in accord with Federal law), or by eliminating the adverse impact. These options have always been present under Federal law, 29 CFR 1607.3; 41 CFR 60-3.3(a); and the Federal Executive Agency Guidelines, 41 FR 51734 (November 23, 1976). The December 30 draft guidelines, however, clarified the nature of the two options open to users.

Psychologists expressed concern that the December 30 draft of section 6A encouraged the use of invalid procedures as long as there is no adverse impact. Employers added the concern that the section might encourage the use of illegal procedures not having an adverse impact against the groups who have historically suffered discrimination (minorities, women), even if they have an adverse impact on a different group (whites, males).

Section 6A was not so intended, and we have revised it to clarify the fact that illegal acts purporting to be affirmative action are not the goal of the agencies or of the guidelines; and that any employee selection procedure must be lawful and should be as job related as possible. The delineation of examples of alternative procedures was eliminated to avoid the implication that particular procedures are either prescribed or are necessarily appropriate. The basic thrust of section 6A, that elimination of adverse impact is an alternative to validation, is retained.

The inclusion of excerpts from the 1976 Equal Employment Opportunity Coordinating Council Policy Statement on Affirmative Action in section 13B of the December 30 draft was criticized as not belonging in a set of guidelines for the validation of selection procedures. Section 13 has been revised. The general statement of policy in support of voluntary affirmative action, and the reaffirmation of the policy statement have been retained, but this statement itself is now found in the appendix to the guidelines.

General Principles

This section appears designed to supplement the eight sections of the Overview by addressing six legal and five technical issues that attracted substantial attention during the comment period after the Guidelines' initial publication. The arguments thus overlap major portions of the Overview and of the offical Guidelines text. This portion of the Analysis attempts to avoid repetition of prior comments in analyzing the agencies' arguments.

1. Relationship Between Validation and Elimination of Adverse Impact and Affirmative Action

The agencies open their defense of the concept that elimination of adverse impact is a lawful alternative to validation by observing that federal EEO law "generally" requires no validity evidence for a selection procedure that does not have adverse impact. For this proposition, *Griggs* is cited. As previously noted, this statement is accurate only if restricted to paper and pencil testing; in other contexts, numerous court decisions show that federal judges are capable of approaching the question of job-relatedness in a practical, common sense manner that is very different from the either/or approach of the Guidelines.

Thus a third "option" exists, which in legal terms might be called a factual showing of job-relatedness, where a selection procedure has all the appearance of being job-related and the circumstances suggest no reason to suspect discriminatory implementation. *Furnco Construction Co. v. Waters* is mentioned above in this connection; in *Furnco,* the Supreme Court accepted an employer's argument that refusal to hire unknown bricklayers at the job site for jobs requiring very sophisticated bricklaying skills was job-related. *Smith v. Olin Chemical, supra,* also appears in an earlier discussion; in *Olin* the Fifth Circuit accepted the job-relatedness of an employer's refusal to hire a black applicant who had a bad back for a job that required digging. There are similar cases in which courts have accepted the job-relatedness of standards that some minority group members or women alleged were discriminatory, such as physical agility (police), *Harless v. Duck,* 14 FEP Cases 1616 (N.D. Ohio 1977), a two-year college degree (museum guard), the ability to converse in English (hotel employee), having a neat appearance (supermarket clerk), or having a PhD (university professor), *Campbell v. Ramsay,* 484 F.Supp. 190 (E.D. Ark. 1980). It should be added that employers mounting a "common sense" defense should be sure that the job-relatedness of the procedure in question is self-apparent. Public employers operating under merit selection laws requiring selection of the "best qualified" may not be as able to rely on this kind of job-relatedness showing in lieu of formal validation.

The cases are not confined to situations in which the court accepted the obvious job-relatedness of a single job qualification. For example, in *Vanguard Justice Society v. Hughes,* 471 F.Supp. 670 (D. Md. 1979), the plaintiffs challenged the Baltimore police department's entire hiring and promotion system. While the court sustained their attacks on entry level and sergeant promotion examinations, it was unsympathetic to the attack on selection of high-ranking officers. The judge acknowledged that promotions above captain were completely tied to subjective determinations, but cited numerous cases to support the proposition that courts tend to tolerate subjective criteria as a function of the complexity of a job. Where there is no evidence that the subjective criteria are used to mask discrimination, the job-relatedness of such criteria may be accepted by the courts on the basis of their reasonableness.

The omission of yet a "fourth" option is perhaps an oversight: no mention is made that employers may seek to use procedures validated elsewhere where they discover that their own procedures have adverse impact. This option is, in fact, available, although the agencies have erected formidable, and in some respects professionally unrecognized, barriers to the transportability of validated selection procedures. See the discussion of Section 7 in Part III.

The agencies state that elimination of adverse impact as an alternative to validation has "always" been present under federal law. This is simply not true. Such an alternative was not mentioned in the 1966 EEOC Guidelines and its legality under §1981 as well as Title VII is at least doubtful. That is, it is one thing to use an unvalidated procedure having no adverse impact, but it is quite another thing to alter a procedure of unknown validity that has adverse impact with the express intention of reducing the number of successful whites or males in order to eliminate the adverse impact. While "reverse discrimination" is hardly the issue it was

GENERAL PRINCIPLES:
ITEM 1

1. *Relationship between validation and elimination of adverse impact, and affirmative action.* Federal equal employment opportunity law generally does not require evidence of validity for a selection procedure if there is no adverse impact; e.g., *Griggs* v. *Duke Power Co.*, 401 U.S. 424. Therefore, a user has the choice of complying either by providing evidence of validity (or otherwise justifying use in accord with Federal law), or by eliminating the adverse impact. These options have always been present under Federal law, 29 CFR 1607.3; 41 CFR 60-3.3(a); and the Federal Executive Agency Guidelines, 41 FR 51734 (November 23, 1976). The December 30 draft guidelines, however, clarified the nature of the two options open to users.

Psychologists expressed concern that the December 30 draft of section 6A encouraged the use of invalid procedures as long as there is no adverse impact. Employers added the concern that the section might encourage the use of illegal procedures not having an adverse impact against the groups who have historically suffered discrimination (minorities, women), even if they have an adverse impact on a different group (whites, males).

Section 6A was not so intended, and we have revised it to clarify the fact that illegal acts purporting to be affirmative action are not the goal of the agencies or of the guidelines; and that any employee selection procedure must be lawful and should be as job related as possible. The delineation of examples of alternative procedures was eliminated to avoid the implication that particular procedures are either prescribed or are necessarily appropriate. The basic thrust of section 6A, that elimination of adverse impact is an alternative to validation, is retained.

The inclusion of excerpts from the 1976 Equal Employment Opportunity Coordinating Council Policy Statement on Affirmative Action in section 13B of the December 30 draft was criticized as not belonging in a set of guidelines for the validation of selection procedures. Section 13 has been revised. The general statement of policy in support of voluntary affirmative action, and the reaffirmation of the policy statement have been retained, but this statement itself is now found in the appendix to the guidelines.

GENERAL PRINCIPLES:
ITEM 2

2. *The "bottom line" (section 4C).* The guidelines provide that when the overall selection process does not have an adverse impact the Government will usually not examine the individual components of that process for adverse impact or evidence of validity. The concept is based upon the view that the Federal Government should not generally concern itself with individual components of a selection process, if the overall effect of that process is nonexclusionary. Many commenters criticized the ambiguity caused by the word "generally" in the December 30 draft of section 4C which provided, "the Federal enforcement agencies * * * generally will not take enforcement action based upon adverse impact of any component" of a process that does not have an overall adverse impact. Employer groups stated the position that the "bottom line" should be a rule prohibiting enforcement action by Federal agencies with respect to all or any part of a selection process where the bottom line does not show adverse impact. Civil rights and some labor union representatives expressed the opposing concerns that the concept may be too restrictive, that it may be interpreted as a matter of law, and that it might allow certain discriminatory conditions to go unremedied.

The guidelines have been revised to clarify the intent that the bottom line concept is based upon administrative and prosecutorial discretion. The Federal agencies cannot accept the recommendation that they never inquire into or take enforcement action with respect to any component procedure unless the whole process of which it is a part has an adverse impact. The Federal enforcement agencies believe that enforcement action may be warranted in unusual circumstances, such as those involving other discriminatory practices, or particular selection procedures which have no validity and have a clear adverse impact on a national basis. Other unusual circumstances may warrant a high level agency decision to proceed with enforcement actions although the "bottom line" has been satisfied. At the same time the agencies adhere to the bottom line concept of allocating resources primarily to those users whose overall selection processes have an adverse impact. See overview, above, part III.

thought to be prior to *United Steelworkers of America v. Weber,* 443 U.S. 193 (1979), such deliberate reduction of the representation of one race or sex through manipulation of an unvalidated procedure seems risky. What if the whites/males show that the original procedure *was* job related and that the employer's modifications have destroyed its job-relatedness?

Although this section is titled "Relationship Between Validation and Elimination of Adverse Impact and Affirmative Action," there is no real effort to describe such a relationship. The agencies merely note that there was criticism of their inclusion of the 1976 EEOCC Policy Statement on Affirmative Action in the text of the draft Guidelines, that a general affirmation of their support for voluntary affirmative action has been retained and that the detailed statement of policy has been relegated to an "appendix".[18] The implication is that there

is a relationship between voluntary affirmative action and the Guidelines and this is stated elsewhere in the text. Voluntary affirmative action *is* desirable but this is not sufficient grounds to endorse (and, by implication, to require) such actions in a document purporting to set forth minimum criteria for compliance with laws regarding discrimination. There is *no obligation* under Title VII to engage in affirmative action and this has been stated so often that the agencies can hardly dispute it. Whether in the text or in the appendix, the 1976 EEOCC Statement includes statements of tenuous legality altogether. See discussion of Section 17, Part III. The Statement is, therefore, inappropriate for inclusion in or attachment to the Guidelines.

For a general discussion of the legal status of the Guidelines' position on use of alternatives, see the material in Section 6A in Part III.

2. The "Bottom Line" (Section 4C)

As already indicated, contrary to the agencies' statement here, the "bottom line" concept has been adopted by the courts as a controlling legal principle rather than as a nonbinding expression of policy regarding the agencies' exercise of prosecutorial discretion. The fundamental basis for the statistical discrimination cases upon which the concept of adverse impact relies is that the results of entire selection processes are examined on a job-by-job, job family or departmental basis. The relative rate of selection or a comparison of workforce representation and relevant external availability is the critical factor, *Lee v. City of Richmond,* 456 F.Supp. 756 (E.D. Va. 1978). (See discussion of Points II and III in the "Overview".) Where there is no overall ad-

verse impact, the *Griggs* analysis is inapplicable. This does not mean that the agencies are then altogether precluded from scrutinizing discriminatory components: the *McDonnell Douglas v. Green* analysis, showing disparate treatment, is available where there is the appearance of intent to discriminate in the use or maintenance of a component. But disparate treatment is outside the scope of the Guidelines; the agencies themselves acknowledge that only adverse impact calls the Guidelines into play.[19]

For a more extensive discussion of "bottom line" issues, see the material on Points II and III of the Overview and the material on Section 4C in Part III.

WARNING: As this volume went to press, the Second Circuit, in *Teal v. State of Connecticut,* 25 FEP Cases 529 (2d Cir. 1981), issued a ruling that, in effect, found the "bottom line" inconsistent with Title VII. See the discussion on page 97.

---

[18]The "appendix" appears as Section 17 of the Guidelines.

[19]This is not to say that job-relatedness defense to a *McDonnell Douglas prima facie* case cannot be shown by validation performed in compliance with the Guidelines. Validation could furnish an excellent partial defense, except that it does not meet the "intent" aspects of a *McDonnell Douglas* case and it is only one means of defending against a *prima facie* case of disparate treatment. See Section 11 in Part III.

GENERAL PRINCIPLES: ITEM 3

3. *Investigation of alternative selection procedures and alternative methods of use (section 3B)*. The December 30 draft included an obligation on the user, when conducting a validity study, to investigate alternative procedures and uses, in order to determine whether there are other procedures which are substantially equally valid, but which have less adverse impact. The American Psychological Association stated:

"We would concur with the drafters of the guidelines that it is appropriate in the determination of a selection strategy to consider carefully a variety of possible procedures and to think carefully about the question of adverse impact with respect to each of these procedures. Nevertheless, we feel it appropriate to note that a rigid enforcement of these sections, particularly for smaller employers, would impose a substantial and expensive burden on these employers."

Since a reasonable consideration of alternatives is consistent with the underlying principle of minimizing adverse impact consistent with business needs, the provision is retained.

Private employer representatives challenged earlier drafts of these guidelines as being inconsistent with the decision of the Supreme Court in *Albemarle Paper Co.* v. *Moody*, 422 U.S. 405. No such inconsistency was intended. Accordingly, the first sentence of section 3B was revised to paraphrase the opinion in the *Albemarle* decision, so as to make it clear that section 3B is in accord with the principles of the *Albemarle* decision.

Section 3B was further revised to clarify the intent of the guidelines that the obligation to investigate alternative procedures is a part of conducting a validity study, so that alter-native procedures should be evaluated in light of validity studies meeting professional standards, and that section 3B does not impose an obligation to search for alternatives if the user is not required to conduct a validity study.

Just as, under section 3B of the guidelines, a user should investigate alternative selection procedures as a part of choosing and validating a procedure, so should the user investigate alternative uses of the selection device chosen to find the use most appropriate to his needs. The validity study should address the question of what method of use (screening, grouping, or rank ordering) is appropriate for a procedure based on the kind and strength of the validity evidence shown, and the degree of adverse impact of the different uses.

GENERAL PRINCIPLES: ITEM 4

4. *Establishment of cutoff scores and rank ordering*. Some commenters from civil rights groups believed that the December 30 draft guidelines did not provide sufficient guidance as to when it was permissible to use a selection procedure on a ranking basis rather than on a pass-fail basis. They also objected to section 5G in terms of setting cutoff scores. Other comments noted a lack of clarity as to how the determination of a cutoff score or the use of a procedure for ranking candidates relates to adverse impact.

As we have noted, users are not required to validate procedures which do not have an adverse impact. However, if one way of using a procedure (e.g., for ranking) results in greater adverse impact than another way (e.g., pass/fail), the procedure must be validated for that use. Similarly, cutoff scores which result in adverse impact should be justified. If the use of a validated procedure for ranking results in greater adverse impact than its use as a screening device, the evidence of validity and utility must be sufficient to warrant use of the procedures as a ranking device.

A new section 5G has been added to clarify these concepts. Section 5H (formerly section 5G) addresses the choice of a cutoff score when a procedure is to be used for ranking.

GENERAL PRINCIPLES: ITEM 5

5. *Scope: Requests for exemptions for certain classes of users*. Some employer groups and labor organizations (e.g., academic institutions, large public employers, apprenticeship councils) argued that they should be exempted from all or some of the provisions of these guidelines because of their special needs. The intent of Congress as expressed in Federal equal employment opportunity law is to apply the same standards to all users, public and private.

These guidelines apply the same principles and standards to all employers. On the other hand, the nature of the procedures which will actually meet those principles and standards may be different for different employ-ers, and the guidelines recognize that fact. Accordingly, the guidelines are applicable to all employers and other users who are covered by Federal equal employment opportunity law.

Organizations of handicapped persons objected to excluding from the scope of these guidelines the enforcement of laws prohibiting discrimination on the basis of handicap, in particular the Rehabilitation Act of 1973, sections 501, 503, and 504. While this issue has not been addressed in the guidelines, nothing precludes the adoption of the principles set forth in these guidelines for other appropriate situations.

Licensing and certification boards raised the question of the applicability of the guidelines to their licensing and certification functions. The guidelines make it clear that licensing and certification are covered "to the extent" that licensing and certification may be covered by Federal equal employment opportunity law.

Voluntary certification boards, where certification is not required by law, are not users as defined in section 16 with respect to their certifying functions and therefore are not subject to these guidelines. If an employer relies upon such certification in making employment decisions, the employer is the user and must be prepared to justify, under Federal law that reliance as it would any other selection procedure.

3. Investigation of Alternative Selection Procedures and Alternative Methods of Use (Section 3B)

See the discussions of alternatives in the material relating to Point V of the Overview and Sections 3B and 6A in Part III of the Analysis.

4. Establishment of Cutoff Scores and Rank Ordering

The strict requirement of justifying ranking appears to violate both professional and legal concepts as to the employer's ability to choose employees on the basis of their relative qualifications, but the courts have been receptive to this provision.

See the material on justification of rank ordering and setting of cutoff scores in the discussion of Sections 3B, 5G, 5H, 14B (6), 14C (9) and 14D (1) in Part III.

5. Scope: Requests for Exemptions for Certain Classes of Users

The agencies' failure to take a firm position regarding the applicability of the Guidelines to licensing and certification boards is incorrect, as the weight of authority suggests that such boards are neither "employers" nor "employment agencies" within the meaning of Title VII and, therefore, cannot be subject to the Guidelines. It is true that *Puntolillo v. New Hampshire Racing Commission*, 375 F.Supp. 1089 (D. N.H. 1974), held that Title VII applied to a state licensing commission that allegedly denied a license and the use of stall space to a driver-trainer of horses because of his ethnic background. Similarly, in *Gill v. Monroe County Department of Social Services*, 79 F.R.D. 316 (W.D. N.Y. 1978), state departments of social services and civil service were held to be within Title VII because they controlled access to employment by a county's social services department. But these cases stand virtually alone. The closest parallel is *Sibley Memorial Hospital v. Wilson*, 488 F.2d 1338 (D.C. Cir. 1973), where a hospial that controlled the access of private nurses to employment by patients was held liable under Title VII for refusing to refer a male private nurse to female patients. A scattering of other cases have found Title VII liability in the absence of a direct employment relationship where the defendant controlled the plaintiff's access to employment and allegedly behaved in a discriminatory manner.

These cases are in the minority. In *Tyler v. Vickery*, 517 F.2d 1089 (5th Cir. 1975), *cert. denied*, 426 U.S. 940 (1976), the court declared that Title VII "does not apply [to the Georgia Board of Bar Examiners] by its terms, of course, because the [Board] is neither an 'employer'; an 'employment agency' nor a 'labor organiza-

tion' within the meaning of the statute." The court expressly rejected application of EEOC's testing guidelines to the Board's activities as a measure of constitutional compliance. The same rationale is applied to bar examinations in *Richardson v. McFadden*, 540 F.2d 744 (4th Cir. 1976); *Lewis v. Hartsock*, 18 FEP Cases 831 (S.D. Ohio, 1976); *Woodard v. Virginia Board of Bar Examiners*, 420 F.Supp. 211 (E.D. Va. 1976), *aff'd.*, 598 F.2d 1345 (4th Cir. 1979); *Delgado v. McTighe*, 442 F.Supp. 725 (E.D. Pa. 1977). In *EEOC v. Supreme Court of New Mexico*, 19 FEP Cases 448 (D.N.M. 1977), the court held that EEOC is without the power to investigate a charge that the state bar examination discriminates against minorities and women.

In *Lavender-Cabellero v. Department of Consumer Affairs*, 458 F.Supp. 213 (S.D. N.Y 1978), the agency that licensed process servers in New York City was held to be outside Title VII because it was not an employer. *Puntolillo* was distinguished as involving a state agency's exercise of proprietary rather than regulatory functions; the Racing Commission exercised sufficient control over maintenance and operation of the race track to justify treating it as an employer. A similar conclusion was reached in *NOW v. Waterfront Commission*, 468 F.Supp. 317 (S.D. N.Y. 1979), even though the Commission registered longshoremen and licensed hiring agents.

The agencies correctly exclude voluntary certification boards from the scope of the Guidelines. But requiring employers who rely upon such certification to justify that reliance is unrealistic. Hospitals cannot validate the examinations given by the national medical specialty boards, but they cannot afford to ignore the existence of such credentials.

GENERAL PRINCIPLES:
ITEM 6

6. *The "Four-Fifths Rule of Thumb"* (*section 4D*). Some representatives of employers and some professionals suggest that the basic test for adverse impact should be a test of statistical significance, rather than the four-fifths rule. Some civil rights groups, on the other hand, still regard the four-fifths rule as permitting some unlawful discrimination.

The Federal agencies believe that neither of these positions is correct.

The great majority of employers do not hire, promote, or assign enough employees for most jobs to warrant primary reliance upon statistical significance. Many decisions in day-to-day life are made on the basis of information which does not have the justification of a test of statistical significance. Courts have found adverse impact without a showing of statistical significance. *Griggs* v. *Duke Power Co.*, supra; *Vulcan Society of New York* v.

CSC of N.Y., 490 F. 2d 387, 393 (2d Cir. 1973); *Kirkland* v. *New York St. Dept. of Corr. Serv.*, 520 F. 2d 420, 425 (2d Cir. 1975).

Accordingly, the undersigned believe that while the four-fifths rule does not define discrimination and does not apply in all cases, it is appropriate as a rule of thumb in identifying adverse impact.

GENERAL PRINCIPLES:
TECHNICAL STANDARDS
ITEMS 7-11

Technical Standards

7. *Criterion-related validity* (*section 14B*). This section of the guidelines found general support among the commenters from the psychological profession and, except for the provisions concerning test fairness (sometimes mistakenly equated with differential prediction or differential validity), generated relatively little comment.

The provisions of the guidelines concerning criterion-related validity studies call for studies of fairness of selection procedures where technically feasible.

Section 14B(8). Some psychologists and employer groups objected that the concept of test fairness or unfairness has been discredited by professionals and pointed out that the term is commonly misused. We recognize that there is serious debate on the question of test fairness; however, it is accepted professionally that fairness should be examined where feasible. The A.P.A. standards for educational and psychological tests, for example, direct users to explore the question of fairness on finding a difference in group performances (section E9, pp. 43–44). Similarly the concept of test fairness is one which is closely related to the basic thrust of Federal equal employment opportunity law; and that concept was endorsed by the Supreme Court in *Albemarle Paper Co.* v. *Moody*, 422 U.S. 405.

Accordingly, we have retained in the guidelines the obligation upon users to investigate test fairness where it is technically feasible to do so.

8. *Content validity.* The Division of Industrial and Organizational Psychology of A.P.A. correctly perceived that the provisions of the draft guidelines concerning content validity, with their emphasis on observable work behaviors or work products, were "greatly concerned with minimizing the inferential leap between test and performance." That division expressed the view that the draft guidelines neglected situations where a knowledge, skill or ability is necessary to an outcome but where the work behavior cannot be replicated in a test. They recommended that the section be revised.

We believe that the emphasis on observable work behaviors or observable work products is appropriate; and that in order to show content validity, the gap between the test and performance on the job should be a small one. We recognize, however, that content validity may be appropriate to support a test which measures a knowledge, skill, or ability which is a necessary prerequisite to the performance of the job, even though the test might not be close enough to the work behavior to be considered a work sample, and the guidelines have been revised appropriately. On the other hand, tests of mental processes which are not directly observable and which may be difficult to determine on the basis of observable work behaviors or work products should not be supported by content validity.

Thus, the Principles for the Validation and Use of Personnel Selection Procedures (Division of Industrial and Organizational Psychology, American Psychological Association, 1975, p. 10), discuss the use of content validity to support tests of "specific items of knowledge, or specific job skills;" but call attention to the inappropriateness of attempting to justify tests for traits or constructs on a content validity basis.

9. *Construct validity* (*section 14D*). Business groups and professionals expressed concern that the construct validity requirements in the December 30 draft were confusing and technically inaccurate. As section 14D indicates, construct validity is a relatively new procedure in the field of personnel selection and there is not yet substantial guidance in the professional literature as to its use in the area of employment practices. The provisions on construct validity have been revised to meet the concerns expressed by the A.P.A. The construct validity section as revised clarifies what is required by the Federal enforcement agencies at this stage in the development of construct validity. The guidelines leave open the possibility that different evidence of construct validity may be accepted in the future, as new methodologies develop and become incorporated in professional standards and other professional literature.

10. *Documentation* (*section 15*). Commenters stated that the documentation section did not conform to the technical requirements of the guidelines or was otherwise inadequate. Section 15 has been clarified and two significant changes have been made to minimize the recordkeeping burden. (See overview, part VIII.)

11. *Definitions* (*section 16*). The definition of work behavior in the December 30, 1977 draft was criticized by the A.P.A. and others as being too vague to provide adequate guidance to those using the guidelines who must identify work behavior as a part of any validation technique. Other comments criticized the absence or inadequacies of other definitions, expecially "adverse impact." Substantial revisions of and additions to this section were therefore made.

6. The "Four-Fifths Rule of Thumb" (Section 4D)

See the discussion of the "four-fifths" rule in the material dealing with Point II of the Overview ("Adverse Impact") and with Section 4D in Part III.

Technical Standards

For discussion of the technical issues involved in General Principles 7 through 11, see the material regarding the appropriate section of the Guidelines in Part III.

PART III

Text of the
UNIFORM GUIDELINES
ON EMPLOYEE SELECTION
PROCEDURES

The ground covered by the prefatory "Supplementary Materials" (the "Overview of the 1978 Guidelines" and the "Analysis of Comments") is so comprehensive that points covered in the following discussion need be made only briefly in the analysis of the actual text of the Guidelines. Many matters, however, are not clearly raised in the prefatory material and are addressed below. Matters pertinent both to Guidelines text and Overview material are cross-referenced.

PART III: Guidelines Text—With Comprehensive Commentary, Including Legal and Professional Analyses

DOCUMENTATION OF IMPACT AND VALIDITY EVIDENCE

Executive Summary
General Principles

Sec. 1. Statement of Purpose

A. *Need for Uniformity: Issuing Agencies*

The EEO agencies' acknowledgment of the need for a uniform approach to the use of tests and other selection procedures is shared by employers and professional industrial psychologists. On the other hand, even though the agencies claim that there is consistency between the Guidelines and "Validation standards generally accepted by the psychological profession" (Q & A 1), the courts have tended to defer to the latter, as well as to congressional intent and a general rule of reasonableness, when provisions in government guidelines have been shown to be inconsistent with such standards.

B. *Purpose of Guidelines*

The purpose of assisting employers and others to comply with federal antidiscrimination law is appropri-ate and the statement that validation is not required in the absence of adverse impact is accurate. Professional standards encourage the use of valid selection procedures in all situations. The intended application of the Guidelines to religious discrimination, however, is incorrect.

C. *Relation to Prior Guidelines*

The statements contending that the Guidelines "have been built upon court decisions" and that they "are intended to be consistent with existing law" do not reflect the fact that there are inconsistencies between the Guidelines' provisions and a number of decisions rendered in Title VII related court cases. Also, this section fails to afford "grandfather" protection to validation studies made in accordance with earlier guidelines then in effect, or before any guidelines were in place.

Sec. 2. Scope

A. *Application of Guidelines*

The Guidelines are only directly applicable to the antidiscrimination provisions of Title VII, Executive Order 11246 and a number of statutes prohibiting discrimination by public sector employers. Compliance with the Guidelines does not assure that an employer is meeting its affirmative action obligations.

B. *Employment Decisions*

The claim that the Guidelines apply to tests and other selection procedures which are used as a basis for all "employment decisions" is probably too broad because the Guidelines can only be applied to selection procedures that lend themselves to a statistical measurement of adverse impact. The failure expressly to exclude licensing and certifying boards from coverage here and in Section 1B is inappropriate.

C. *Selection Procedures*

As the agencies state, the Guidelines "apply only to selection procedures used as a basis for making employment decisions" and therefore do not pertain directly to seniority systems. The endorsement of selection according to relative qualifications is appropriate, but since the agencies failed to address the issue of "bona fide merit systems" in the Guidelines, this topic must await judicial resolution. Also, in excluding "recruitment practices" from Guidelines coverage, the agencies fail to mention how these practices differ substantively from "selection procedures used as a basis for making employment decisions". Rather, this exclusion is inappropriately discussed in terms of the relationship which may exist between recruitment practices and the fulfillment of affirmative action obligations.

D. *Limitations*

The exclusion of the Age Discrimination in Employment Act and the Rehabilitation Act from Guidelines coverage is appropriate, although there is a possibility that the Guidelines may eventually influence the administration of those statutes. The failure to exclude the post-Civil War Civil Rights statutes (especially 42 U.S.C. §1981) from Guidelines coverage is incorrect.

Sec. 3. Discrimination Defined: Relationship Between Use of Selection Procedures and Discrimination

A. *Procedure Having Adverse Impact Constitutes Discrimination Unless Justified*

The proposition that a procedure having an "adverse impact" constitutes discrimination is consistent with the principles of *Griggs v. Duke Power Co.* if it is understood that (1) adverse impact establishes only a *prima facie* case of discrimination rather than *proof* of discrimination, (2) the differences in impact between minority and majority groups must be substantial and (3) court cases subsequent to *Griggs* have often allowed demonstrations of job-relatedness which reflected neither formal validation acceptable by the profession nor the specific requirements necessary to achieve validation in accordance with the Guidelines. Moreover, professional standards regarding formal validation are far more flexible than is the Guidelines' approach.

B. *Consideration of Suitable Alternative Selection Procedures*

The principle underlying Section 3B is reasonably

E. *Indian Preference Not Affected*

The exclusion of Indian preference legislation from Guidelines coverage is correct, but veterans' preferences should also have been mentioned.

appropriate. If an employer has a choice between two known, available and equally valid and useful selection procedures, the one chosen should be that which has the least adverse impact. An inappropriate provision in Section 3B imposes upon the user (employer) the burden of *searching* for alternative procedures and alternative methods of using validated procedures with less adverse impact when there exists a procedure at hand which has been validated. This latter provision is inconsistent as a strict requirement with the flexibility of professional practice, although a reasonable search for a valid alternative is generally appropriate. Moreover, since information about comparative validity and comparative degrees of adverse impact is often unobtainable, compliance with these provisions may be impossible to demonstrate. Professional principles stress maximizing the validity of selection procedures.

Comments on professional objections to the required justification for method of use are found at Section 5G.

Sec. 4. Information on Impact

A. *Records Concerning Impact*

It is inappropriate to require maintenance of data that is the burden of a plaintiff to produce in the first instance, although it may be informative, from a user's viewpoint, to monitor the "bottom line" impact of selection procedures.

B. *Applicable Race, Sex and Ethnic Groups for Recordkeeping*

The requirement that adverse impact records be kept on all sex and ethnic groups (no matter how small) is excessive because adverse impact calculations are required only for groups constituting two percent or more of the relevant labor market.

C. *Evaluation of Selection Rates: The "Bottom Line"*

As stated in the analysis of the Overview, the adoption of the "bottom line" principle—i.e., that the impact of components of an overall selection process will

not be examined if the overall procedure does not have adverse impact—is an appropriate feature of the Guidelines. However, the agencies have reserved a broad and undefined right to disregard the "bottom line" principle in any "circumstances" which they alone determine to be "unusual". Thus, even if an overall selection procedure meets the "bottom line", the agencies can, at their discretion, require the user to justify the individual components of that process by declaring the circumstances to be "unusual". The agencies have failed to appropriately document their need for such broad discretionary power in applying the "bottom line" principle, especially in light of the fact that Section 4C contains only two specific "unusual circumstances" which will destroy "bottom line" coverage. The list of components that the agencies state will require special attention despite a safe bottom line is legally questionable. Also, many employers feel that "bottom line" protection should be available when utilization matches the qualified labor market, especially when affirmative action efforts have distorted applicant flow data. This section apparently confuses the "bottom line" concept with measurement by "applicant flow/pool of eligibles" data. The section also raises serious questions about the definition of "applicant".

D. *Adverse Impact and the "Four-Fifths Rule"*

The provision that adverse impact will generally be found only when the selection rate for the least successful group is less than four-fifths (80 percent) of that of the most successful group is an appropriate rule of thumb. There is in this section, however, an implication that adverse impact may only be measured in terms of applicant flow/pool of eligibles data rather than by comparisons with relevant qualified area workforce statistics. If this is the agencies' intention, then because of the ambiguity surrounding the definition of "applicant", the utility of both the four-fifths rule and the "bottom line" concept will suffer. It also should be noted that most employers believe that the four-fifths rule is meaningful only when statistical significance supports the inference of adverse impact, although the agencies reject a rule of statistical significance. The statement that adverse impact will not be found if a change of race or sex of one person would eliminate the adverse impact is an inappropriate substitute. In addition, it is improper for the agencies to draw an inference of adverse impact when an employer does not keep the records required by Section 4A and there is "underutilization", as provided in this section. Many also feel that it is similarly inappropriate to transport impact data from other users when an employer's data are too small to be reliable but indicate adverse impact.

E. *Consideration of Users' Equal Employment Opportunity Posture*

The statement that the agencies will consider employers' general EEO posture is appropriate. However, this section over-emphasizes the employer's obligation to meet goals to the point that no mention is made of the good faith efforts required to meet them and it inappropriately limits the consideration of EEO posture to "the job or group of jobs in question".

Sec. 5. General Standards for Validation Studies

A. *Acceptable Types of Validity Studies*

The statement that the agencies permit reliance upon criterion-related, content or construct validity is appropriate. However, the contention that the three approved aspects of validity studies are co-equal is inconsistent with the validation sections of the Guidelines, which emphasize criterion-related validity over the others. This emphasis is inconsistent with professional opinion. Also, although provision is made for consideration of new strategies of validation, it is inappropriate to require these strategies to await agency evaluation even after "they become accepted by the psychological profession".

B. *Criterion-Related, Content and Construct Validity*

The Guidelines link proof of validity closely to "job performance" and fail to mention the importance of other considerations such as tenure, rate of progress, success in training programs, etc. This incorrectly implies that job performance is the only acceptable criterion.

C. *Guidelines are Consistent with Professional Standards*

Contrary to the agency's declaration, there are major inconsistencies between the Guidelines and professional standards.

D. *Need for Documentation of Validity*

E. *Accuracy and Standardization*

Section 5D states that full documentation for a validation study, as set forth in Section 15, is required for any selection procedure having an adverse impact and which is part of a selection process having an overall adverse impact. What this section fails to mention, however, is that the job-relatedness of a procedure may often be accepted by a court without formal validation. The agencies acknowledge the existence of this option in Section 6. Although accuracy and standardization are appropriate requirements in Section 5E, the level of documentation required by Section 15 exceeds that which is required by the profession for scientific inquiry.

F. *Caution Against Selection on Basis of Knowledges, Skills or Ability Learned in Brief Orientation Period*

This general rule is appropriate, but fails to give guidance for those cases in which employers cannot practically use even short training periods because of cost or safety factors. Rigid application of this section could undermine the usefulness of content validity and discourage the hiring of experienced candidates.

65

G. *Method of Use of Selection Procedures*

The requirement of Section 5G that an employer must separately justify the method in which scores on a validated procedure are used (i.e., pass/fail vs. ranking) exceeds professional opinion and practice. This requirement also reduces the practicability for some employers of using content validated procedures in most situations, especially where the procedure is not clearly a work sample. Some courts have utilized this requirement in cases involving content-valid procedures, but only in a context where the adverse impact of the method used (i.e., ranking) was substantial.

H. *Cutoff Scores*

Requiring that cutoff scores be set so as to reflect "normal expectations of acceptable proficiency" hampers employers from improving the quality of their workforce and is therefore neither legally justified nor professionally condoned.

I. *Use of Selection Procedures for Higher Level Jobs*

Section 5I permitting, under limited circumstances, the use of selection procedures which test for qualifications needed in jobs at a higher level than the one being filled is generally appropriate, but this section fails to recognize the difference between non-managerial and managerial as well as some other jobs in this context and fails to recognize that there are many variables (such as productivity, costs, etc.) which are relevant to specific selection situations requiring the consideration of qualifications of higher level jobs.

J. *Interim Use of Selection Procedures*

This section permits use of selection procedures while they are being validated if there is "substantial evidence of validity". This implies that the agencies will not take enforcement action while the study is being completed, which is appropriate. However, from a professional perspective, if there is "substantial evidence of validity" for a procedure from other sources, a user's failure to show validity for the procedure locally would most probably be due to technical inadequacies of the study rather than to a "true" lack of validity for that procedure. Another problem is the statement that this provision will not provide a defense in any legal action. Some employers believe that this deprives the "interim use" section of much of its practical value.

K. *Review of Validity Studies for Currency*

Section 5K deviates from professional standards in stating that the validation strategy used and changes in the relevant labor market are two factors which can affect currency. Currency is potentially affected by major changes in the job. Otherwise, the general requirement to review validity studies for currency is appropriate.

Sec. 6. Use of Selection Procedures Which Have Not Been Validated

A. *Use of Alternative Selection Procedures to Eliminate Adverse Impact*

This section provides that employers may eliminate adverse impact or implement an affirmative action plan by utilizing alternative procedures which are "as job related as possible". It can be noted, however, that it is possible for this strategy to result in illegal preferential action. Also, the agencies fail to identify examples of such procedures in this section.

B. *Where Validity Studies Cannot or Need Not Be Performed*
   (1) *Where informal or unscored procedures are used*
   (2) *Where formal and scored procedures are used*

This section acknowledges that there are circumstances in which an employer either cannot or need not utilize formal validation studies. Section B1 provides that where informal or unscored procedures having adverse impact are involved, the adverse impact should be eliminated or the procedure modified so that it can be validated or the procedure should be "otherwise justified" under federal law. This section fails to relate the fact that some courts have allowed showings of job-relatedness in the absence of formal validation. Section B (2), dealing with formal, scored procedures, fails to mention the possibility of transporting validity evidence from other users as an option in lieu of the recommended, though professionally inappropriate, "modification" of such procedures.

Sec. 7. Use of Other Validity Studies

A. *Validity Studies Not Conducted by the User*
B. *Use of Criterion-Related Validity Evidence from Other Sources*
   (1) *Validity evidence*
   (2) *Job similarity*
   (3) *Fairness evidence*
C. *Validity Evidence from Multi-Unit Study*

D. *Other Significant Variables*

Section 7 appropriately permits the "transportation" of validity studies conducted by other users and test publishers, but it contains the following shortcomings:

1. It fails to consider the problems of small employers who, as a matter of economics and practical necessity, must rely primarily on transported validity evidence.

2. The burden of proving the validity of transported procedures is too severe. Also, this section exceeds professional principles in its requirements for showing job similarity.

3. A "grandfather clause" is omitted, which apparently precludes the transportability of studies undertaken in accordance with earlier guidelines or before there were any guidelines in place.

4. The requirement for examining "fairness" is without sufficient professional support to warrant its inclusion. Also, since only criterion-related studies are mentioned specifically in 7B, there exists an implication that only criterion-related studies may be transported, even though the profession recognizes the possibility of transporting all three types of validity evidence.

5. Although Section 7C appropriately encourages multi-unit validation studies, it also refers to an exception that will be made in cases where undefined "variables" are likely to affect validity "significantly". Although Q and A 66 gives examples of such variables, most of them are professionally unsupportable. Section 7D also refers to such undefined "variables" and prohibits transportation of validity evidence where these "variables" are detected. The agencies fail to provide a rationale for the existence of these variables and similarly fail to demonstrate how it is that they are "likely to affect validity significantly".

Sec. 8. Cooperative Studies

A. *Encouragement of Cooperative Studies*
B. *Standards for Use of Cooperative Studies*

This section appropriately encourages the use of cooperative (consortium) studies by employers. However, as in Section 7, the agencies again make reference to professionally unsupported variables "which are likely to affect validity significantly".

Sec. 9. No Assumption of Validity

A. *Unacceptable Substitutes for Evidence of Validity*

B. *Encouragement of Professional Supervision*

In this section the agencies appropriately disallow the use of "general reputation" and other "casual" reports of validity as a substitute for validity evidence. The courts, however, have allowed demonstrations of job-relatedness without formal validity evidence in a number of situations. The encouragement of professional supervision is appropriate, but the emphasis placed upon conducting a "thorough job analysis" is not only inconsistent with other sections of the Guidelines, but also inconsistent with professional practice which is more flexible about the kind of job analysis that is appropriate under different circumstances.

Sec. 10. Employment Agencies and Employment Services

A. *Where Selection Procedures Are Devised by Agency*

B. *Where Selection Procedures Are Devised Elsewhere*

Section 10 and Q & A 63 do not appropriately distinguish the obligations and responsibilities of employment agencies from those of the employers utilizing them. While Q & A 63 imposes requirements on employers with respect to monitoring employment agency practices, selection procedures, impact data and validity evidence, Section 10 itself requires the employment agencies to comply with the Guidelines when adverse impact exists. Also, since many employment agencies are very small, it will probably be difficult for them to meet the recordkeeping and validation requirements imposed by Section 10.

Sec. 11. Disparate Treatment

Section 11 appropriately distinguishes between disparate treatment and adverse impact/validation, but inappropriately grants preferential treatment to persons who have been subject to earlier discrimination. This is inconsistent with Supreme Court decisions which have held that prior disparate treatment is *not* a legal basis for later preferential treatment. It is true, however, that employers generally may not subject identifiable victims of prior discrimination to standards more stringent than those imposed upon non-discriminatees during the period of discrimination. Otherwise employers are free to upgrade their standards.

Sec. 12. Retesting of Applicants

Encouragement of retesting of applicants is professionally acceptable within limits whenever alternate forms are available. It must be noted, however, that such situations are relatively unusual and retesting is often not technically feasible.

Sec. 13. Affirmative Action

A. *Affirmative Action Obligation*

B. *Encouragement of Voluntary Affirmative Action Programs*

This section appropriately notes that the affirmative action obligations of government contractors are not covered or affected by these Guidelines and that validation is not in itself "affirmative action". Section 13 B encourages other employers to adopt such programs voluntarily and endorses a policy statement on affirmative action for governmental employers which appears as an "appendix" labeled Section 17. These provisions are not, in substance, consistent with the purpose of the Guidelines.

Technical Standards

Sec. 14. Technical Standards for Validity Studies

This section appropriately allows the use of professionally developed validation techniques other than the three officially approved strategies. The language in this section is, however, inconsistent with that in Section 5 and with several of the Qs and As.

A. *Validity Studies Should Be Based on Review of Information About the Job*

Section 14A correctly states that a full job analysis is not necessary for certain performance measures used in criterion-related validity studies. It also is appropriately flexible regarding the method of conducting a job analysis.

B. *Technical Standards for Criterion-Related Validity Studies*

(1) *Technical feasibility*

Section 14B(1) appropriately permits job grouping and encourages the determination of technical feasibility for criterion-related validity studies. There are, however, two areas of inconsistency with professional standards: (1) the implication in this section that the only factor to be considered for feasibility is sample size and (2) the limitation of job groups to those jobs which have "substantially the same major work behaviors".

(2) *Analysis of the job*

Section B(2) provides for a review of job information and the determination of relevant measures of work behavior or performance. While this section's concern with rater bias appears noteworthy, it implies that rating bias can be quantified, which is contrary to professional opinion.

(3) *Criterion measures*

Section B(3) includes an appropriate discussion of criterion measures, but inappropriately suggests that only criterion-related studies are sufficient to show a relationship between job success and training success. Also, the agencies fail to provide a rationale for why they single out paper and pencil tests as criterion measures in need of close review.

(4) *Representativeness of the sample*

The basic requirement of Section B(4) is that the sample of subjects in a study should be representative of the "relevant labor market", including its racial, sexual and ethnic proportions. There is very little professional support for this concept, because it is derived from the theories of "differential validity" and "fairness" which a majority of professionals consider untenable. See Section 14B (8). In the opinion of many professionals, however, questions of sample "representativeness" are most appropriately addressed in terms of score distributions rather than any other characteristic.

(5) *Statistical relationships*

This section appropriately requires a statistically significant demonstration of the relationship between performance on the selection procedures and criterion measures.

(6) *Operational use of selection procedures*

Section B(6) lists several factors that should be considered in determining whether a procedure is appropriate for use. While generally appropriate, this section's primary emphasis on degree of adverse impact is inconsistent with professional principles.

(7) *Overstatement of validity evidence*

This section appropriately notes that validity evidence must not be overstated, as where a few statistically significant criterion measures are relied upon when many have been studied and validity has not been established for most of them. It should be noted, however, that commonly accepted statistical corrections (e.g., correction for criterion unreliability) are not viewed by the profession as techniques which overstate validity.

(8) *Fairness*

a. *Unfairness defined*
b. *Investigation of fairness*
c. *General considerations in fairness investigations*

The "fairness" concept assumes that if a selection procedure does not produce results that reflect "parity" for group membership in the test population, there is reason to study the "fairness" of the procedure for each group to see if the procedure is equally predictive for each. The agencies' inclusion of the "fairness" concept in the Guidelines is legally indefensible and professionally unsupported. Parity is not required by Title VII, and a selection procedure valid under professional standards is sufficient to meet any legally required showing of job-relatedness in most circumstances. The "fairness" concept is closely linked to the professionally discredited statistical concept of "differential validity". There is no professionally agreed-upon model for evaluating "fairness". The further introduction of the concept of item unfairness in the Qs and As is similarly unjustified professionally. In practice, however, the conditions under which the Guidelines require fairness studies will probably seldom occur.

d. *When "unfairness" is shown*

This section, B(8)(d), relates three ways of dealing with unfairness: changing the method of use of the procedure, using a different validated procedure or deleting portions of the procedure that are the source of the unfairness. Such reactions will either invalidate the procedure or harm minorities more than whites, as the little evidence of unfairness that exists suggests that "passing" scores for minorities would have to be set higher than those set for whites.

e. *Technical feasibility of fairness studies*

This section correctly implies that "fairness" studies are rarely technically feasible, especially for smaller employers.

f. *Continued use of selection procedures when fairness studies are not feasible*

This section allows continued use of a selection procedure where a fairness study is not technically feasible except where the infeasibility allegedly results from *prior* discriminatory practices. The exception is legally unjustified.

C. *Technical Standards for Content Validity Studies*

(1) *Appropriateness of content validity studies*

The statement that content validity can support a selection procedure which is "a representative sample of the content of the job" is accurate only if it is clear that it is appropriate to use a content valid procedure which is a representative sample of one or more critical work behaviors of the job rather than of the entire job. The statement that content validity is not appropriate for knowledges, skills or abilities which an employee will be expected to learn on the job is inconsistent with professional opinion. The total exclusion of personal qualities from content validation apparently ignores legal and professional support for a broader reading of "abilities" than is permitted by the Guidelines.

(2) *Job analysis for content validity*

This section emphasizes a "task-oriented" job analysis of observable behavior, although the Section 16 definition of "work behavior" appropriately includes mental as well as physical components of work behavior. The emphasis on critical work behaviors, however, is consistent with professional opinion.

(3) *Development of selection procedures*

This section appropriately permits the development of selection procedures from job analysis and the use of procedures previously developed by the user, other users, or publishers.

(4) *Standards for demonstrating content validity*

This section inappropriately emphasizes that a test or other selection procedure must mirror the specific observable behavioral contents of the job with virtual replication of manner and setting. This is inconsistent with professional standards, which go beyond a work-sample approach in order to identify critical knowledges, skills and abilities, as acknowledged elsewhere in Section 14C.

(5) *Reliability*

Reliability is a professionally accepted matter of concern and it is appropriate to produce statistical estimates, when possible, as suggested here.

(6) *Prior training or experience*

This section obligates employers who require prior training or experience for a job to justify all such requirements as virtual replication of job content. Although the profession recognizes the necessity for showing some relationship between experience requirements and job content, the level required by the Guidelines exceeds professional standards.

(7) *Content validity of training success*

This section appropriately requires training programs to be relevant to job content, but again reflects a professionally unacceptable emphasis on virtual identicalness of the selection procedure and observable work behavior.

(8) *Operational use*

The emphasis on the observable, as noted above, is inconsistent with professional opinion.

(9) *Ranking based on content validity studies*

This section requires an employer to justify separately ranking of candidates on the basis of a content validated procedure. This is inconsistent with professional principles and, in effect, requires a criterion-related study if a content valid test is to be useful.

D. *Technical Standards for Construct Validity Studies*

(1) *Appropriateness of construct validity studies*
(2) *Job analysis for construct validity*
(3) *Relationship to the job*
(4) *Use of construct validity study without new criterion-related evidence*
a. *Standards for use*
b. *Determination of common work behaviors*

The Guidelines for construct validity given in Section 14D tend to preclude the use of this method of validation except as a strategy subordinate to criterion-related validation. This approach is a subject of professional debate. The implication given in Section 14D is that the construct method is quite new, very difficult and little understood. This is professionally incorrect.

Sec. 15. Documentation of Impact and Validity Evidence

A. *Required Information*

It is incorrect to require the maintenance of impact data for every job (Q and A 27) and incorrect to suggest that all instances of adverse impact trigger the necessity for having validity evidence. See Section 5B and Section 6. Concern with discrimination in job assignment patterns fails to consider all of the variables which can impact on job assignments.

(1) *Simplified recordkeeping for users with less than 100 employees*

This section fails to offer this option to large employers' small facilities and jobs with relatively few incumbents. Also, the ambiguity surrounding the meaning of "applicant" may make it difficult to meet the requirements of this section.

> (2) *Information on impact*
>> a. *Collection of information on impact*

The requirement that data be maintained on all groups is contrary to professional recommendations and legal requirements. (See also Section 4B.)

>> b. *When adverse impact has been eliminated in the total selection process*

The agencies fail to provide a rationale for why impact data on components must be kept for two years after overall adverse impact has been eliminated.

>> c. *When data are insufficient to determine impact*

Impact data cumulated over many years would be of questionable value because economic and population changes, among others, may readily contaminate it.

> (3) *Documentation of validity evidence*
>> a. *Types of evidence*

This section notes the different requirements that follow for the several validity strategies.

>> b. *Form of report*

The presence of a limited "grandfather" clause for pre-Guideline studies is appropriate.

>> c. *Completeness*

It is appropriate that users are given an opportunity to explain the absence of "essential" information.

B. *Criterion-Related Validity Studies*

Section 15B contains a total of 32 "essential items". If applied literally, this section would probably never be satisfied. Also, new substantive requirements are included in this section, which purports to list only documentation standards. These added requirements include:

—a requirement in Section 15B (8) for data on every group which is a factor in the labor market and not just the group which was included in the study;

—a requirement in Section 15B (10) for reporting "utility" as well as validity.

> (1) *User(s), location(s) and date(s) of study*

This could be a difficult record to maintain by "date(s)" and "location(s)" because the person conducting a validity study gathers a knowledge of job requirements in many ways, from many sources and at different times.

> (2) *Problem and setting*

The encouragement of narrative explanation of a study's purpose is consistent with professional recommendations.

> (3) *Job analysis or review of job information*

Because of ambiguities, it is possible for a professionally performed job analysis to fail to meet the requirements of Section 15B (3).

> (4) *Job titles and codes*

This requirement is not inappropriate, but no rationale is provided for why D.O.T. codes are necessary, especially since job analysis results or a review of job information must be included anyway.

> (5) *Criterion measures*

Although there may be some overlap with Section 15 B (2) in the required narrative rationale for the choice of criterion measures, the requirement itself is appropriate as is the required description of the mechanics of data collection. However, the requirement that "appraisal forms" and "instructions to raters" be included in the records kept exceeds professional recommendations.

> (6) *Sample description*

A description of the research sample is essential, as indicated here, but some of the "desirable" data exceed those recommended in professional standards.

> (7) *Description of selection procedures*

An explicit description of selection procedures is appropriate, but it would generally be unprofessional to submit the actual procedures themselves unless certain conditions are met. (See Section 15B (7) in text.)

> (8) *Techniques and results*

This section appropriately requires a description of methods of analyzing data, but inappropriately includes a requirement that measures of "central tendency" and of "dispersion" be reported for each sex, race and ethnic group that is a significant factor in the relevant labor market. It is professionally appropriate to include data only for each group which is of sufficient size in the study sample to make such reporting reliable. The requirement for studies of test "fairness" is likewise inappropriate. (See Section 14B (8).)

> (9) *Alternative procedures investigated*

While professional practice may include an investigation of various techniques, there are legal and professional objections to the type of search for alternatives required by the Guidelines. (See Section 6A.)

> (10) *Uses and applications*

Professional standards dictate that the research undertaken should support the method of use recommended by the researcher. The requirement that different methods of use be examined for comparative adverse impact is inconsistent with professional standards as is the implication that method of use should be unchanged regardless of changes in such things as the economy, needs of the employer, etc.

71

(11) *Source data*

Although some specific requirements of this section exceed professional standards, it is correct in principle to require researchers to record pertinent data on individual sample members for a reasonable period of time.

(12) *Contact person*

Furnishing information about the contact person is an appropriate requirement.

(13) *Accuracy and completeness*

Attention to matters of accuracy and completeness is professionally appropriate.

C. *Content Validity Studies*

Section 15C is similar in its strengths and weaknesses to Section 15B. Some issues that employers should be aware of include:

(1) It requires a total of 19 "essential items", making literal compliance difficult to achieve.

(2) New substantive requirements are included in this section, which purports to list only documentation standards. These include:

—a requirement that the employer justify time limits for job performance,

—a requirement that utility studies be conducted.

In most respects, the documentation requirements in this section parallel those for criterion-related studies and the commentary in Section 15B adequately pertains to the requirements of Section 15C. Additionally, it can be noted that comparing the validity of alternatives is meaningless when applied to content validity, the job analysis requirements exceed those required by the profession as applied to content validation and (as discussed in Section 14A and elsewhere) the required, though professionally unsupported, justification for ranking as a method of use removes content validity from the status of equality with other validation strategies which the Guidelines claim it should have.

D. *Construct Validity Studies*

The commentary in Section 15B and 15C adequately pertain to documentation requirements for construct validity studies. Additionally, however, this section inappropriately emphasizes observable behavior in the job analysis section and fails to recognize that construct validation may rely, in part, on studies not conducted by the user.

E. *Evidence of Validity from Other Studies*

(1) *Evidence from criterion-related validity studies*

It is appropriate to require evidence that external studies are relevant, but otherwise the requirements here (such as a full description of job behaviors) exceed those required by the profession.

(2) *Evidence from content validity studies*

See Sections 14C (3) and 15C.

(3) *Evidence from construct validity studies*

See Section 15E (1).

F. *Evidence of Validity from Cooperative Studies*

This section inappropriately requires that the provisions of Section 15E be satisfied.

G. *Selection for Higher Level Jobs*

This section incorrectly implies that employers have a definite program of progression which virtually all employees experience. This is inappropriate for many employers, especially at the managerial level, where general categories rather than specific positions are more useful for study purposes. Therefore, the requirements in this section call for specific data which may not be pertinent to many employers.

H. *Interim Use of Selection Procedures*

Comments pertinent here have been made elsewhere. See Section 5H and, for criterion-related studies, see Section 14B (8) (f).

Sec. 16. Definitions

Some definitions are incomplete and some are incorrect. Their impact on the substantive requirements of the Guidelines is noted in the commentary above where appropriate.

Appendix
Sec. 17. Policy Statement on Affirmative Action

The desirability of affirmative action for most employers is not an issue, but the Appendix is of questionable propriety for Guidelines intending to set forth minimum standards for Title VII compliance. Moreover, a number of concepts in the statement are legally unsound and/or inconsistent with other Guidelines' provisions.

General Principles

GENERAL PRINCIPLES
SECTION 1A:
UNIFORMITY

SECTION 1. *Statement of purpose.—A. Need for uniformity—Issuing agencies.* The Federal government's need for a uniform set of principles on the question of the use of tests and other selection procedures has long been recognized. The Equal Employment Opportunity Commission, the Civil Service Commission, the Department of Labor, and the Department of Justice jointly have adopted these uniform guidelines to meet that need, and to apply the same principles to the Federal Government as are applied to other employers.

I. PURPOSE AND SCOPE

1. Q. What is the purpose of the Guidelines?

A. The guidelines are designed to aid in the achievement of our nation's goal of equal employment opportunity without discrimination on the grounds of race, color, sex, religion or national origin. The Federal agencies have adopted the Guidelines to provide a uniform set of principles governing use of employee selection procedures which is consistent with applicable legal standards and validation standards generally accepted by the psychological profession and which the Government will apply in the discharge of its responsibilities.

3. Q. Who is covered by the Guidelines?

A. The Guidelines apply to private and public employers, labor organizations, employment agencies, apprenticeship committees, licensing and certification boards (see Question 7), and contractors or subcontractors, who are covered by one or more of the following provisions of Federal equal employment opportunity law: Title VII of the Civil Rights Act of 1964, as amended by the Equal Employment Opportunity Act of 1972 (hereinafter Title VII); Executive Order 11246, as amended by Executive Orders 11375 and 12086 (hereinafter Executive Order 11246); the State and Local Fiscal Assistance Act of 1972, as amended; Omnibus Crime Control and Safe Streets Act of 1968, as amended; and the Intergovernmental Personnel Act of 1970, as amended. Thus, under Title VII, the Guidelines apply to the Federal Government with regard to Federal employment. Through Title VII they apply to most private em-

ployers who have 15 or more employees for 20 weeks or more a calendar year, and to most employment agencies, labor organizations and apprenticeship committees. They apply to state and local governments which employ 15 or more employees, or which receive revenue sharing funds, or which receive funds from the Law Enforcement Assistance Administration to impose and strengthen law enforcement and criminal justice, or which receive grants or other federal assistance under a program which requires maintenance of personnel standards on a merit basis. They apply through Executive Order 11246 to contractors and subcontractors of the Federal Government and to contractors and subcontractors under federally-assisted construction contracts.

SECTION 1B:
PURPOSE

B. *Purpose of guidelines.* These guidelines incorporate a single set of principles which are designed to assist employers, labor organizations, employment agencies, and licensing and certification boards to comply with requirements of Federal law prohibiting employment practices which discriminate on grounds of race, color, religion, sex, and national origin. They are designed to provide a framework for determining the proper use of tests and other selection procedures. These guidelines do not require a user to conduct validity studies of selection procedures where no adverse impact results. However, all users are encouraged to use selection procedures which are valid, especially users operating under merit principles.

II. ADVERSE IMPACT, THE BOTTOM LINE AND AFFIRMATIVE ACTION

9. Q. Do the Guidelines require that only validated selection procedures be used?

A. No. Although validation of selection procedures is desirable in personnel management, the Uniform Guidelines require users to produce evidence of validity only when the selection procedure adversely affects the opportunities of a race, sex, or ethnic group for hire, transfer, promotion, retention or other employment decision. If there is no adverse impact, there is no validation requirement under the Guidelines. Sections 1B and 3A. See also, Section 6A.

General Principles

Section 1. Statement of Purpose

1A. Need for Uniformity–Issuing Agencies

LEGAL ANALYSIS

Federal uniformity in this field is universally desired, but the courts have also recognized that government standards must be flexible and consistent with professional recommendations, court precedent and "reason". When asked to choose between the widely criticized 1970 EEOC Guidelines and the more realistic 1976 Federal Executive Agency Guidelines, the courts elected to follow the latter. See, e. g., *Friend v. Leidinger; Commonwealth v. O'Neill,* 465 F. Supp. 451 (E.D. Pa. 1979). In addition, where government guidelines have diverged from professionally acceptable standards (i.e., the 1974 Standards for Educational and Psychological Tests of the American Psychological Association (APA), the American Educational Research Association and the National Council on Measurement in Education, and the 1975 APA Division 14 Principles for the Validation and Use of Personnel Selection Procedures), courts have deferred to professional standards in preference to the guidelines. *United States v. South Carolina,* 445 F. Supp. 1094 (D.S.C. 1977), *aff'd. mem.* 434 U.S. 1026 (1978); *White v. City of Suffolk,* 460 F. Supp. 516 (E.D. Va. 1978). The present Uniform Guidelines have been criticized in a lengthy opinion by the Second Circuit Court of Appeals, *Guardians Association v. Civil Service Commission,* 23 FEP Case 909 (2d Cir., 1980), for excessive rigidity. The Court expressly stated that the Guidelines are merely one kind of expert opinion, that of the government agencies that drafted the Guidelines, and that their authority must be tempered by the courts' view of Congressional intent and a general standard of reasonableness. This appears to refute the claims for Guidelines superiority reflected in Q and A 40. See Sections 1C and 5C, below.

PROFESSIONAL ANALYSIS

Professionals encourage uniformity in the setting of minimum compliance guidelines by government agencies. The history of the Guidelines and the need for uniformity are set out in Parts I and II.

1B. Purpose of Guidelines

LEGAL ANALYSIS

The attempt to develop a simple set of principles "to assist" employers and others "to comply with requirements of Federal law prohibiting" discriminatory employment practices is appropriate and necessary. For reasons stated in the material addressed to the Overview: General Principle 5 and to the prefatory "Adoption of Employee Selection Procedures" in Part II of the Analysis, coverage of race, national origin and sex discrimination by the Guidelines is undisputed. Mention of discrimination based on religion in connection with the Guidelines, however, is questionable. There is no precedent for a statistical approach to religious discrimination and therefore adverse impact analysis is not appropriate in the context of Title VII religious discrimination law, even if it were possible to maintain such statistics.

PROFESSIONAL ANALYSIS

This section defines the purpose of the Guidelines as providing the framework for proper use of selection procedures based on either validation or the absence of adverse impact. Professional standards deal only with the question of validation. Concerns for the presence or absence of adverse impact and accompanying affirmative action principles are legitimate corporate goals and may be endorsed by professionals in their role as corporate citizens. However, when acting in their role as professionals, industrial psychologists endorse and encourage the use of valid selection procedures in all situations. The greater the validity (i.e., formal, professionally acceptable showing of job-relatedness) of selection procedures, the greater the likelihood that qualified individuals, regardless of group membership,

75

SECTION 1B: PURPOSE

B. *Purpose of guidelines.* These guidelines incorporate a single set of principles which are designed to assist employers, labor organizations, employment agencies, and licensing and certification boards to comply with requirements of Federal law prohibiting employment practices which discriminate on grounds of race, color, religion, sex, and national origin. They are designed to provide a framework for determining the proper use of tests and other selection procedures. These guidelines do not require a user to conduct validity studies of selection procedures where no adverse impact results. However, all users are encouraged to use selection procedures which are valid, especially users operating under merit principles.

II. ADVERSE IMPACT, THE BOTTOM LINE AND AFFIRMATIVE ACTION

9. Q. Do the Guidelines require that only validated selection procedures be used?

A. No. Although validation of selection procedures is desirable in personnel management, the Uniform Guidelines require users to produce evidence of validity only when the selection procedure adversely affects the opportunities of a race, sex, or ethnic group for hire, transfer, promotion, retention or other employment decision. If there is no adverse impact, there is no validation requirement under the Guidelines. Sections 1B and 3A. See also, Section 6A.

SECTION 1C: RELATION TO PRIOR GUIDELINES

C. *Relation to prior guidelines.* These guidelines are based upon and supersede previously issued guidelines on employee selection procedures. These guidelines have been built upon court decisions, the previously issued guidelines of the agencies, and the practical experience of the agencies, as well as the standards of the psychological profession. These guidelines are intended to be consistent with existing law.

SECTION 2A: APPLICATION

SEC. 2. *Scope.*—A. *Application of guidelines.* These guidelines will be applied by the Equal Employment Opportunity Commission in the enforcement of title VII of the Civil Rights Act of 1964, as amended by the Equal Employment Opportunity Act of 1972 (hereinafter "Title VII"); by the Department of Labor, and the contract compliance agencies until the transfer of authority contemplated by the President's Reorganization Plan No. 1 of 1978, in the administration and enforcement of Executive Order 11246, as amended by Executive Order 11375 (hereinafter "Executive Order 11246"); by the Civil Service Commission and other Federal agencies subject to section 717 of Title VII; by the Civil Service Commission in exercising its responsibilities toward State and local governments under section 208(b)(1) of the Intergovernmental-Personnel Act; by the Department of Justice in exercising its responsibilities under Federal law; by the Office of Revenue Sharing of the Department of the Treasury under the State and Local Fiscal Assistance Act of 1972, as amended; and by any other Federal agency which adopts them.

will be selected to perform particular jobs maximizing the overall productivity of the organization. This is not to deny the acceptance of affirmative action principles as a legitimate corporate objective, but rather to point out that professional standards encourage the development of selection procedures that enhance the likelihood of selecting· persons whose qualifications will enable them to succeed in the opportunities made available to them.

The discussion of Section 14 and 15 later in Part III

demonstrates that the agencies' view of validity differs in many ways from that recognized by the profession. Moreover, the agencies' endorsement of the use of valid selection procedures is qualified by the provisions of Section 6 of the Guidelines endorsing the use of non-validated selection procedures having little adverse impact as an alternative to validation, a practice that is not consistent with professional recommendations. See Q and A 9.

1C. Relation to Prior Guidelines ——————————————————————————

LEGAL ANALYSIS

The Guidelines are undoubtedly "built upon" some court decisions, but some provisions seem contrary to other court decisions of at least equal authority.

The failure of the Guidelines to provide "grandfather" protection for validation studies which were completed prior to the issuance of guidelines or that complied with prior guidelines in effect at the time such studies were performed is of concern, although perhaps ameliorated by the partial "grandfather" clause applicable to validation reports in Section 15A (3) (b), Form of Report. This omission of protection could render decades of valuable research useless and already has been seized upon by at least one court —*Allen v. City of Mobile*— to invalidate a test developed and used several years prior to the adoption of the Uniform Guidelines. The danger is that employers may be pressured to replace existing selection procedures with

newer procedures whose only superiority is their greater conformance to current Guidelines. It also may be noted that the very fact that the present Guidelines are inconsistent with the EEOC's initial interpretations of federal requirements in the 1966 Guidelines undermines their authority as agency interpretations having "great weight" with the courts. See *General Electric Co. v. Gilbert,* 429 U.S. 125 (1976).

PROFESSIONAL ANALYSIS

In Section 5C, the agencies state that the Guidelines are intended to be consistent with professional standards and here they indicate that the Guidelines are "built upon" professional standards, among other sources. As is shown in the comments on Section 5C and elsewhere, however, the Guidelines are not always consistent with professional standards in significant respects.

Section 2. Scope

2A. Application of Guidelines ——————————————————————————

LEGAL ANALYSIS

See the discussion of the scope of the Guidelines in Part I of the Legal and Professional Analysis and in the Overview material in Part II of the Analysis.

As discussed in Part I, the issue of validation is separate from that of affirmative action. Compliance with the validation requirements may not satisfy all of a government contractor's obligations under E.O. 11246, particularly with respect to affirmative action. For example, an employer validates a test in compliance with the requirements of the Guidelines. The use of this test,

however, results in adverse impact. Validation insulates the employer against "affected class" liability, provided the test is properly used, but it does not necessarily provide a defense against the employer's failure to meet goals and timetables established under E.O. 11246 and other affirmative action requirements. Affirmative action commitments may require more than a showing that the selection procedures are job-related — for example, the employer may be faulted by OFCCP for failure to promote in a manner likely to attract minority or female candidates.

SECTION 2B:
EMPLOYMENT DECISIONS

B. *Employment decisions.* These guidelines apply to tests and other selection procedures which are used as a basis for any employment decision. Employment decisions include but are not limited to hiring, promotion, demotion, membership (for example, in a labor organization), referral, retention, and licensing and certification, to the extent that licensing and certification may be covered by Federal equal employment opportunity law. Other selection decisions, such as selection for training or transfer, may also be considered employment decisions if they lead to any of the decisions listed above.

5. Q. Do the Guidelines apply only to written tests?

A. No. They apply to all selection procedures used to make employment decisions, including interviews, review of experience or education from application forms, work samples, physical requirements, and evaluations of performance. Sections 2B and 16Q, and see Question 6.

6. Q. What practices are covered by the Guidelines?

A. The Guidelines apply to employee selection procedures which are used in making employment decisions, such as hiring, retention, promotion, transfer, demotion, dismissal or referral. Section 2B. Employee selection procedures include job requirements (physical, education, experience), and evaluation of applicants or candidates on the basis of application forms, interviews, performance tests, paper and pencil tests, performance in training programs or probationary periods, and any other procedures used to make an employment decision whether administered by the employer or by an employment agency. See Section 2B.

7. Q. Do the Guidelines apply to the licensing and certification functions of state and local governments?

A. The Guidelines apply to such functions to the extent that they are covered by Federal law. Section 2B. The courts are divided on the issue of such coverage. The Government has taken the position that at least some kinds of licensing and certification which deny persons access to employment opportunity may be enjoined in an action brought pursuant to Section 707 of the Civil Rights Act of 1964, as amended.

LEGAL ANALYSIS

Q and A 6 is perhaps misleading. It suggests that the Guidelines apply to all ''selection procedures'', but the Guidelines really apply only to selection procedures that lend themselves to statistical measurement of adverse impact. For example, where certain information on application forms is not actually used in selection decisions, it would be impossible to determine whether such information had adverse impact. This also is often true with such information as interviewer comments.

Even though the inclusion of licensing and certifying activities is now accompanied by a qualification that the extension of coverage to licensing and certification boards is limited to the extent that licensing and certifying may be covered by federal equal employment opportunity law, the continued inclusion of any of these activities in any form in the Guidelines is questionable. See Q and A 7 and also the discussion in Part II, Analysis of Comments, General Principle 5, ''Requests for Exemptions for Certain Classes of Users''.

SECTION 2C:
SELECTION PROCEDURES

C. *Selection procedures.* These guidelines apply only to selection procedures which are used as a basis for making employment decisions. For example, the use of recruiting procedures designed to attract members of a particular race, sex, or ethnic group, which were previously denied employment opportunities or which are currently underutilized, may be necessary to bring an employer into compliance with Federal law, and is frequently an essential element of any effective affirmative action program; but recruitment practices are not considered by these guidelines to be selection procedures. Similarly, these guidelines do not pertain to the question of the lawfulness of a seniority system within the meaning of section 703(h), Executive Order 11246 or other provisions of Federal law or regulation, except to the extent that such systems utilize selection procedures to determine qualifications or abilities to perform the job. Nothing in these guidelines is intended or should be interpreted as discouraging the use of a selection procedure for the purpose of determining qualifications or for the purpose of selection on the basis of relative qualifications, if the selection procedure had been validated in accord with these guidelines for each such purpose for which it is to be used.

31. Q. Section 6A authorizes the use of alternative selection procedures to eliminate adverse impact, but does not appear to address the issue of validity. Thus, the use of alternative selection procedures without adverse impact seems to be presented as an option in lieu of validation. Is that its intent?

A. Yes. Under Federal equal employment opportunity law the use of any selection procedure which has an adverse impact on any race, sex or ethnic group is discriminatory unless the procedure has been properly validated, or the use of the procedure is otherwise justified under Federal law. *Griggs* v. *Duke Power Co.,* 401 U.S. 424 (1971); Section 3A. If a selection procedure has an adverse impact, therefore, Federal equal employment opportunity law authorizes the user to choose lawful alternative procedures which eliminate the adverse impact rather than demonstrating the validity of the original selection procedure.

Many users, while wishing to validate all of their selection procedures, are not able to conduct the validity studies immediately. Such users have the option of choosing alternative techniques which eliminate adverse impact, with a view to providing a basis for determining subsequently which selection procedures are valid and have as little adverse impact as possible.

Apart from Federal equal employment opportunity law, employers have economic incentives to use properly validated selection procedures. Nothing in Section 6A should be interpreted as discouraging the use of properly validated selection procedures; but Federal equal employment opportunity law does not require validity studies to be conducted unless there is adverse impact. See Section 2C.

80. Q. Under content validity, may a selection procedure for entry into a job be justified on the grounds that the knowledges, skills or abilities measured by the selection procedure are prerequisites to successful performance in a training program?

A. Yes, but only if the training material and the training program closely approximate the content and level of difficulty of the job and if the knowledges, skills or abilities are not those taught in the training program. For example, if training materials are at a level of reading difficulty substantially in excess of the reading difficulty of materials used on the job, the Guidelines would not permit justification on a content validity basis of a reading test based on those training materials for entry into the job.

Under the Guidelines a training program itself is a selection procedure if passing it is a prerequisite to retention or advancement. See Section 2C and 14C(17). As such, the content of the training program may only be justified by the relationship between the program and critical or important behaviors of the job itself, or through a demonstration of the relationship between measures of performance in training and measures of job performance.

Under the example given above, therefore, where the requirements in the training materials exceed those on the job, the training program itself could not be validated on a content validity basis if passing it is a basis for retention or promotion.

SECTION 2:
LIMITATIONS

D. *Limitations.* These guidelines apply only to persons subject to Title VII, Executive Order 11246, or other equal employment opportunity requirements of Federal law. These guidelines do not apply to responsibilities under the Age Discrimination in Employment Act of 1967, as amended, not to discriminate on the basis of age, or under sections 501, 503, and 504 of the Rehabilitation Act of 1973, not to discriminate on the basis of handicap.

SECTION 2:
INDIAN PREFERENCE

E. *Indian preference not affected.* These guidelines do not restrict any obligation imposed or right granted by Federal law to users to extend a preference in employment to Indians living on or near an Indian reservation in connection with employment opportunities on or near an Indian reservation.

2C. Selection Procedures

The endorsement of relative qualifications and the disclaimer of Guidelines' applicability to the operation of seniority systems is appropriate, but it should be noted that §703 (h) of Title VII also exempts *bona fide* merit systems. Clarification of the latter exception is needed, but will probably require judicial assistance. It may be added that there is some question as to whether it is appropriate to utilize Guidelines' analysis to determine whether a Civil Service or private seniority or merit system is "bona fide" within the meaning of *Teamsters v. United States.*

Note the definition of "Selection Procedure" in Section 16Q.

Since applicant flow data are crucial in adverse impact determinations and recruitment practices may radically affect applicant flow, it is hard to see how recruitment practices can fail to be a consideration in a review of selection procedure effects, despite their exclusion in this Section. The recruiting example used in Section C is unfortunate. On the basis of this Section, an unwary

employer's special recruitment effort on behalf of a particular group could be used as arguable evidence that it had "previously denied employment opportunities" to that group. Moreover, an employer's efforts to specifically recruit a particular group should not necessarily be construed as an attempt "to bring [the] employer into compliance with federal law". The employer may already be in compliance with the law but may be undertaking voluntary affirmative action under E.O. 11246 or a similar program. Special recruiting activities may also result in an unrepresentatively large minority applicant population, thus distorting adverse impact statistics.

For further discussion of applicant flow issues, see Section 4C, below.

PROFESSIONAL ANALYSIS

It is consistent with professional standards to recognize that selection procedures may be used "for the purpose of determining qualifications" and for "selection on the basis of relative qualifications".

2D. Limitations

LEGAL ANALYSIS

The applicability of the Guidelines to 42 U.S.C. §1981 is not clear, as "adverse impact" analysis is of very limited utility under a statute that most courts have found to require proof of intent to discriminate in order to make out a *prima facie* case, rather than the statistical showing of adverse impact which alone triggers the Guidelines.

Since requirements related to age and handicap legislation are not covered by these Guidelines, different requirements could exist, particularly in the area of physical ability testing, although the Guidelines will most likely be an important influence in the developing case law under legislation prohibiting discrimination on the basis of age or handicap. See the discussion of the scope of the Guidelines in the Overview, Part II of this Analysis.

2E. Indian Preference Not Affected

LEGAL ANALYSIS

The Guidelines state that they do not restrict any obligation to extend a preference to American Indians for employment opportunity on or near an Indian reservation. Indian preference statutes have been recognized as constituting something other than a form of racial pref-

erence. *Morton v. Mancari,* 417 U.S. 535 (1974). Although the Guidelines do not mention veterans' preferences, these too are outside the scope of the Guidelines and have been upheld by the courts as subject not to the *Griggs* test of adverse impact but to an "invidious intent" test. *Personnel Administrator of Massachusetts v. Feeney,* 442 U.S. 256 (1979).

SECTION 3: PROCEDURES, ETC.

Sec. 3. *Discrimination defined: Relationship between use of selection procedures and discrimination.*—A. *Procedure having adverse impact constitutes discrimination unless justified.* The use of any selection procedure which has an adverse impact on the hiring, promotion, or other employment or membership opportunities of members of any race, sex, or ethnic group will be considered to be discriminatory and inconsistent with these guidelines, unless the procedure has been validated in accordance with these guidelines, or the provisions of section 6 below are satisfied.

9. Q. Do the Guidelines require that only validated selection procedures be used?

A. No. Although validation of selection procedures is desirable in personnel management, the Uniform Guidelines require users to produce evidence of validity only when the selection procedure adversely affects the opportunities of a race, sex, or ethnic group for hire, transfer, promotion, retention or other employment decision. If there is no adverse impact, there is no validation requirement under the Guidelines. Sections 1B and 3A. See also, Section 6A.

31. Q. Section 6A authorizes the use of alternative selection procedures to eliminate adverse impact, but does not appear to address the issue of validity. Thus, the use of alternative selection procedures without adverse impact seems to be presented as an option in lieu of validation. Is that its intent?

A. Yes. Under Federal equal employment opportunity law the use of any selection procedure which has an adverse impact on any race, sex or ethnic group is discriminatory unless the procedure has been properly validated, or the use of the procedure is otherwise justified under Federal law. *Griggs* v. *Duke Power Co.*, 401 U.S. 424 (1971); Section 3A. If a selection procedure has an adverse impact, therefore, Federal equal employment opportunity law authorizes the user to choose lawful alternative procedures which eliminate the adverse impact rather than demonstrating the validity of the original selection procedure.

Many users, while wishing to validate all of their selection procedures, are not able to conduct the validity studies immediately. Such users have the option of choosing alternative techniques which eliminate adverse impact, with a view to providing a basis for determining subsequently which selection procedures are valid and have as little adverse impact as possible.

Apart from Federal equal employment opportunity law, employers have economic incentives to use properly validated selection procedures. Nothing in Section 6A should be interpreted as discouraging the use of properly validated selection procedures; but Federal equal employment opportunity law does not require validity studies to be conducted unless there is adverse impact. See Section 2C.

34. Q. Can a user send its validity evidence to an enforcement agency before a review, so as to assure its validity?

A. No. Enforcement agencies will not review validity reports except in the context of investigations or reviews. Even in those circumstances, validity evidence will not be reviewed without evidence of how the selection procedure is used and what impact its use has on various race, sex, and ethnic groups.

36. Q. How can users justify continued use of a procedure on a basis other than validity?

A. Normally, the method of justifying selection procedures with an adverse impact and the method to which the Guidelines are primarily addressed, is validation. The method of justification of a procedure by means other than validity is one to which the Guidelines are not addressed. See Section 6B. In *Griggs* v. *Duke Power Co.*, 401 U.S. 424, the Supreme Court indicated that the burden on the user was a heavy one, but that the selection procedure could be used if there was a "business necessity" for its continued use; therefore, the Federal agencies will consider evidence that a selection procedure is necessary for the safe and efficient operation of a business to justify continued use of a selection procedure.

37. Q. Is the demonstration of a rational relationship (as that term is used in constitutional law) between a selection procedure and the job sufficient to meet the validation requirements of the Guidelines?

A. No. The Supreme Court in *Washington* v. *Davis*, 426 U.S. 229 (1976) stated that different standards would be applied to employment discrimination allegations arising under the Constitution than would be applied to employment discrimination allegations arising under Title VII. The *Davis* case arose under the Constitution, and no Title VII violation was alleged. The Court applied a traditional constitutional law standard of "rational relationship" and said that it would defer to the "seemingly reasonable acts of administrators and executives." However, it went on to point out that under Title VII, the appropriate standard would still be an affirmative demonstration of the relationship between the selection procedure and measures of job performance by means of accepted procedures of validation and it would be an "insufficient response to demonstrate some rational basis" for a selection procedure having an adverse impact. Thus, the mere demonstration of a rational relationship between a selection procedure and the job does not meet the requirement of Title VII of the Civil Rights Act of 1964, or of Executive Order 11246, or the State and Local Fiscal Assistance Act of 1972, as amended (the revenue sharing act) or the Omnibus Crime Control and Safe Streets Act of 1968, as amended, and will not meet the requirements of these Guidelines for a validity study. The three validity strategies called for by these Guidelines all require evidence that the selection procedure is related to successful performance on the job. That evidence may be obtained through local validation or through validity studies done elsewhere.

41. Q. When should a validity study be carried out?

A. When a selection procedure has adverse impact on any race, sex or ethnic group, the Guidelines generally call for a validity study or the elimination of adverse impact. See Sections 3A and 6, and Questions 9, 31, and 36. If a selection procedure has adverse impact, its use in making employment decisions without adequate evidence of validity would be inconsistent with the Guidelines. Users who choose to continue the use of a selection procedure with an adverse impact until the procedure is challenged increase the risk that they will be found to be engaged in discriminatory practices and will be liable for back pay awards, plaintiffs' attorneys' fees, loss of Federal contracts, subcontracts or grants, and the like. Validation studies begun on the eve of litigation have seldom been found to be adequate. Users who choose to validate selection procedures should consider the potential benefit from having a validation study completed or well underway before the procedures are administered for use in employment decisions.

Section 3. Discrimination Defined: Relationship Between Use of Selection Procedures and Discrimination

3A. Procedure Having Adverse Impact Constitutes Discrimination Unless Justified

LEGAL ANALYSIS

Section 3A provides that it is discriminatory for an employer to use "any selection procedure" having an "adverse impact" on the employment opportunities of members of "any" race, sex or ethnic group unless the procedure "has been validated in accordance with these guidelines" or the employer has "satisfied" the provisions of Section 6. Section 6 permits an employer to use unvalidated selection procedures which will eliminate adverse impact or, where validation techniques cannot or need not be utilized, to use procedures which are as job-related as possible and which minimize or eliminate adverse impact. Leaving legal objections to Section 6 aside, as they are discussed later in connection with that section, the balance of this section is a reasonable statement of the principles of *Griggs v. Duke Power Co.* and its progeny, subject to the following observations:

• "Adverse impact", as developed in the case law and defined in Section 16B, requires at least a "substantial" and statistically significant difference in selection rates between groups. As a rule of thumb, the "four-fifths rule" set forth in Section 4D may be interpreted as the agencies' application of the legal requirement that "substantially" different selection rates are necessary to establish "adverse impact". Under most circumstances, however, such differences should meet a threshold requirement of being statistically significant at the .05 level. See also comments in Part II, "Overview", Point II, "Adverse Impact".

• The statement that an adverse impact on "any" race, sex or ethnic group will be considered discriminatory unless justified is too broad. It is difficult to imagine that an employer could be called upon to demonstrate the validity of a selection procedure that may have an adverse impact on any one of our numerous ethnic and racial groups, assuming that data were available to show impact on a group for which statistics are not required on the Annual EEO-1 Report. See also Q and A 87 and the discussion of recordkeeping in Sections 15 A, 15A (1) and 15A (2), below.

• Under some circumstances, the courts have been most receptive to showings of job-relatedness without formal validation as a common-sense legal approach. In particular, it may be noted that few cases involving selection procedures other than tests have sought to invoke the Guidelines or their predecessors. See, e. g., *New York City Transit Authority v. Beazer; Furnco Construction Co. v. Waters; Friend v. Leidinger; EEOC v. North Hills Passavant Hospital,* 466 F. Supp. 783 (W.D. Pa. 1979); *Vanguard Justice Society v. Hughes; Anderson v. U.S. Steel Corp.,* 19 FEP Cases 1215 (N.D. Cal. 1979).

See also Sections 5D and 6B, below, and comments in Part II, above, "Overview", Point IV, "Where Adverse Impact Exists: The Basic Options".

PROFESSIONAL ANALYSIS

The only validation recognized by this Section is validation "in accordance with these Guidelines". As elsewhere demonstrated, however, the Section 15 documentation requirements exceed the standards set forth in the Principles of the American Psychological Association's Division of Industrial and Organizational Psychology ("Division 14"). Even if this were not true, the APA's *Standards* and the Division's *Principles* state with regard to the literal application of their respective standards:

> A final caveat is necessary in view of the prominence of testing issues in litigation. This document is prepared as a technical guide for those within the sponsoring professions; it is not written as law. What is intended is a set of standards to be used in part for self-evaluation by test developers and test users. *An evaluation of their competence does not rest on the literal satisfaction of every relevant provision of this document.* The individual standards are statements of ideals or goals, some having priority over others. Instead, an evaluation of competence depends on the degree to which the intent of this document has been satisfied by the test developer or user. (Emphasis added.)

This succinct statement of professional opinion as to the relative flexibility of technical standards contrasts with the rigid approach found in the "essential" requirements of Section 15.

The alternative to validation stated in Section 3A is, as already noted, compliance with Section 6. As shown below, Section 6 is in some respects inconsistent with professional standards and does not prescribe a professionally acceptable alternative to validation.

83

SECTION 3B:
SUITABLE ALTERNATIVES

B. *Consideration of suitable alternative selection procedures.* Where two or more selection procedures are available which serve the user's legitimate interest in efficient and trustworthy workmanship, and which are substantially equally valid for a given purpose, the user should use the procedure which has been demonstrated to have the lesser adverse impact. Accordingly, whenever a validity study is called for by these guidelines, the user should include, as a part of the validity study, an investigation of suitable alternative selection procedures and suitable alternative methods of using the selection procedure which have as little adverse impact as possible, to determine the appropriateness of using or validating them in accord with these guidelines. If a user has made a reasonable effort to become aware of such alternative procedures and validity has been demonstrated in accord with these guidelines, the use of the test or other selection procedure may continue until such time as it should reasonably be reviewed for currency. Whenever the user is shown an alternative selection procedure with evidence of less adverse impact and substantial evidence of validity for the same job in similar circumstances, the user should investigate it to determine the appropriateness of using or validating it in accord with these guidelines. This subsection is not intended to preclude the combination of procedures into a significantly more valid procedure, if the use of such a combination has been shown to be in compliance with the guidelines.

48. Q. Do the Guidelines call for a user to consider and investigate alternative selection procedures when conducting a validity study?

A. Yes. The Guidelines call for a user, when conducting a validity study, to make a reasonable effort to become aware of suitable alternative selection procedures and methods of use which have as little adverse impact as possible, and to investigate those which are suitable. Section 3B.

An alternative procedure may not previously have been used by the user for the job in question and may not have been extensively used elsewhere. Accordingly, the preliminary determination of the suitability of the alternative selection procedure for the user and job in question may have to be made on the basis of incomplete information. If on the basis of the evidence available, the user determines that the alternative selection procedure is likely to meet its legitimate needs, and is likely to have less adverse impact than the existing selection procedure, the alternative should be investigated further as a part of the validity study. The extent of the investigation should be reasonable. Thus, the investigation should continue until the user has reasonably concluded that the alternative is not useful or not suitable, or until a study of its validity has been completed. Once the full validity study has been completed, including the evidence concerning the alternative procedure, the user should evaluate the results of the study to determine which procedure should be used. See Section 3B and Question 50.

49. Q. Do the Guidelines call for a user *continually* to investigate "suitable alternative selection procedures and suitable alternative methods of using the selection procedure which have as little adverse impact as possible"?

A. No. There is no requirement for continual investigation. A reasonable investigation of alternatives is called for by the Guidelines as a part of any validity study. Once the study is complete and validity has been found, however, there is generally no obligation to conduct further investigations, until such time as a new study is called for. See, Sections 3B and 5K. If a government agency, complainant, civil rights organization or other person having a legitimate interest shows such a user an alternative procedure with less adverse impact and with substantial evidence of validity for the same job in similar circumstances, the user is obliged to investigate only the particular procedure which has been presented. Section 3B.

50. Q. In what circumstances do the Guidelines call for the use of an alternative selection procedure or an alternative method of using the procedure?

A. The alternative selection procedure (or method of use) should be used when it has less adverse impact and when the evidence shows that its validity is substantially the same or greater for the same job in similar circumstances. Thus, if under the original selection procedure the selection rate for black applicants was only one half (50 percent) that of the selection rate for white applicants, whereas under the alternative selection procedure the selection rate for blacks is two-thirds (67 percent) that of white applicants, the new alternative selection procedure should be used when the evidence shows substantially the same or greater validity for the alternative than for the original procedure. The same principles apply to a new user who is deciding what selection procedure to institute.

51. Q. What are the factors to be considered in determining whether the validity for one procedure is substantially the same as or greater than that of another procedure?

A. In the case of a criterion-related validity study, the factors include the importance of the criteria for which significant relationships are found, the magnitude of the relationship between selection procedure scores and criterion measures, and the size and composition of the samples used. For content validity, the strength of validity evidence would depend upon the proportion of critical and/or important job behaviors measured, and the extent to which the selection procedure resembles actual work samples or work behaviors. Where selection procedures have been validated by different strategies, or by construct validity, the determination should be made on a case by case basis.

52. Q. The Guidelines require consideration of alternative procedures and alternative methods of use, in light of the evidence of validity and utility and the degree of adverse impact of the procedure. How can a user know that any selection procedure with an adverse impact is lawful?

A. The Uniform Guidelines (Section 5G) expressly permit the use of a procedure in a manner supported by the evidence of validity and utility, even if another method of use has a lesser adverse impact. With respect to consideration of alternative selection procedures, if the user made a reasonable effort to become aware of alternative procedures, has considered them and investigated those which appear suitable as a part of the validity study, and has shown validity for a procedure, the user has complied with the Uniform Guidelines. The burden is then on the person challenging the procedure to show that there is another procedure with better or substantially equal validity which will accomplish the same legitimate business purposes with less adverse impact. Section 3B. See also, *Albemarle Paper Co. v. Moody,* 422 U.S. 405.

3B. Consideration of Suitable Alternative Selection Procedures

LEGAL ANALYSIS

Section 3B opens with a reasonable statement: assuming that a user can choose between two selection procedures which serve the user's interest in effective employee selection and which are ''substantially equally valid'' for that purpose, the user should select the one having less adverse impact. Aside from professional concerns about the ''substantially equally valid'' standard, the proposition makes sense in the abstract. It is difficult to imagine that employers could justify the conscious adoption of a procedure having more adverse impact than another known procedure that serves their purposes equally well. The major difficulty is that the proposition is wholly hypothetical: selection procedures do not come neatly labeled as to degree of validity and degree of adverse impact on applicant or employee populations. Not even the federal EEO agencies have been able to make concrete suggestions for finding such data for many of the most common jobs in the economy.

In addition to requiring persons conducting validation studies to investigate ''suitable alternative selection procedures'', Section 3B of the Guidelines adds a new provision that they also search for ''suitable alternative methods of using the selection procedure'' which have ''as little adverse impact as possible''. This new and wholly different proposition places on the employer the burden of maximizing opportunities for minorities and women and appears to be inconsistent with the approach of *Furnco Construction v. Waters* and *Keene State College v. Sweeney.* Yet the Second and Eighth Circuit Courts of Appeal have been receptive to the Guidelines' requirement in cases involving content validity defenses, as has the federal court in Kentucky: *Guardians Association v. Civil Service Commission; Louisville Black Police Officers Orgn. v. City of Louisville* 20 F.E.P. Cases 1195 (D. Ky. 1979); *Firefighters Institute for Racial Equality v. City of St. Louis,* 616 F.2d 350 (8th Cir. 1980).

The agencies claim that placing the burden of seeking less adverse alternatives on the user is consistent with *Albemarle Paper Co. v. Moody,* but *Albemarle* places the burden of demonstrating the availability of a less adverse alternative on the plaintiff in a Title VII case. It is one way in which a plaintiff can rebut the employer's showing of job-relatedness and it is no more than evidence from which triers of fact may infer that the showing of job-relatedness is pretextual. This will always be a fact question, as there are numerous factors that defy a simplistic approach. For example, the rea-

sonableness of assuming the employer's knowledge of the less adverse alternative procedure, the degree of difference in its impact and the comparative predictiveness of the two procedures are all thorny issues going to the effectiveness of a plaintiff's effort to show that an employer's use of a validated selection procedure is, nevertheless, a pretext for discrimination. *Spurlock v. United Air Lines Inc.* suggests that cost and other business considerations may be legitimate factors in determining whether to seek less adverse alternatives. While the district courts in *Dickerson v. U.S. Steel* and *Allen v. City of Mobile* appear to support the required search for less adverse alternatives, the *Furnco* holding suggests that the Supreme Court would not endorse a requirement that employers seek procedures that maximize the opportunity of minorities and women if a validity study supports the present use. See also *New York City Transit Authority v. Beazer.*

The District Court decision in *Allen v. City of Mobile* admittedly endorses the required search for equally valid, less adverse alternatives. To the extent that this decision is inconsistent with *Albemarle, Furnco* and *Keene State,* of course, it cannot stand. But, in fact, *City of Mobile* is a special case, not to be viewed as an accurate statement of legal requirements. The complete absence of minorities in the job category involved, the ''eve of trial'' validation study, the judge's apparent suspicion that the validation study was inadequate, despite the failure of the plaintiffs to present evidence to that effect, all suggest that the result was inevitable. The judge seemingly took advantage of a technical deviation from the Guidelines to achieve a result that he felt was required by justice and it would be rash to conclude that he would overturn a proper validation study in another case merely because there was no evidence of a search for equally valid, less adverse alternatives.

A similar explanation underlies the result in *Dickerson v. U.S. Steel,* in which the judge in effect castigated the employer for spending large sums of money to validate examinations where validity was unconvincing. The judge apparently discerned a discriminatory motive from the decision to validate rather than to seek better selection devices. It is again clear that the judge was not convinced that the tests in question were very good, although they had been nominally validated and the plaintiffs' ''expert'' witnesses had themselves been insufficiently convincing to overturn the validation studies. To the extent that the *Dickerson* case goes beyond its special context, however, it is plainly inconsistent

SECTION 3B:
SUITABLE ALTERNATIVES

B. *Consideration of suitable alternative selection procedures.* Where two or more selection procedures are available which serve the user's legitimate interest in efficient and trustworthy workmanship, and which are substantially equally valid for a given purpose, the user should use the procedure which has been demonstrated to have the lesser adverse impact. Accordingly, whenever a validity study is called for by these guidelines, the user should include, as a part of the validity study,. an investigation of suitable alternative selection procedures and suitable alternative methods of using the selection procedure which have as little adverse impact as possible, to determine the appropriateness of using or validating them in accord with these guidelines. If a user has made a reasonable effort to become aware of such alternative procedures and validity has been demonstrated in accord with these guidelines, the use of the test or other selection procedure may continue until such time as it should reasonably be reviewed for currency.

Whenever the user is shown an alternative selection procedure with evidence of less adverse impact and substantial evidence of validity for the same job in similar circumstances, the user should investigate it to determine the appropriateness of using or validating it in accord with these guidelines. This subsection is not intended to preclude the combination of procedures into a significantly more valid procedure, if the use of such a combination has been shown to be in compliance with the guidelines.

---

53. Q. Are the Guidelines consistent with the decision of the Supreme Court in *Furnco Construction Corp.* v. *Waters,* — *U.S.* —, 98 S. Ct. 2943 (1978) where the Court stated: "Title VII * * * does not impose a duty to adopt a hiring procedure that maximizes hiring of minority employees."

A. Yes. The quoted statement in *Furnco* v. *Waters* was made on a record where there was no adverse impact in the hiring process, no different treatment, no intentional discrimination, and no contractual obligations under E.O. 11246. Section 3B of the Guidelines is predicated upon a finding of adverse impact. Section 3B indicates that, when two or more selection procedures are available which serve a legitimate business purpose with substantially equal validity, the user should use the one which has been demonstrated to have the lesser adverse impact. Part V of the Overview of the Uniform Guidelines, in elaborating on this principle, states: "Federal equal employment opportunity law has added a requirement to the process of validation. In conducting a validation study, the employer should consider available alternatives which will achieve its legitimate purpose with lesser adverse impact."

Section 3B of the Guidelines is based on the principle enunciated in the Supreme Court decision in *Albermarle Paper Co.* v. *Moody,* 422 U.S. 405 (1975) that, even where job relatedness has been proven, the availability of other tests or selection devices which would also serve the employer's legitimate interest in "efficient and trustworthy workmanship" without a similarly undesirable racial effect would be evidence that the employer was using its tests merely as a pretext for discrimination.

Where adverse impact still exists, even though the selection procedure has been validated, there continues to be an obligation to consider alternative procedures which reduce or remove that adverse impact if an opportunity presents itself to do so without sacrificing validity. Where there is no adverse impact, the *Furnco* principle rather than the *Albermarle* principle is applicable.

54. Q. How does a user choose which validation strategy to use?

A. A user should select a validation strategy or strategies which are (1) appropriate for the type of selection procedure, the job, and the employment situation, and (2) technically and administratively feasible. Whatever method of validation is used, the basic logic is one of prediction; that is, the presumption that level of performance on the selection procedure will, on the average, be indicative of level of performance on the job after selection. Thus, a criterion-related study, particularly a predictive one, is often regarded as the closest to such an ideal. See American Psychological Association *Standards,* pp. 26-27.

Key conditions for a criterion-related study are a substantial number of individuals for inclusion in the study, and a considerable range of performance on the selection and criterion measures. In addition, reliable and valid measures of job performance should be available, or capable of being developed. Section 14B(1). Where such circumstances exist, a user should consider use of the criterion-related strategy.

Content validity is appropriate where it is technically and administratively feasible to develop work samples or measures of operationally defined skills, knowledges, or abilities which are a necessary prerequisite to observable work behaviors. Content validity is not appropriate for demonstrating the validity of tests of mental processes or aptitudes or characteristics; and is not appropriate for knowledges, skills or abilities which an employee will be expected to learn on the job. Section 14C(1)

The application of a construct validity strategy to support employee selection procedures is newer and less developed than criterion-related or content validity strategies. Continuing research may result in construct validity becoming more widely used. Because construct validity represents a generalization of findings, one situation in which construct validity might hold particular promise is that where it is desirable to use the same selection procedures for a variety of jobs. An overriding consideration in whether or not to consider construct validation is the availability of an individual with a high level of expertise in this field.

In some situations only one kind of validation study is likely to be appropriate. More than one strategy may be possible in other circumstances, in which case administrative considerations such as time and expense may be decisive. A combination of approaches may be feasible and desirable.

Supplemental Questions and Answers

91. Q. What constitutes a "reasonable investigation of alternatives" as that phrase is used in the Answer to Question 49?

A. The Uniform Guidelines call for a reasonable investigation of alternatives for a proposed selection procedure as a part of any validity study. See Section 3B and Questions 48 and 49. A reasonable investigation of alternatives would begin with a search of the published literature (test manuals and journal articles) to develop a list of currently available selection procedures that have in the past been found to be valid for the job in question or for similar jobs. A further review would then be required of all selection procedures at least as valid as the proposed procedure to determine if any offer the probability of lesser adverse impact. Where the information on the proposed selection procedure indicates a low degree of validity and high adverse impact, and where the published literature does not suggest a better alternative, investigation of other sources (for example, professionally-available, unpublished research studies) may also be necessary before continuing use of the proposed procedure can be justified. In any event, a survey of the enforcement agencies alone does not constitute a reasonable investigation of alternatives. Professional reporting of studies of validity and adverse impact is encouraged within the constraints of practicality.

with *Griggs,* not to mention *Furnco* and *Keene State College.*

Whatever the legal posture of the required search, it is illusory: barring special circumstances, if employers know of "equally valid" procedures, they will use them rather than go to the expense of validating procedures whose validity is unknown. Also, practically speaking, a "search" could become unduly expensive, as validation studies of several procedures might be involved and such studies might be inaccessible. *U.S. v. South Carolina* suggests that cost may be a relevant factor in determining the reasonableness of validation studies.

An article on workforce productivity by Schmidt, 32 *Personnel Psychology,* p. 272, cited in the Professional Analysis below, illustrates the economic significance of even very small differences in validities between two procedures. Its utility example uses a figure of $1,641,658 at a validity of 0.52. If the validity is changed to 0.50 (a figure the agencies might call "substantially equal"), the result is a loss of $63,333, as the utility figure drops to $1,578,325.

PROFESSIONAL ANALYSIS

The required use of procedures having less adverse impact if their validity is "substantially" equal is professionally questionable. Although increased utility may properly be compared with the magnitude of increased adverse impact, use of a more valid selection device is generally considered professionally desirable, since such an instrument is more likely to select those with a higher probability of job success. More to the point, even "small increases in the validity of selection procedures will result in considerable benefit." Cronbach and Gleser, *Tests and Personnel Decisions,* 53 (1965). See also, Schmidt, et al., "The Impact of Valid Selection Procedures on Workforce Productivity", *Personnel Psychol.,* Vol. 2, p. 272 (1979); Anastasi, *Psychological Testing,* Chapter 3 (3rd. ed. 1968). Thus, the alternative's validity should be at least equal to that of the user's.

It is true that when an employer undertakes a validity study, the employer should investigate alternative selection procedures. The purpose is to identify the procedure or combination of procedures that will *maximize validity and thereby increase utility.* The search for alternative selection procedures also may include the investigation of adverse impact because of legal or other extra-professional considerations, but adverse impact statistics, if available and interpretable at all, should not under normal circumstances take precedence over valid-

ity statistics. By maximizing validity, the employer maximizes equal employment opportunity be enhancing the likelihood of selecting candidates who will succeed on the job.

Section 3B also contains a new provision not found in any previous documents and one which is inconsistent with professional practice. This new requirement stipulates that not only are employers and users required to seek out and if necessary validate suitable alternatives; they also must consider alternative "methods" of *using* validated selection procedures so as to minimize the degree of adverse impact.

In conducting a validation study, the professional's responsibility is first to seek out instruments with the highest probability of predicting success in the job in question. These determinations typically are made on the basis of existing validity evidence and professional judgment. At the conclusion of a validity study and based on the statistical information derived from the study, or on the information gathered from demonstrating the relationship between the content of a procedure and the content of the job, the professional's responsibility is to determine and recommend the use which maximizes objectivity, efficiency, practical utility and workforce quality.

An approach to utility that accounts for intangible, as well as tangible costs, is found in Dunnette, M. D., *Personnel Selection and Placement* (Belmont, CA, 1966). In selecting the method of use of a selection procedure, the employer also should consider the costs associated with incorrect selection errors, whether they be "false negatives" or "false positives". "False negatives" are errors in which the employer fails to select someone who would have been successful on the job. "False positives" are errors in which an employer selects an individual who later fails to do the job adequately. In managerial, professional and supervisory positions, such selection errors may be particularly costly in terms of lost clients, high turnover of capable subordinate staff, length of time until the employee becomes proficient, etc. In other positions such as firefighter, consequences associated with false positive selection errors may be disastrous, such as loss of life.

Basically, the professional is required to make recommendations on the basis of data. If a criterion-related validity study has been conducted and the procedure involved shown to be valid, the evidence almost always indicates that there is a linear relationship between scores achieved on the test or tests and success in the job in question. In content validity work, given the typ-

87

SECTION 3B:
SUITABLE ALTERNATIVES

B. *Consideration of suitable alternative selection procedures.* Where two or more selection procedures are available which serve the user's legitimate interest in efficient and trustworthy workmanship, and which are substantially equally valid for a given purpose, the user should use the procedure which has been demonstrated to have the lesser adverse impact. Accordingly, whenever a validity study is called for by these guidelines, the user should include, as a part of the validity study,. an investigation of suitable alternative selection procedures and suitable alternative methods of using the selection procedure which have as little adverse impact as possible, to determine the appropriateness of using or validating them in accord with these guidelines. If a user has made a reasonable effort to become aware of such alternative procedures and validity has been demonstrated in accord with these guidelines, the use of the test or other selection procedure may continue until such time as it should reasonably be reviewed for currency. Whenever the user is shown an alternative selection procedure with evidence of less adverse impact and substantial evidence of validity for the same job in similar circumstances, the user should investigate it to determine the appropriateness of using or validating it in accord with these guidelines. This subsection is not intended to preclude the combination of procedures into a significantly more valid procedure, if the use of such a combination has been shown to be in compliance with the guidelines.

SECTION 4A:
RECORDS
CONCERNING IMPACT

SEC. 4. *Information on impact.*—A. *Records concerning impact.* Each user should maintain and have available for inspection records or other information which will disclose the impact which its tests and other selection procedures have upon employment opportunities of persons by identifiable race, sex, or ethnic group as set forth in subparagraph B below in order to determine compliance with these guidelines. Where there are large numbers of applicants and procedures are administered frequently, such information may be retained on a sample basis, provided that the sample is appropriate in terms of the applicant population and adequate in size.

16. Q. Should adverse impact determinations be made for all groups regardless of their size?

A. No. Section 15A(2) calls for annual adverse impact determinations to be made for each group which constitutes either 2% or more of the total labor force in the relevant labor area, or 2% or more of the applicable workforce. Thus, impact determinations should be made for any employment decision for each group which constitutes 2% or more of the labor force in the relevant labor area. For hiring, such determination should also be made for groups which constitute more than 2% of the applicants; and for promotions, determinations should also be made for those groups which constitute at least 2% of the user's workforce. There are record keeping obligations for all groups, even those which are less than 2%. See Question 86.

83. Q. Is the requirement in the Guidelines that users maintain records of the race, national origin, and sex of employees and applicants constitutional?

A. Yes. For example, the United States Court of Appeals for the First Circuit rejected a challenge on constitutional and other grounds to the Equal Employment Opportunity Commission regulations requiring State and local governmental units to furnish information as to race, national origin and sex of employees. *United States* v. *New Hampshire,* 539 F. 2d 277 (1st Cir. 1976), *cert. denied,* sub nom. *New Hampshire* v. *United States,* 429 U.S. 1023. The Court held that the recordkeeping and reporting requirements promulgated under Title VII of the Civil Rights Act of 1964, as amended, were reasonably necessary for the Federal agency to determine whether the state was in compliance with Title VII and thus were authorized and constitutional. The same legal principles apply to. recordkeeping with respect to applicants.

Under the Supremacy Clause of the Constitution, the Federal law requiring maintenance of records identifying race, sex and national origin overrides any contrary provision of State law. See Question 8.

The agencies recognize, however, that such laws have been enacted to prevent misuse of this information. Thus, employers should take appropriate steps to ensure proper use of all data. See Question #88.

84. Q. Is the user obliged to keep records which show whether its selection processes have an adverse impact on race, sex, or ethnic groups?

A. Yes. Under the Guidelines users are obliged to maintain evidence indicating the impact which their selection processes have on identifiable race, sex or ethnic groups. Sections 4 A and B. If the selection process for a job does have an adverse impact on one or more such groups, the user is expected to maintain records showing the impact for the individual procedures. Section 15A(2).

86. Q. Should applicant and selection information be maintained for race or ethnic groups constituting less than 2% of the labor force and the applicants?

A. Small employers and other small users are not obliged to keep such records. Section 15A(1). Employers with more than 100 employees and other users required to file EEO-1 *et seq.* reports should maintain records and other information upon which impact determinations could be made, because section 15A2 requires the maintenance of such information for "any of the groups for which records are called for by section 4B above." See also, Section 4A.

No user, regardless of size, is required to make adverse impact determinations for race or ethnic groups constituting less than 2% of the labor force and the applicants. See Question 16.

(See also Questions and Answers 17, 87 and 88 on page 90.)

ical work situation, an assumption usually can be made that those who show greater mastery of the content being measured also will be among the better performers. In both instances, the professional's responsibility is to make recommendations on the basis of the validity evidence. The Section 3B implication that users may or should adjust data-based use of validated procedures in order to make group-membership based decisions ignores the data and is inconsistent with professional standards. See also Section 5G.

Section 4. Information on Impact

4A. Records Concerning Impact

LEGAL ANALYSIS

Although the desirability of maintaining "adverse impact" data is not disputed, it is not a requirement of Title VII to maintain these data. OFCCP, however, as an aspect of its enforcement of the EEO clause in federal contracts, may require impact data and may elect to do so in its compliance regulations. But such a requirement is out of place in the Uniform Guidelines. It is well established that the burden is on a plaintiff to demonstrate adverse impact and that validation of a test is not required prior to its implementation, as the fundamental legal issue is whether the test is in fact valid if it has adverse impact. *U.S. v. Georgia Power Co.*, 474 F.2d 906 (5th Cir., 1973); *Cooper v. Allen,* 467 F.2d 836 (5th Cir., 1972). The Guidelines, therefore, can recommend that adverse impact data be maintained, but an employer's failure to determine whether adverse impact exists, although very unwise, is not a violation of law.

The section does not expressly state that bottom line impact data are normally the only impact data that need be collected. Indeed, it implies the opposite by stating that records must be kept showing the impact of "tests and other selection procedures". Records need not be maintained for tests that are merely components of an overall selection process having no adverse impact. Sufficient records should be kept, however, to permit reconstruction of the effect of process components in the event that the overall process ultimately shows adverse impact.

SECTION 4B:
RACE, SEX
AND ETHNIC GROUPS

B. *Applicable race, sex, and ethnic groups for recordkeeping.* The records called for by this section are to be maintained by sex, and the following races and ethnic groups: Blacks (Negroes), American Indians (including Alaskan Natives), Asians (including Pacific Islanders), Hispanic (including persons of Mexican, Puerto Rican, Cuban, Central or South American, or other Spanish origin or culture regardless of race), whites (Caucasians) other than Hispanic, and totals. The race, sex, and ethnic classifications called for by this section are consistent with the Equal Employment Opportunity Standard Form 100, Employer Information Report EEO-1 series of reports. The user should adopt safeguards to insure that the records required by this paragraph are used for appropriate purposes such as determining adverse impact, or (where required) for developing and monitoring affirmative action programs, and that such records are not used improperly. See sections 4E and 17(4), below.

17. Q. In determining adverse impact, do you compare the selection rates for males and females, and blacks and whites, or do you compare selection rates for white males, white females, black males and black females?

A. The selection rates for males and females are compared, and the selection rates for the race and ethnic groups are compared with the selection rate of the race or ethnic group with the highest selection rate. Neutral and objective selection procedures free of adverse impact against any race, sex or ethnic group are unlikely to have an impact against a subgroup. Thus there is no obligation to make comparisons for subgroups (e.g., white male, white female, black male, black female). However, there are obligations to keep records (see Question 87), and any apparent exclusion of a subgroup may suggest the presence of discrimination.

87. Q. Should information be maintained which identifies applicants and persons selected both by sex and by race or ethnic group?

A. Yes. Although the Federal agencies have decided not to require computations of adverse impact by subgroups (white males, black males, white females, black females—see Question 17), the Guidelines call for record keeping which allows identification of persons by sex, combined with race or ethnic group, so as to permit the identification of discriminatory practices on any such basis. Section 4A and 4B.

88. Q. How should a user collect data on race, sex or ethnic classifications for purposes of determining the impact of selection procedures?

A. The Guidelines have not specified any particular procedure, and the enforcement agencies will accept different procedures that capture the necessary information. Where applications are made in person, a user may maintain a log or applicant flow chart based upon visual observation, identifying the number of persons expressing an interest, by sex and by race or national origin; may in some circumstances rely upon personal knowledge of the user; or may rely upon self-identification. Where applications are not made in person and the applicants are not personally known to the employer, self-identification may be appropriate. Wherever a self-identification form is used, the employer should advise the applicant that identification by race, sex and national origin is sought, not for employment decisions, but for record-keeping in compliance with Federal law. Such self-identification forms should be kept separately from the application, and should not be a basis for employment decisions; and the applicants should be so advised. See Section 4B.

90

4B. Applicable Race, Sex and Ethnic Groups for Recordkeeping

Data must be collected by subgroups (i.e., white males, black females) and for all groups, even those constituting less than two percent of the relevant labor market if the employer has over 100 employees, even though such data are not used to calculate adverse impact. Adverse impact is calculated for each sex and for each ethnic or racial group that constitutes more than two percent of the relevant labor market.

An employer who honors the Guidelines' requirement for gathering race, national origin and sex data on applicants may violate state laws and other regulations regarding pre-employment inquiries unless special precautions are taken. What needs to be emphasized is the distinction between what Title VII requires as opposed to what an employer might otherwise do voluntarily. It is worth noting that federal agencies are not yet permitted to collect data on candidates who are Federal employees or on outside applicants who are Federal employees.

Q & A 87 confounds Section 4B in calling for recordkeeping ". . . which allows identification of persons by sex, *combined with race or ethnic group*, so as to permit the identification of discriminatory practices on any such basis." Obviously, the more comparisons a plaintiff can make, the greater the likelihood that adverse impact will be established for some group.

See also the discussion of Sections 4A, 15A, 15A (1) and 15A (2), below.

The omission of an exception for keeping records on groups constituting less than two percent of the employer's workforce or the appropriate labor market is inexplicable. Question and Answer 87 requires the maintenance of records for all groups, even those constituting less than two percent of the relevant labor market. This recordkeeping requirement seems unreasonable, since adverse impact calculations are mandated only for groups constituting two percent or more of the relevant labor market.

In connection with Q & A 88 and the issue of visual identification versus self-report, the interim guidelines for federal agencies state that self-report is preferable to visual identification. Given the pitfalls of both methods, it is well that the agencies do not state a preference in the Uniform Gudielines.

C. *Evaluation of selection rates. The "bottom line."* If the information called for by sections 4A and B above shows that the total selection process for a job has an adverse impact, the individual components of the selection process should be evaluated for adverse impact. If this information shows that the total selection process does not have an adverse impact, the Federal enforcement agencies, in the exercise of their administrative and prosecutorial discretion, in usual circumstances, will not expect a user to evaluate the individual components for adverse impact, or to validate such individual components, and will not take enforcement action based upon adverse impact of any component of that process, including the separate parts of a multipart selection procedure or any separate procedure that is used as an alternative method of selection. However, in the following circumstances the Federal enforcement agencies will expect a user to evaluate the individual components for adverse impact and may, where appropriate, take enforcement action with respect to the individual components: (1) where the selection procedure is a significant factor in the continuation of patterns of assignments of incumbent employees caused by prior discriminatory employment practices, (2) where the weight of court decisions or administrative interpretations hold that a specific procedure (such as height or weight requirements or no-arrest records) is not job related in the same or similar circumstances. In unusual circumstances, other than those listed in (1) and (2) above, the Federal enforcement agencies may request a user to evaluate the individual components for adverse impact and may, where appropriate, take enforcement action with respect to the individual component.

13. Q. Is adverse impact determined on the basis of the overall selection process or for the components in that process?

A. Adverse impact is determined first for the overall selection process for each job. If the overall selection process has an adverse impact, the adverse impact of the individual selection procedure should be analyzed. For any selection procedures in the process having an adverse impact which the user continues to use in the same manner, the user is expected to have evidence of validity satisfying the Guidelines. Sections 4C and 5D. If there is no adverse impact for the overall selection process, in most circumstances there is no obligation under the Guidelines to investigate adverse impact for the components, or to validate the selection procedures used for that job. Section 4C. But see Question 25.

15. Q. What is meant by the terms "applicant" and "candidate" as they are used in the Uniform Guidelines?

A. The precise definition of the term "applicant" depends upon the user's recruitment and selection procedures. The concept of an applicant is that of a person who has indicated an interest in being considered for hiring, promotion, or other employment opportunities. This interest might be expressed by completing an application form, or might be expressed orally, depending upon the employer's practice.

The term "candidate" has been included to cover those situations where the initial step by the user involves consideration of current employees for promotion, or training, or other employment opportunities, without inviting applications. The procedure by which persons are identified as candidates is itself a selection procedure under the Guidelines.

A person who voluntarily withdraws formally or informally at any stage of the selection process is no longer an applicant or candidate for purposes of computing adverse impact. Employment standards imposed by the user which discourage disproportionately applicants of a race, sex or ethnic group may, however, require justification. Records should be kept for persons who were applicants or candidates at any stage of the process.

25. Q. Are there any circumstances in which the employer should evaluate components of a selection process, even though the overall selection process results in no adverse impact?

A. Yes, there are such circumstances: (1) Where the selection procedure is a significant factor in the continuation of patterns of assignments of incumbent employees caused by prior discriminatory employment practices. Assume, for example, an employer who traditionally hired blacks as employees for the "laborer" department in a manufacturing plant, and traditionally hired only whites as skilled craftsmen. Assume further that the employer in 1962 began to use a written examination not supported by a validity study to screen incumbent employees who sought to enter the apprenticeship program for skilled craft jobs. The employer stopped making racial assignments in 1972. Assume further that for the last four years, there have been special recruitment efforts aimed at recent black high school graduates and that the selection process, which includes the written examination, has resulted in the selection of black applicants for apprenticeship in approximately the same rates as white applicants.

In those circumstances, if the written examination had an adverse impact, its use would tend to keep incumbent black employees in the laborer department, and deny them entry to apprenticeship programs. For that reason, the enforcement agencies would expect the user to evaluate the impact of the written examination, and to have validity evidence for the use of the written examination if it has an adverse impact.

(2) Where the weight of court decisions or administrative interpretations holds that a specific selection procedure is not job related in similar circumstances.

For example, courts have held that because an arrest is not a determination of guilt, an applicant's arrest record by itself does not indicate inability to perform a job consistent with the trustworthy and efficient operation of a business. Yet a no arrest record requirement has a nationwide adverse impact on some minority groups. Thus, an employer who refuses to hire applicants solely on the basis of an arrest record is on notice that this policy may be found to be discriminatory. *Gregory* v. *Litton Industries,* 472 F. 2d 631 (9th Cir., 1972) (excluding persons from employment solely on the basis of arrests, which has an adverse impact, held to violate Title VII). Similarly, a minimum height requirement disproportionately disqualifies women and some national origin groups, and has been held not to be job related in a number of cases. For example, in *Dothard* v. *Rawlinson,* 433 U.S. 321 (1977), the Court held that height and weight requirements not shown to be job related were violative of Title VII. Thus an employer using a minimum height requirement should have evidence of its validity.

(3) In addition, there may be other circumstances in which an enforcement agency may decide to request an employer to evaluate components of a selection process, but such circumstances would clearly be unusual. Any such decision will be made only at a high level in the agency. Investigators and compliance officers are not authorized to make this decision.

LEGAL ANALYSIS

This subject is discussed at some length in the material dealing with the third point in the Overview in Part II of the Legal and Professional Analysis. As a general proposition, employers welcome the adoption of the "bottom line" concept by the agencies.

The agencies suggest that a "high-level agency decision" will be required before enforcement will be brought in situations where the "bottom line" has been satisfied, but there is no useful explanation as to what "unusual" circumstances the agencies envision as justifying such a decision. Nor do they explain what guidance will be given to lower level agency compliance personnel as to what degree they will be permitted to impose additional data-gathering responsibility upon employers with respect to components where the bottom line has no adverse impact. Such additional data gathering requirements pertaining to component selection procedures should properly be imposed only after "high level" review. From a practical point of view, a clear "bottom line" should assure more than freedom from agency prosecution; it should assure freedom from unreasonable and unnecessary paper work.

The discussion also does not address another problem raised by the "high level" decision to examine components. Will the agencies communicate with each other at high levels before proceeding with enforcement action despite a satisfactory bottom line? The use of the singular in the text suggests not, but the alternative is reimposition of the very inconsistency the Uniform Guidelines are designed to eliminate. Hopefully, the OFCCP-EEOC Memorandum of Understanding will help control this problem.

Another difficulty with this section is the requirement that components be evaluated where they continue patterns of assignment of incumbents "caused by prior discriminatory employment practices". There is no indication who determines whether prior practices were "discriminatory" or when and how such a determination is made. Nor is there an indication why analysis of the impact of a component will be appropriate where the present "bottom line" is satisfactory. If the "discrimination" amounts to a Title VII violation and is the subject of a timely charge under that statute, then the "bottom line" would be irrelevant in any case, since remedial measures would be fully available to eradicate the effects of past discrimination as to the affected individuals. *U.S. v. Teamsters*. The same might be true under the Executive Order. If there is no present discrimination, the continued use of an employment practice that may have been used in an earlier period (when, perhaps, the bottom line was not satisfactory) is without legal significance. And the existence of victims of past discrimination cannot relate in any way to the operation of "bottom line" principles regarding selection procedures themselves. If the overall process does not discriminate, then the agencies are precluded from examining components. In any event, the existence of past discriminatees is irrelevant to the present functioning of the selection process. The concept here appears inconsistent with *United Air Lines, Inc. v. Evans* 431 U.S. 553 (1977), where the Supreme Court ruled that actions predating a timely Title VII charge filing period are not unlawful and their later effects do not constitute a Title VII violation.

It is difficult to understand what the agencies have in mind: if the bottom line is "clean", the impact of the components on minorities as a group, let alone on specific persons who have been discriminated against in the past, will be unknown. As remedying past discrimination is simply outside the scope of the Guidelines, the inclusion of the first bottom line exception seems inconsistent and unjustified.

Employers must also question the agencies' example of a component that they will attack regardless of satisfactory bottom line statistics: practices that "have a clear adverse impact on a national basis" and "no validity". The courts have not accepted this exception. *EEOC v. Navajo Oil Corp.; Friend v. Leidinger; Robinson v. City of Dallas,* 514 F.2d 1271 (5th Cir., 1975). Indeed, the agencies' conclusion assumes that a validation study has been unsuccessfully attempted and the results ignored, so that the practice has "no validity". This is highly unlikely, as any employer having the sophistication to attempt validation of an employment practice would usually heed the results of the validation study.

The agencies seem to have something else in mind, however: the transportability of *in*validity. But in order to transport invalidity, the same criteria required in the transportability section of the Guidelines (Section 7) should apply, especially the similarity of job analyses results. Further, a showing of adverse impact on the relevant population must be made. *EEOC v. Navajo Oil Corp.* The cases cited in the Answer to Question 25 do not stand for the proposition that a component may be attacked even though the "bottom line" is satisfactory. They show only that in some instances courts have been

SECTION 4C: "BOTTOM LINE"

C. *Evaluation of selection rates. The "bottom line."* If the information called for by sections 4A and B above shows that the total selection process for a job has an adverse impact, the individual components of the selection process should be evaluated for adverse impact. If this information shows that the total selection process does not have an adverse impact, the Federal enforcement agencies, in the exercise of their administrative and prosecutorial discretion, in usual circumstances, will not expect a user to evaluate the individual components for adverse impact, or to validate such individual components, and will not take enforcement action based upon adverse impact of any component of that process, including the separate parts of a multipart selection procedure or any separate procedure that is used as an alternative method of selection. However, in the following circumstances the Federal enforcement agencies will expect a user to evaluate the individual components for adverse impact and may, where appropriate, take enforcement action with respect to the individual components: (1) where the selection procedure is a significant factor in the continuation of patterns of assignments of incumbent employees caused by prior discriminatory employment practices, (2) where the weight of court decisions or administrative interpretations hold that a specific procedure (such as height or weight requirements or no-arrest records) is not job related in the same or similar circumstances. In unusual circumstances, other than those listed in (1) and (2) above, the Federal enforcement agencies may request a user to evaluate the individual components for adverse impact and may, where appropriate, take enforcement action with respect to the individual component.

94

willing to use national statistics to challenge selection procedures in a specific employment setting.

In summary, this provision operates as an attempt to prohibit certain facially neutral tests, hiring criteria and employment practices by diluting the legal principle of the bottom line.

The second listed exception to the bottom line—"where the weight of court decisions or administrative interpretations" hold that a procedure is not job-related—is equally groundless. First, as noted above, *Navajo Oil* and the weight of court decisions is to the contrary. Second, there is no authority whatever for the agencies to use "administrative interpretations" to rule out any selection procedure. Finally, court decisions questioning such criteria have always done so in a context where the bottom line was far from satisfactory so that the component (height, weight, arrest record) was legitimately under scrutiny.

The agencies' "exceptions" to the bottom line may lead to inter-agency and even intra-agency inconsistency in enforcement. A strong argument could be made that the discussion of "applicant" and "candidate" in Q & A 15 is inconsistent with *Hill v. Western Electric Co.,* 596 F.2d 99 (4th Cir.), *cert. denied,* 444 U.S. 924 (1979), in which the Fourth Circuit adopted a realistic view of which persons are counted for making impact determinations for bottom line purposes.

See also the discussion of Section 16I, which defines "enforcement action" and thereby indicates the real scope of the bottom line.

PROFESSIONAL ANALYSIS

Conceptually, the "bottom line" means that an employer should not be required to demonstrate the validity of selection procedures where placement of women and minorities is consistent with the availability of qualified persons. Availability in this context means the representation of qualified women or minorities in the relevant labor market. It is a different concept from "applicant pool" or "applicant flow" (e.g., the people who actually show up looking for a job), yet it is not mentioned in Section 4C. In fact, Section 4D strongly implies that adverse impact will be defined in terms of applicant flow alone, regardless of the interest or fundamental qualifications of the applicants involved.

Of particular concern here is the possibility that an employer's vigorous "affirmative action" efforts or reputation for "fair" treatment may inflate the number of minorities or women in the applicant pool, but not necessarily the percentage who are qualified. The employer is expected to match the artificially inflated "availability" estimate represented by the applicant pool.

An additional problem created by the emphasis on applicant flow is the definition of what constitutes an applicant for a particular job. As defined in Q & A 15, an "applicant" may be anyone who might have been considered for a job, regardless of interest or qualifications. This is unworkable. Rather, a "bona fide" applicant should be defined as a person who personally completed and filed with an employer a formal written application for a specific job for which the employer was accepting applications on the date and at the place of receipt of the applications, and a job for which the person was minimally qualified. A person who makes formal or informal inquiry about employment opportunities in general or about specific jobs for which the employer is not currently accepting applications cannot be a bona fide applicant because he or she is not actually being considered for a job. Likewise, a person referred to an employer by a third party is not considered to be a bona fide applicant as defined above. Moreover, an "applicant" must complete all steps necessary for consideration for the job applied for until turned down or accepted and must be identifiable as to race, ethnic group and sex. "Drop-outs" should not be counted. See also the discussion of "applicant" in connection with Section 15A (1), below.

Many organizations, in keeping with recommended affirmative action procedures, do not require specification of interest in a specific job as part of the applicant process. Thus, it is difficult, if not impossible, to identify the applicants for a specific job in order to conduct the analysis of selection rate differences. The Guidelines imply that applicants are all those people who might have been considered for the job in question, whether or not they actually were considered or would have been interested or minimally qualified if they had been. Conducting a series of selection rate comparison analyses in such circumstances means that while individuals are counted as "accepts" only once, they may be counted as "rejects" a number of times, leading to the overestimation of adverse impact. This is especially true to the extent the "applicant" group includes a large number of individuals whose interests and qualifications are marginal (a likely event where an organization has aggressively pressed an open applications policy as part of an affirmative action plan). Again, the emphasis on applicant flow will penalize employers with a history of effective affirmative action, although the Guidelines do provide that greater differences in selection rates (than

95

SECTION 4C: "BOTTOM LINE"

C. *Evaluation of selection rates. The "bottom line."* If the information called for by sections 4A and B above shows that the total selection process for a job has an adverse impact, the individual components of the selection process should be evaluated for adverse impact. If this information shows that the total selection process does not have an adverse impact, the Federal enforcement agencies, in the exercise of their administrative and prosecutorial discretion, in usual circumstances, will not expect a user to evaluate the individual components for adverse impact, or to validate such individual components, and will not take enforcement action based upon adverse impact of any component of that process, including the separate parts of a multipart selection procedure or any separate procedure that is used as an alternative method of selection. However, in the following circumstances the Federal enforcement agencies will expect a user to evaluate the individual components for adverse impact and may, where appropriate, take enforcement action with respect to the individual components: (1) where the selection procedure is a significant factor in the continuation of patterns of assignments of incumbent employees caused by prior discriminatory employment practices, (2) where the weight of court decisions or administrative interpretations hold that a specific procedure (such as height or weight requirements or no-arrest records) is not job related in the same or similar circumstances. In unusual circumstances, other than those listed in (1) and (2) above, the Federal enforcement agencies may request a user to evaluate the individual components for adverse impact and may, where appropriate, take enforcement action with respect to the individual component.

under the "four-fifths rule") may be tolerated where an employer has undertaken an affirmative action program. See Section 4D.

A reasonable reaction from employers would be to restrict applications and include in the analyses only those individuals identified as qualified applicants for each specific job. See, *Williams v. Tallahassee Motors, Inc.*, 607 F.2d 689 (5th Cir. 1979). These problems are paralleled, and indeed amplified, in determining pools of eligible candidates to measure the impact of promotional and other procedures affecting current employees.

Another problem arising from the agencies' attempt to reserve the right to examine the individual components of a selection system even if there is no overall adverse impact is that maintaining data on components could become incredibly burdensome. If an employer considered 5,000 job applicants during the course of a year, then 5,000 dispositions would have been reached on all candidates, with each disposition requiring a data element. But what if, for example, six components entered into each selection decision (e.g., three tests, two interviews and a reference check)? To examine each component would require $6 \times 5,000$ or 30,000 data elements. This is despite the fact that these components may not be interpreted individually in making selection decisions.

It may be asked whether the converse to the transportability of invalidity is also recognized by the agencies. Where court decisions uphold a specific selection procedure as "job-related", may employers use it in similar circumstances without themselves examining its validity? An example might be a high school graduation requirement for police officers. This is a logical corollary to Section 4C, but Section 7 shows that the agencies take a narrow view of transportability of positive validity evidence.

See also the discussion in Part II, "Overview", Point III, "Is Adverse Impact to Be Measured by the Overall Process?" and Point 2 of the Analysis of Comments.

WARNING: As this volume went to press, the Second Circuit Court of Appeals in New York decided a major case involving the "bottom line". In *Teal v. State of Connecticut,* 25 FEP Cases 529 (2d Cir. 1981), the court ruled, in effect, that the "bottom line" proposal is inconsistent with Title VII. The case involved a pass-fail examination that screened out blacks at a disproportionate rate. However, the employer applied "Affirmative Action" proposals to assure that a greater percentage of blacks than whites among those passing the written test were ultimately selected for employment. The result was a satisfactory "bottom line", but the court ruled that the blacks who failed the test and were not considered for employment could establish a *prima facie* case of discrimination based upon the test's disparate impact. The decision conflicts with other court decisions and the issue will undoubtedly be resolved ultimately by the Supreme Court.

D. *Adverse impact and the "four-fifths rule."* A selection rate for any race, sex, or ethnic group which is less than four-fifths (⅘) (or eighty percent) of the rate for the group with the highest rate will generally be regarded by the Federal enforcement agencies as evidence of adverse impact, while a greater than four-fifths rate will generally not be regarded by Federal enforcement agencies as evidence of adverse impact. Smaller differences in selection rate may nevertheless constitute adverse impact, where they are significant in both statistical and practical terms or where a user's actions have discouraged applicants disproportionately on grounds of race, sex, or ethnic group. Greater differences in selection rate may not constitute adverse impact where the differences are based on small numbers and are not statistically significant, or where special recruiting or other programs cause the pool of minority or female candidates to be atypical of the normal pool of applicants from that group. Where the user's evidence concerning the impact of a selection procedure indicates adverse impact but is based upon numbers which are too small to be reliable, evidence concerning the impact of the procedure over a longer period of time and/or evidence concerning the impact which the selection procedure had when used in the same manner in similar circumstances elsewhere may be considered in determining adverse impact. Where the user has not maintained data on adverse impact as required by the documentation section of applicable guidelines, the Federal enforcement agencies may draw an inference of adverse impact of the selection process from the failure of the user to maintain such data, if the user has an underutilization of a group in the job category, as compared to the group's representation in the relevant labor market or, in the case of jobs filled from within, the applicable work force.

10. Q. What is adverse impact?

A. Under the Guidelines adverse impact is a substantially different rate of selection in hiring, promotion or other employment decision which works to the disadvantage of members of a race, sex or ethnic group. Sections 4D and 16B. See Questions 11 and 12.

11. Q. What is a substantially different rate of selection?

A. The agencies have adopted a rule of thumb under which they will generally consider a selection rate for any race, sex, or ethnic group which is less than four-fifths (4/5ths) or eighty percent (80%) of the selection rate for the group with the highest selection rate as a substantially different rate of selection. See Section 4D. This "4/5ths" or "80%" rule of thumb is not intended as a legal definition, but is a practical means of keeping the attention of the enforcement agencies on serious discrepancies in rates of hiring, promotion and other selection decisions.

For example, if the hiring rate for whites other than Hispanics is 60%, for American Indians 45%, for Hispanics 48%, and for Blacks 51%, and each of these groups constitutes more than 2% of the labor force in the relevant labor area (see Question 16), a comparison should be made of the selection rate for each group with that of the highest group (whites). These comparisons show the following impact ratios: American Indians 45/60 or 75%; Hispanics 48/60 or 80%; and Blacks 51/60 or 85%. Applying the 4/5ths or 80% rule of thumb, on the basis of the above information alone, adverse impact is indicated for American Indians but not for Hispanics or Blacks.

12. Q. How is adverse impact determined?

A. Adverse impact is determined by a four step process.

(1) calculate the rate of selection for each group (divide the number of persons selected from a group by the number of applicants from that group).

(2) observe which group has the highest selection rate.

(3) calculate the impact ratios, by comparing the selection rate for each group with that of the highest group (divide the selection rate for a group by the selection rate for the highest group).

(4) observe whether the selection rate for any group is substantially less (i.e., usually less than 4/5ths or 80%) than the selection rate for the highest group. If it is, adverse impact is indicated in most circumstances. See Section 4D.

For example:

Applicants	Hires	Selection rate Percent hired
80 White	48	48/80 or 60%
40 Black	12	12/40 or 30%

A comparison of the black selection rate (30%) with the white selection rate (60%) shows that the black rate is 30/60, or one-half (or 50%) of the white rate. Since the one-half (50%) is less than 4/5ths (80%) adverse impact is usually indicated.

The determination of adverse impact is not purely arithmetic however; and other factors may be relevant. See, Section 4D.

14. Q. The Guidelines designate the "total selection process" as the initial basis for determining the impact of selection procedures. What is meant by the "total selection process"?

A. The "total selection process" refers to the combined effect of all selection procedures leading to the final employment decision such as hiring or promoting. For example, appraisal of candidates for administrative assistant positions in an organization might include initial screening based upon an application blank and interview, a written test, a medical examination, a background check, and a supervisor's interview. These in combination are the total selection process. Additionally, where there is more than one route to the particular kind of employment decision, the total selection process encompasses the combined results of all routes. For example, an employer may select some applicants for a particular kind of job through appropriate written and performance tests. Others may be selected through an internal upward mobility program, on the basis of successful performance in a directly related trainee type of position. In such a case, the impact of the total selection process would be the combined effect of both avenues of entry.

18. Q. Is it usually necessary to calculate the statistical significance of differences in selection rates when investigating the existence of adverse impact?

A. No. Adverse impact is normally indicated when one selection rate is less than 80% of the other. The federal enforcement agencies normally will use only the 80% (⅘ths) rule of thumb, except where large numbers of selections are made. See Questions 20 and 22.

19. Q. Does the ⅘ths rule of thumb mean that the Guidelines will tolerate up to 20% discrimination?

A. No. The ⅘ths rule of thumb speaks only to the question of adverse impact, and is not intended to resolve the ultimate question of unlawful discrimination. Regardless of the amount of difference in selection rates, unlawful discrimination may be present, and may be demonstrated through appropriate evidence. The ⅘ths rule merely establishes a numerical basis for drawing an initial inference and for requiring additional information.

With respect to adverse impact, the Guidelines expressly state (section 4D) that differences in selection rates of less than 20% may still amount to adverse impact where the differences are significant in both statistical and practical terms. See Question 20. In the absence of differences which are large enough to meet the ⅘ths rule of thumb or a test of statistical significance, there is no reason to assume that the differences are reliable, or that they are based upon anything other than chance.

20. Q. Why is the ⅘ths rule called a rule of thumb?

A. Because it is not intended to be controlling in all circumstances. If, for the sake of illustration, we assume that nationwide statistics show that use of an arrest record would disqualify 10% of all Hispanic persons but only 4% of all whites other than Hispanic (hereafter non-Hispanic), the selection rate for that selection procedure is 90% for Hispanics and 96% for non-Hispanics. Therefore, the ⅘ rule of thumb would not indicate the presence of adverse impact (90% is approximately 94% of 96%). But in this example, the information is based upon nationwide statistics, and the sample is large enough to yield statistically significant results, and the dif-

4D. Adverse Impact and the "Four-Fifths Rule"

See the discussion of Adverse Impact in Part II of the Legal and Professional Analysis, both in the "Overview" and the "Analysis of Comments".

The agencies' proposed handling of employers who fail to maintain impact data is unrealistic, as noted in connection with Section 4A, above. Drawing an inference of adverse impact where there is "underutilization" is of doubtful utility. The agencies should simply require that appropriate data be prepared. To infer underutilization in jobs filled from within based on internal workforce data is especially undesirable and unrealistic. First, it operates as a disincentive to hiring minorities and females in entry level jobs. Second, the courts recognize that internal workforce statistics do not give an accurate measure of availability for promotion, as experience, interest and other elements must properly be considered in determining the makeup of the pool of eligible candidates. *Hill v. Western Electric Co.,* 596 F.2d 99 (4th Cir., 1979).

As already indicated, the courts have been very receptive to the "four-fifths" rule. See, e. g., *Moore v. Southwestern Bell Telephone Co.,* 593 F.2d 607 (5th Cir., 1979); *Jackson v. Nassau County Civil Service Commission,* 424 F.Supp. 1162 (E.D.N.Y. 1976). Employers agree that a rule is necessary, but employers and professionals also believe that the rule is only meaningful when statistical significance supports the inference of adverse impact. It is incorrect to state (as is done in the Analysis of Comments in Part II) that employers endorse statistical significance *in place of* the four-fifths rule; employers endorse statistical significance *as well as* the four-fifths rule. See the Professional Analysis, below.

The agencies' citation of cases to show that adverse impact has been found without a showing of statistical significance is misleading. Statistical significance was not an issue in those cases — at most, they use external statistics where internal statistics might have lacked statistical significance. No case has rejected an employer's defenses based upon lack of statistical significance and many have accepted such a defense. *Williams v. Tallahassee Motors, Inc.* and cases cited therein; *Friend v. Leidinger; Morita v. Southern California Permanente Medical Group,* 541 F.2d 217 (9th Cir., 1976); *Harper v. Trans World Airlines,* 525 F.2d 409 (8th Cir., 1975); *Vanguard Justice Society v. Hughes,* 471 F.Supp. 670 (D.Md. 1979); *EEOC v. Virginia Chemicals,* 19 FEP Cases 425 (E.D.Va. 1978); *Lee v. City of Richmond; Johnson v. Fulton Sylphon Division of Robertshaw Controls Co.,* 439 F.Supp. 658 (E.D.Tenn. 1977);

Haskell v. Rice University, 19 FEP Cases 1209 (S.D.Tex. 1979); *Rich v. Martin-Marietta Corp.,* 467 F.Supp. 587 (D. Colo. 1979); *Castaneda v. Partida,* 430 U.S. 482 (1977); *Mayor of Philadelphia v. Educational Equality League,* 415 U.S. 605 (1974).

Where numbers are too small to yield a statistically significant showing of adverse impact, they will probably also be too small to make the conduct of a professionally acceptable criterion-related or construct validation study feasible.

The four-fifths or 80 percent rule originated in 1972 as part of the California Fair Employment Practice Commission's 1972 "Guidelines on Employee Selection Procedures". It was suggested at that time as a rule of thumb to determine whether observed differences were practically significant, as well as statistically significant. The concern was that with fairly large samples, almost any difference would be statistically significant and the 80 percent rule would provide some guidance as to whether differences were large enough to merit investing a compliance agency's limited time and resources. The 80 percent rule thus originated as an ancillary standard to supplement a statistically significant finding of adverse impact, but in the current Guidelines it is the central test of adverse impact.

The appeal of the 80 percent rule is its simplicity of calculation. However, because it is a ratio of ratios, it is unaffected by sample size and there is no way to determine the degree to which the observed differences could have occurred by chance alone. The 80 percent rule is affected by the size of the selection rates in question: with larger selection rates, large differences are tolerated; with small selection rates, only small differences are tolerated. Indeed, with small selection rates, the 80 percent rule will show adverse impact differences which, given even modest sample size (e.g., 100-200 applicants), have a high probability of occurring by chance alone. For example, if the majority group's selection rate is 10 percent, a difference of only two percent is tolerated. Thus, if there are 100 white applicants and 30 black applicants, if 10 whites are selected (a rate of 10 percent), blacks must be selected at a rate of at least eight percent (i.e., four-fifths of 10 percent); in terms of numbers, this means that at least three blacks must be selected to avoid adverse impact, as anything less than eight percent (2.4 where the pool is 30) will constitute adverse impact. Yet statistically, there is no significance to a difference of one where the selection rate is eight percent out of 30. In effect, especially as

99

ference (Hispanics are 2½ times as likely to be disqualified as non-Hispanics) is large enough to be practically significant. Thus, in this example the enforcement agencies would consider a disqualification based on an arrest record alone as having an adverse impact. Likewise, in *Gregory* v. *Litton Industries*, 472 F. 2d 631 (9th Cir., 1972), the court held that the employer violated Title VII by disqualifying persons from employment solely on the basis of an arrest record, where that disqualification had an adverse impact on blacks and was not shown to be justified by business necessity.

On the other hand, a difference of more than 20% in rates of selection may not provide a basis for finding adverse impact if the number of persons selected is very small. For example, if the employer selected three males and one female from an applicant pool of 20 males and 10 females, the ⅘ths rule would indicate adverse impact (selection rate for women is 10%; for men 15%; ¹⁰/₁₅ or 66⅔% is less than 80%), yet the number of selections is too small to warrant a determination of adverse impact. In these circumstances, the enforcement agency would not require validity evidence in the absence of additional information (such as selection rates for a longer period of time) indicating adverse impact. For recordkeeping requirements, see Section 15A(2)(c) and Questions 84 and 85.

21. Q. Is evidence of adverse impact sufficient to warrant a validity study or an enforcement action where the numbers involved are so small that it is more likely than not that the difference could have occurred by chance? For example:

Applicants	Not hired	Hired	Selection rate percent hired
80 White	64	16	20
20 Black	17	3	15

White Selection Rate...	20
Black Selection Rate	15

15 divided by 20=75% (which is less than 80%).

A. No. If the numbers of persons and the difference in selection rates are so small that it is likely that the difference could have occurred by chance, the Federal agencies will not assume the existence of adverse impact, in the absence of other evidence. In this example, the difference in selection rates is too small, given the small number of black applicants, to constitute adverse impact in the absence of other information (see Section 4D). If only one more black had been hired instead of a white the selection rate for blacks (20%) would be higher than that for whites (18.7%). Generally, it is inappropriate to require validity evidence or to take enforcement action where the number of persons and the difference in selection rates are so small that the selection of one different person for one job would shift the result from adverse impact against one group to a situation in which that group has a higher selection rate than the other group.

On the other hand, if a lower selection rate continued over a period of time, so as to constitute a pattern, then the lower selection rate would constitute adverse impact, warranting the need for validity evidence.

22. Q. Is it ever necessary to calculate the statistical significance of differences in selection rates to determine whether adverse impact exists?

A. Yes. Where large numbers of selections are made, relatively small differences in selection rates may nevertheless constitute adverse impact if they are both statistically and practically significant. See Section 4D and Question 20. For that reason, if there is a small difference in selection rates (one rate is more than 80% of the other), but large numbers of selections are involved, it would be appropriate to calculate the statistical significance of the difference in selection rates.

23. Q. When the ⅘th rule of thumb shows adverse impact, is there adverse impact under the Guidelines?

A. There usually is adverse impact, except where the number of persons selected and the difference in selection rates are very small. See Section 4D and Questions 20 and 21.

24. Q. Why do the Guidelines rely primarily upon the ⅘ths rule of thumb, rather than tests of statistical significance?

A. Where the sample of persons selected is not large, even a large real difference between groups is likely not to be confirmed by a test of statistical significance (at the usual .05 level of significance). For this reason, the Guidelines do not rely primarily upon a test of statistical significance, but use the ⅘ths rule of thumb as a practical and easy-to-administer measure of whether differences in selection rates are substantial. Many decisions in day-to-day life are made without reliance upon a test of statistical significance.

84. Q. Is the user obliged to keep records which show whether its selection processes have an adverse impact on race, sex, or ethnic groups?

A. Yes. Under the Guidelines users are obliged to maintain evidence indicating the impact which their selection processes have on identifiable race, sex or ethnic groups. Sections 4 A and B. If the selection process for a job does have an adverse impact on one or more such groups, the user is expected to maintain records showing the impact for the individual procedures. Section 15A(2).

85. Q. What are the recordkeeping obligations of a user who cannot determine whether a selection process for a job has adverse impact because it makes an insufficient number of selections for that job in a year?

A. In such circumstances the user should collect, maintain, and have available information on the impact of the selection process and the component procedures until it can determine that adverse impact does not exist for the overall process or until the job has changed substantially. Section 15A(2)(c).

selection rates drop below 50 percent, the 80 percent rule will identify trivial differences which have a high probability of occurring by pure chance as indicating adverse impact. Since selection rates above 50 percent are unusual, rates of 20 to 30 percent are common and rates of 10 percent are by no means unusual, statistically insignificant adverse impact conclusions are likely to occur frequently under the 80 percent rule.

Although computation of appropriate inferential statistics would be somewhat more complicated than computation of the selection rate, it can be accomplished with a hand calculator. As the Guidelines elsewhere recognize, a .05 level of significance is professionally acceptable as a general standard for statistical significance. The agencies' concession that adverse impact will not be found where a change of group identity of one person would change the adverse impact is a poor substitute for a rule of statistical significance. In such circumstances, a shift in impact by changing the identity of two or three would almost invariably indicate that the sample is too small to measure adverse impact in a meaningful way.

An additional feature of Section 4D must be addressed. "Where the user's evidence concerning the impact of a selection procedure indicates adverse impact, but is based on numbers which are too small to be reliable . . . evidence concerning the impact which the selection procedure had when *used in the same manner in similar circumstances elsewhere* may be considered in determining adverse impact." (Emphasis added.) The burden of implementing and demonstrating the applicability of this special rule for transporting impact figures should be on the enforcement agencies and will require much more than a simple showing of job title similarity.

E. *Consideration of user's equal employment opportunity posture.* In carrying out their obligations, the Federal enforcement agencies will consider the general posture of the user with respect to equal employment opportunity for the job or group of jobs in question. Where a user has adopted an affirmative actiōn program, the Federal enforcement agencies will consider the provisions of that program, including the goals and timetables which the user has adopted and the progress which the user has made in carrying out that program and in meeting the goals and timetables. While such affirmative action programs may in design and execution be race, color, sex, or ethnic conscious, selection procedures under such programs should be based upon the ability or relative ability to do the work.

29. Q. What is the relationship between affirmative action and the requirements of the Uniform Guidelines?

A. The two subjects are different, although related. Compliance with the Guidelines does not relieve users of their affirmative action obligations, including those of Federal contractors and subcontractors under Executive Order 11246. Section 13.

The Guidelines encourage the development and effective implementation of affirmative action plans or programs in two ways. First, in determining whether to institute action against a user on the basis of a selection procedure which has adverse impact and which has not been validated, the enforcement agency will take into account the general equal employment opportunity posture of the user with respect to the job classifications for which the procedure is used and the progress which has been made in carrying out any affirmative action program. Section 4E. If the user has demonstrated over a substantial period of time that it is in fact appropriately utilizing in the job or group of jobs in question the available race, sex or ethnic groups in the relevant labor force, the enforcement agency will generally exercise its discretion by not initiating enforcement proceedings based on adverse impact in relation to the applicant flow. Second, nothing in the Guidelines is intended to preclude the use of selection procedures, consistent with Federal law, which assist in the achievement of affirmative action objectives. Section 13A. See also, Questions 30 and 31.

30. Q. When may a user be race, sex or ethnic-conscious?

A. The Guidelines recognize that affirmative action programs may be race, sex or ethnic conscious in appropriate circumstances, (See Sections 4E and 13; See also Section 17, Appendix). In addition to obligatory affirmative action programs (See Question 29), the Guidelines encourage the adoption of voluntary affirmative action programs. Users choosing to engage in voluntary affirmative action are referred to EEOC's Guidelines on Affirmative Action (44 F.R. 4422, January 19, 1979). A user may justifiably be race, sex or ethnic-conscious in circumstances where it has reason to believe that qualified persons of specified race, sex or ethnicity have been or may be subject to the exclusionary effects of its selection procedures or other employment practices in its work force or particular jobs therein. In establishing long and short range goals, the employer may use the race, sex, or ethnic classification as the basis for such goals (Section 17(3) (a)).

In establishing a recruiting program, the employer may direct its recruiting activities to locations or institutions which have a high proportion of the race, sex, or ethnic group which has been excluded or underutilized (section 17(3) (b)). In establishing the pool of qualified persons from which final selections are to be made, the employer may take reasonable steps to assure that members of the excluded or underutilized race, sex, or ethnic group are included in the pool (Section 17(3) (e)).

Similarly, the employer may be race, sex or ethnic-conscious in determining what changes should be implemented if the objectives of the programs are not being met (Section 17(3) (g)).

Even apart from affirmative action programs a user may be race, sex or ethnic-conscious in taking appropriate and lawful measures to eliminate adverse impact from selection procedures (Section 6A).

31. Q. Section 6A authorizes the use of alternative selection procedures to eliminate adverse impact, but does not appear to address the issue of validity. Thus, the use of alternative selection procedures without adverse impact seems to be presented as an option in lieu of validation. Is that its intent?

A. Yes. Under Federal equal employment opportunity law the use of any selection procedure which has an adverse impact on any race, sex or ethnic group is discriminatory unless the procedure has been properly validated, or the use of the procedure is otherwise justified under Federal law. *Griggs* v. *Duke Power Co.*, 401 U.S. 424 (1971); Section 3A. If a selection procedure has an adverse impact, therefore, Federal equal employment opportunity law authorizes the user to choose lawful alternative procedures which eliminate the adverse impact rather than demonstrating the validity of the original selection procedure.

Many users, while wishing to validate all of their selection procedures, are not able to conduct the validity studies immediately. Such users have the option of choosing alternative techniques which eliminate adverse impact, with a view to providing a basis for determining subsequently which selection procedures are valid and have as little adverse impact as possible.

Apart from Federal equal employment opportunity law, employers have economic incentives to use properly validated selection procedures. Nothing in Section 6A should be interpreted as discouraging the use of properly validated selection procedures; but Federal equal employment opportunity law does not require validity studies to be conducted unless there is adverse impact. See Section 2C.

4E. Consideration of User's Equal Employment Opportunity Posture

Although it calls for a subjective judgment without articulated standards, this section of the Guidelines is appropriate and helpful to employers engaging in voluntary affirmative action. However, the agencies limit themselves to consideration of EEO posture only for "the job or group of jobs in question"; this seems too narrow, as overall EEO posture is surely relevant to a decision on taking enforcement action against an employer. Further, the agencies should consider more than goal achievement—as provided in the applicable OFCCP regulations, good faith efforts rather than actual numerical results are often the touchstone for measuring EEO compliance.

SECTION 5A: ACCEPTABLE VALIDITY STUDIES

SEC. 5. *General standards for validity studies.—A. Acceptable types of validity studies.* For the purposes of satisfying these guidelines, users may rely upon criterion-related validity studies, content validity studies or construct validity studies, in accordance with the standards set forth in the technical standards of these guidelines, section 14 below. New strategies for showing the validity of selection procedures will be evaluated as they become accepted by the psychological profession.

32. Q. What is "validation" according to the Uniform Guidelines?

A. Validation is the demonstration of the job relatedness of a selection procedure. The Uniform Guidelines recognize the same three validity strategies recognized by the American Psychological Association:

(1) Criterion-related validity—a statistical demonstration of a relationship between scores on a selection procedure and job performance of a sample of workers.

(2) Content validity—a demonstration that the content of a selection procedure is representative of important aspects of performance on the job.

(3) Construct validity—a demonstration that (a) a selection procedure measures a construct (something believed to be an underlying human trait or characteristic, such as honesty) and (b) the construct is important for successful job performance.

42. Q. Where can a user obtain professional advice concerning validation of selection procedures?

A. Many industrial and personnel psychologists validate selection procedures, review published evidence of validity and make recommendations with respect to the use of selection procedures. Many of these individuals are members or fellows of Division 14 (Industrial and Organizational Psychology) or Division 5 (Evaluation and Measurement) of the American Psychological Association. They can be identified in the membership directory of that organization. A high level of qualification is represented by a diploma in Industrial Psychology awarded by the American Board of Professional Psychology.

Individuals with the necessary competence may come from a variety of backgrounds. The primary qualification is pertinent training and experience in the conduct of validation research.

Industrial psychologists and other persons competent in the field may be found as faculty members in colleges and universities (normally in the departments of psychology or business administration) or working as individual consultants or as members of a consulting organization.

Not all psychologists have the necessary expertise. States have boards which license and certify psychologists, but not generally in a specialty such as industrial psychology. However, State psychological associations may be a source of information as to individuals qualified to conduct validation studies. Addresses of State psychological associations or other sources of information may be obtained from the American Psychological Association, 1200 Seventeenth Street, NW., Washington, D.C. 20036.

46. Q. Must the same method for validation be used for all parts of a selection process?

A. No. For example, where a selection process includes both a physical performance test and an interview, the physical test might be supported on the basis of content validity, and the interview on the basis of a criterion-related study.

55. Q. Why do the Guidelines recognize only content, construct and criterion-related validity?

A. These three validation strategies are recognized in the Guidelines since they represent the current professional consensus. If the professional community recognizes new strategies or substantial modifications of existing strategies, they will be considered and, if necessary, changes will be made in the Guidelines. Section 5A.

56. Q. Why don't the Uniform Guidelines state a preference for criterion-related validity over content or construct validity?

A. Generally accepted principles of the psychological profession support the use of criterion-related, content or construct validity strategies as appropriate. American Psychological Association *Standards*, E, pp. 25-26. This use was recognized by the supreme Court in *Washington* v. *Davis*, 426 U.S. 229, 247, fn. 13. Because the Guidelines describe the conditions under which each validity strategy is inappropriate, there is no reason to state a general preference for any one validity strategy.

57. Q. Are the Guidelines intended to restrict the development of new testing strategies, psychological theories, methods of job analysis or statistical techniques?

A. No. The Guidelines are concerned with the validity and fairness of selection procedures used in making employment decisions, and are not intended to limit research and new developments. See Question 55.

81. Q. In Section 5, "General Standards for Validity Studies," construct validity is identified as no less acceptable than criterion-related and content validity. However, the specific requirements for construct validity, in Section 14D, seem to limit the generalizability of construct validity to the rules governing criterion-related validity. Can this apparent inconsistency be reconciled?

A. Yes. In view of the developing nature of construct validation for employment selection procedures, the approach taken concerning the generalizability of construct validity (section 14D) is intended to be a cautious one. However, construct validity may be generalized in circumstances where transportability of tests supported on the basis of criterion-related validity would not be appropriate. In establishing transportability of criterion-related validity, the jobs should have substantially the same major work behaviors. Section 7B(2). Construct validity, on the other hand, allows for situations where only some of the important work behaviors are the same. Thus, well-established measures of the construct which underlie particular work behaviors and which have been shown to be valid for some jobs may be generalized to other jobs which have some of the same work behaviors but which are different with respect to other work behaviors. Section 14D(4).

As further research and professional guidance on construct validity in employment situations emerge, additional extensions of construct validity for employee selection may become generally accepted in the profession. The agencies encourage further research and professional guidance with respect to the appropriate use of construct validity.

Section 5. General Standards for Validity Studies

5A. Acceptable Types of Validity Studies

LEGAL ANALYSIS

The agencies are perhaps overreaching their authority in stating that they will "evaluate" new validation strategies as they become accepted by the psychological profession. As noted at Section 1A and elsewhere, the courts are inclined to credit professional judgments about professional matters over agency pronouncements on technical issues.

PROFESSIONAL ANALYSIS

The practical problem resulting from this Section is that organizations may be discouraged from developing new or innovative validation strategies since the agencies recognize only three acceptable alternatives (criterion-related, content and construct), with an apparent preference for the first of the three. Anyone developing and/or adopting a new strategy would be uncertain as to (1) what the agencies will consider to be "acceptance" by the profession, since there is no formal mechanism within the profession for doing so, and (2) what the outcome of the agencies' "evaluation" will be.

Additionally, there is an implication in this Section that only job performance is an acceptable criterion, when other criteria (e.g., successful completion of a training program, responsibility level achieved, absenteeism, turnover, rate of progress, etc.) are professionally acceptable. For example, several candidates might be equally qualified to perform a job but have different probabilities of remaining with the organization for a long period of time. In this case, turnover might be an appropriate criterion.

SECTION 5B:
CRITERION
RELATED VALIDITY

B. *Criterion-related, content, and construct validity.* Evidence of the validity of a test or other selection procedure by a criterion-related validity study should consist of empirical data demonstrating that the selection procedure is predictive of or significantly correlated with important elements of job performance. See section 14B below. Evidence of the validity of a test or other selection procedure by a content validity study should consist of data showing that the content of the selection procedure is representative of important aspects of performance on the job for which the candidates are to be evaluated. See section 14C below. Evidence of the validity of a test or other selection procedure through a construct validity study should consist of data showing that the procedure measures the degree to which candidates have identifiable characteristics which have been determined to be important in successful performance in the job for which the candidates are to be evaluated. See section 14D below.

IV. TECHNICAL STANDARDS

54. Q. How does a user choose which validation strategy to use?

A. A user should select a validation strategy or strategies which are (1) appropriate for the type of selection procedure, the job, and the employment situation, and (2) technically and administratively feasible. Whatever method of validation is used, the basic logic is one of prediction; that is, the presumption that level of performance on the selection procedure will, on the average, be indicative of level of performance on the job after selection. Thus, a criterion-related study, particularly a predictive one, is often regarded as the closest to such an ideal. See American Psychological Association *Standards*, pp. 26-27.

Key conditions for a criterion-related study are a substantial number of individuals for inclusion in the study, and a considerable range of performance on the selection and criterion measures. In addition, reliable and valid measures of job performance should be available, or capable of being developed. Section 14B(1). Where such circumstances exist, a user should consider use of the criterion-related strategy.

Content validity is appropriate where it is technically and administratively feasible to develop work samples or measures of operationally defined skills, knowledges, or abilities which are a necessary prerequisite to observable work behaviors. Content validity is not appropriate for demonstrating the validity of tests of mental processes or aptitudes or characteristics; and is not appropriate for knowledges, skills or abilities which an employee will be expected to learn on the job. Section 14C(1)

The application of a construct validity strategy to support employee selection procedures is newer and less developed than criterion-related or content validity strategies. Continuing research may result in construct validity becoming more widely used. Because construct validity represents a generalization of findings, one situation in which construct validity might hold particular promise is that where it is desirable to use the same selection procedures for a variety of jobs. An overriding consideration in whether or not to consider construct validation is the availability of an individual with a high level of expertise in this field.

In some situations only one kind of validation study is likely to be appropriate. More than one strategy may be possible in other circumstances, in which case administrative considerations such as time and expense may be decisive. A combination of approaches may be feasible and desirable.

SECTION 5C:
CONSISTENCY WITH
PROFESSIONAL STANDARDS

C. *Guidelines are consistent with professional standards.* The provisions of these guidelines relating to validation of selection procedures are intended to be consistent with generally accepted professional standards for evaluating standardized tests and other selection procedures, such as those described in the Standards for Educational and Psychological Tests prepared by a joint committee of the American Psychological Association, the American Educational Research Association, and the National Council on Measurement in Education (American Psychological Association, Washington, D.C., 1974) (hereinafter "A.P.A. Standards") and standard textbooks and journals in the field of personnel selection.

39. Q. Are there any formal requirements imposed by these Guidelines as to who is allowed to perform a validity study?

A. No. A validity study is judged on its own merits, and may be performed by any person competent to apply the principles of validity research, including a member of the user's staff or a consultant. However, it is the user's responsibility to see that the study meets validity provisions of the Guidelines, which are based upon professionally accepted standards. See Question 42.

40. Q. What is the relationship between the validation provisions of the Guidelines and other statements of psychological principles, such as the *Standards for Educational and Psychological Tests*, published by the American Psychological Association (Wash., D.C., 1974) (hereinafter "American Psychological Association *Standards*")?

A. The validation provisions of the Guidelines are designed to be consistent with the generally accepted standards of the psychological profession. These Guidelines also interpret Federal equal employment opportunity law, and embody some policy determinations of an administrative nature. To the extent that there may be differences between particular provisions of the Guidelines and expressions of validation principles found elsewhere, the Guidelines will be given precedence by the enforcement agencies.

5B. Criterion-Related, Content and Construct Validity

LEGAL ANALYSIS

In a criterion-related validity study, scores on the selection procedure are correlated with important elements of job or training behaviors or work outcomes, not only with "job performance" as stated in this section. The courts also have supported the use of other criteria, such as training success, e.g., *Washington v. Davis,* 426 U.S. 229 (1976). See comments on criterion-related, content and construct validity in the analysis of Section 14.

PROFESSIONAL ANALYSIS

The three validation strategies recognized in this section are also recognized by the profession. Unfortunately, however, the requirements for content and construct validation studies in Section 14 of the Uniform Guidelines are inconsistent with published professional standards, as described in the discussion of that Section. Thus, the claim in Section 5 that content and construct validity are accepted equally with criterion validity by the Guidelines is misleading. This is further reinforced by Q and A 54, which suggests a preference for criterion-related validity.

5C. Guidelines Are Consistent with Professional Standards

LEGAL ANALYSIS

The Guidelines are intended "to be consistent with generally accepted professional standards". This is appropriate and probably legally necessary, but the remainder of Section 5C and Q and A 39 and 40 indicate that when that intent is not realized, the agencies will rely on the provisions of the Guidelines rather than on professional standards. The courts, however, are likely to take a dim view of an approach to the Guidelines that treats their provisions as though they were strict regulations. *Guardians Association v. Civil Service Commission,* 23 FEP Cases 909 (2d Cir., 1980)

PROFESSIONAL ANALYSIS

As indicated in the discussion of Section 5A, the basic Guidelines requirements for content and construct validity are not consistent with professional principles in major respects. Furthermore, the Guidelines in their detailed documentation requirements make statements which are not generally endorsed by the profession.

It is worth noting that the APA *Standards* are primarily addressed to test developers, while the major thrust of the Uniform Guidelines is toward test validation. Thus the *Standards* simply do not treat many issues that the Guidelines raise. The Guidelines may therefore be generally consistent with *Standards,* but the absence of overlap does not make the Guidelines "consistent" with many professional principles not fully articulated in the APA *Standards.*

The agencies' point of view is set forth in the response to Question 40, which states that "To the extent that there may be differences between particular provisions of the Guidelines and expressions of validation principles found elsewhere, the Guidelines will be given precedence by the enforcement agencies." This implies that the agencies will not be responsive to professional research or opinion if it is not consistent with their purposes.

SECTION 5D:
NEED FOR
DOCUMENTATION

D. *Need for documentation of validity.* For any selection procedure which is part of a selection process which has an adverse impact and which selection procedure has an adverse impact, each user should maintain and have available such documentation as is described in section 15 below.

13. Q. Is adverse impact determined on the basis of the overall selection process or for the components in that process?

A. Adverse impact is determined first for the overall selection process for each job. If the overall selection process has an adverse impact, the adverse impact of the individual selection procedure should be analyzed. For any selection procedures in the process having an adverse impact which the user continues to use in the same manner, the user is expected to have evidence of validity satisfying the Guidelines. Sections 4C and 5D. If there is no adverse impact for the overall selection process, in most circumstances there is no obligation under the Guidelines to investigate adverse impact for the components, or to validate the selection procedures used for that job. Section 4C. But see Question 25.

25. Q. Are there any circumstances in which the employer should evaluate components of a selection process, even though the overall selection process results in no adverse impact?

A. Yes, there are such circumstances: (1) Where the selection procedure is a significant factor in the continuation of patterns of assignments of incumbent employees caused by prior discriminatory employment practices. Assume, for example, an employer who traditionally hired blacks as employees for the "laborer" department in a manufacturing plant, and traditionally hired only whites as skilled craftsmen. Assume further that the employer in 1962 began to use a written examination not supported by a validity study to screen incumbent employees who sought to enter the apprenticeship program for skilled craft jobs. The employer stopped making racial assignments in 1972. Assume further that for the last four years, there have been special recruitment efforts aimed at recent black high school graduates and that the selection process, which includes the written examination, has resulted in the selection of black applicants for apprenticeship in approximately the same rates as white applicants.

In those circumstances, if the written examination had an adverse impact, its use would tend to keep incumbent black employees in the laborer department, and deny them entry to apprenticeship programs. For that reason, the enforcement agencies would expect the user to evaluate the impact of the written examination, and to have validity evidence for the use of the written examination if it has an adverse impact.

(2) Where the weight of court decisions or administrative interpretations holds that a specific selection procedure is not job related in similar circumstances.

For example, courts have held that because an arrest is not a determination of guilt, an applicant's arrest record by itself does not indicate inability to perform a job consistent with the trustworthy and efficient operation of a business. Yet a no arrest record requirement has a nationwide adverse impact on some minority groups. Thus, an employer who refuses to hire applicants solely on the basis of an arrest record is on notice that this policy may be found to be discriminatory. *Gregory* v. *Litton Industries*, 472 F. 2d 631 (9th Cir., 1972) (excluding persons from employment solely on the basis of arrests, which has an adverse impact, held to violate Title VII). Similarly, a minimum height requirement disproportionately disqualifies women and some national origin groups, and has been held not to be job related in a number of cases. For example, in *Dothard* v. *Rawlinson*, 433 U.S. 321 (1977), the Court held that height and weight requirements not shown to be job related were violative of Title VII. Thus an employer using a minimum height requirement should have evidence of its validity.

(3) In addition, there may be other circumstances in which an enforcement agency may decide to request an employer to evaluate components of a selection process, but such circumstances would clearly be unusual. Any such decision will be made only at a high level in the agency. Investigators and compliance officers are not authorized to make this decision.

SECTION 5E:
ACCURACY AND
STANDARDIZATION

E. *Accuracy and standardization.* Validity studies should be carried out under conditions which assure insofar as possible the adequacy and accuracy of the research and the report. Selection procedures should be administered and scored under standardized conditions.

SECTION 5F:
CAUTION

F. *Caution against selection on basis of knowledges, skills, or ability learned in brief orientation period.* In general, users should avoid making employment decisions on the basis of measures of knowledges, skills, or abilities which are normally learned in a brief orientation period, and which have an adverse impact.

5D. Need for Documentation of Validity

LEGAL ANALYSIS

Section 5D repeats the bottom line formula and appears to endorse the concept that components of a selection process having an unsatisfactory bottom line must be examined for adverse impact. In the event that the component selection procedure has adverse impact, it must be justified as job-related. However, to require the full documentation for a validation study, as set forth in Section 15, for every such procedure is unrealistic and exceeds legal requirements. As pointed out in Part II, "Overview", Point IV, "Where Adverse Impact Exists: The Basic Options", courts frequently accept explanations of job-relatedness without requiring formal validation studies. Furthermore, as the Guidelines themselves acknowledge, validation studies are not always feasible or even necessary under federal law. Section 15, therefore, is not always applicable even where the component has adverse impact and the bottom line is unsatisfactory. While there is a need to document validity when a validation study is undertaken, there is reason to question the scope of Section 5D as a "legal" requirement for all cases where a component of a selection procedure has adverse impact. The Guidelines are not regulations having the full force of law. *Guardians Association v. Civil Service Commission*, 23 FEP Cases 909 (2d Cir., 1980). See also discussion of Section 3A, above, and Section 6B, below.

The documentation requirements were greatly altered between their publication for comment in December 1977 and later versions. There was no opportunity for public comment on these changes.

PROFESSIONAL ANALYSIS

The scientific principle underlying any documentation requirement describing research is that documentation should be sufficient so as to allow an independent investigator to evaluate the research and outcome and, if desired, to replicate the study design to verify the conclusions of the original research. There is a need for documentation; however, the level of documentation required by the Guidelines is excessive, as described in Section 15, below.

5E. Accuracy and Standardization

LEGAL ANALYSIS

The requirement that conditions of a validity study ensure insofar as possible the adequacy and accuracy of the research and resulting report is reasonable. However, the adequacy and accuracy of the research and reports will not necessarily be legally measured by the rigid standards of Sections 14 and 15. The tendency of the courts is to prefer professional standards to those detailed in government guidelines. See Section 1A, above.

PROFESSIONAL ANALYSIS

While a general principle supporting standardized administration and scoring of selection procedures is desirable, absolute standardization of administration will be frequently unattainable. Section 5E, therefore, must be interpreted somewhat flexibly.

5F. Caution Against Selection on Basis of Knowledges, Skills or Abilities Learned in Brief Orientation Period

LEGAL ANALYSIS

There is little reason to think that the courts will be inclined to disagree with the general principle in Section 5F. However, it must be emphasized that the caution against selection on the basis of knowledges, skills or abilities learned in a brief orientation period is prefaced by the phrase "in general". This suggests that employers should be given the opportunity to justify deviations from the principle involved. Examples of such explanations might be: economic (the employer is too small or too marginal economically to give even a brief orientation period); or public policy (safety factors militate in favor of hiring experienced personnel who do not need any training, however brief). In a collective bargaining context, ready definitions may be available under transfer and bumping rights provisions or in related arbitration decisions, but generally the meaning of "brief orientation period" is not very clear.

PROFESSIONAL ANALYSIS

If too rigidly applied, this Section could in effect be-

SECTION 5F: CAUTION

F. Caution against selection on basis of knowledges, skills, or ability learned in brief orientation period. In general, users should avoid making employment decisions on the basis of measures of knowledges, skills, or abilities which are normally learned in a brief orientation period, and which have an adverse impact.

SECTION 5G: METHOD OF USE

G. Method of use of selection procedures. The evidence of both the validity and utility of a selection procedure should support the method the user chooses for operational use of the procedure, if that method of use has a greater adverse impact than another method of use. Evidence which may be sufficient to support the use of a selection procedure on a pass/fail (screening) basis may be insufficient to support the use of the same procedure on a ranking basis under these guidelines. Thus, if a user decides to use a selection procedure on a ranking basis, and that method of use has a greater adverse impact than use on an appropriate pass/fail basis (see section 5H below), the user should have sufficient evidence of validity and utility to support the use on a ranking basis. See sections 3B, 14B (5) and (6), and 14C (8) and (9).

8. Q. What is the relationship between Federal equal employment opportunity law, embodied in these Guidelines, and State and Local government merit system laws or regulations requiring rank ordering of candidates and selection from a limited number of the top candidates?

A. The Guidelines permit ranking where the evidence of validity is sufficient to support that method of use. State or local laws which compel rank ordering generally do so on the assumption that the selection procedure is valid. Thus, if there is adverse impact and the validity evidence does not adequately support that method of use, proper interpretation of such a state law would require validation prior to ranking. Accordingly, there is no necessary or inherent conflict between Federal law and State or local laws of the kind described.

Under the Supremacy Clause of the Constitution (Art. VI, Cl. 2), however, Federal law or valid regulation overrides any contrary provision of state or local law. Thus, if there is any conflict, Federal equal opportunity law prevails. For example, in *Rosenfeld* v. *So. Pacific Co.,* 444 F. 2d 1219 (9th Cir., 1971), the court held invalid state protective laws which prohibited the employment of women in jobs entailing long hours or heavy labor, because the state laws were in conflict with Title VII. Where a State or local official believes that there is a possible conflict, the official may wish to consult with the State Attorney General, County or City attorney, or other legal official to determine how to comply with the law.

47. Q. Is a showing of validity sufficient to assure the lawfulness of the use of a selection procedure?

A. No. The use of the selection procedure must be consistent with the validity evidence. For example, if a research study shows only that, at a given passing score the test satisfactorily screens out probable failures, the study would not justify the use of substantially different passing scores, or of ranked lists of those who passed. See Section 5G. Similarly, if the research shows that a battery is valid when a particular set of weights is used, the weights actually used must conform to those that were established by the research.

52. Q. The Guidelines require consideration of alternative procedures and alternative methods of use, in light of the evidence of validity and utility and the degree of adverse impact of the procedure. How can a user know that any selection procedure with an adverse impact is lawful?

A. The Uniform Guidelines (Section 5G) expressly permit the use of a procedure in a manner supported by the evidence of validity and utility, even if another method of use has a lesser adverse impact. With respect to consideration of alternative selection procedures, if the user made a reasonable effort to become aware of alternative procedures, has considered them and investigated those which appear suitable as a part of the validity study, and has shown validity for a procedure, the user has complied with the Uniform Guidelines. The burden is then on the person challenging the procedure to show that there is another procedure with better or substantially equal validity which will accomplish the same legitimate business purposes with less adverse impact. Section 3B. See also, *Albemarle Paper Co.* v. *Moody,* 422 U.S. 405.

79. Q. What is required to show the content validity of a test of a job knowledge?

A. There must be a defined, well recognized body of information, and knowledge of the information must be prerequisite to performance of the required work behaviors. The work behavior(s) to which each knowledge is related should be identified on an item by item basis. The test should fairly sample the information that is actually used by the employee on the job, so that the level of difficulty of the test items should correspond to the level of difficulty of the knowledge as used in the work behavior. See Section 14C(1) and (4).

come the exception that swallows the rule in the context of content validity. Since learning inevitably occurs on the job, to limit testing for a knowledge, skill or ability on the grounds that subsequent mastery is achieved as a result of learning on the job would be specious.

Self-paced instruction is an excellent case in point. If a candidate such as a computer programmer comes to the hiring gate with some prior knowledge of programming, it is likely that this person would attain proficiency in self-paced individual instruction faster than the candidate who had no prior experience. Since learn-

ing/training is occurring on company time, a plaintiff could be encouraged under Section 5F to argue that it is discriminatory to prefer experienced candidates over inexperienced ones.

Of course, the employer should be able to identify what training is given to employees. Even for the same job, this may vary from location to location. It is professionally appropriate to expect employers to address the training issue when implementing or evaluating a selection system.

5G. Method of Use of Selection Procedures

LEGAL ANALYSIS

Responding to these Guidelines, *Louisville Black Police Officers Orgn. v. City of Louisville* suggests a justification requirement for method of use of content valid procedures only if substantial adverse impact is first demonstrated. The agencies' requirement that method of use be supported by evidence if there is any difference in degree of adverse impact, however, is unwarranted. See also, *Guardians Association v. Civil Service Commission, supra*.

The Congress which enacted Title VII wished to preserve management's ability to hire individuals on the basis of their relative qualifications to do the work. This concern is exemplified by the following excerpt from a memorandum of understanding between Senators Clark and Case, floor managers of Title VII, which is included in the legislative history of the statute. Title VII:

. . . expressly protects the employer's right to insist that any prospective applicant, Negro or white, *must meet the applicable job qualifications*. Indeed, the very purpose of Title VII is to promote hiring on the basis of job qualifications, rather than on the basis of race or color. (Emphasis added.) 110 Cong. Rec. 7247.

Moreover,

There is no requirement in Title VII that employers abandon bona fide qualification tests where, because of differences in background and education, members of some groups are able to perform better on these tests than members of other groups. *An employer may set his qualifications as high as he likes, he may test to determine which applicants have these qualifications, and he may hire, assign, and promote on the basis of test performance.* 110 Cong. Rec. 7213

In *Griggs v. Duke Power Co.*, the Supreme Court affirmed the employer's right to hire on the basis of relative qualifications and this right was more recently reaffirmed in *U.S. v. Teamsters*. As noted in the Professional Analysis, the concept in this Section is essentially tied to affirmative action achievement. This is otherwise legally unobjectionable, but it is out of place in guidelines that set minimum standards for compliance with Title VII, which is a "neutrality" statute.

See also comments at Section 14C (9).

PROFESSIONAL ANALYSIS

The effect of this paragraph, coupled with Section 14 C (9), is to reduce much content validation to a secondary status subject to criterion-related support unless the agencies' pass-fail preference is adopted. This will not be a major issue for most private sector employers, as few use ranked results on tests developed on a content strategy. However, many public sector employers will find that this Section presents problems. This requirement, which is inconsistent with professional opinion, is most particularly aimed at content valid procedures that are not clearly work samples. For most jobs involving typing, for example, a reveiw of information about the job will generally show that the fastest typists are the most desirable. With knowledge or ability tests or typical training success measures, however, it is not possible to make such a showing to justify rank ordering of candidates, and generally only empirical proof (i.e., criterion-related studies) could meet the Guidelines' inappropriate requirement.

The proper use of tests requires weighing a number of interacting factors. Except in the unusual case of

SECTION 5G: METHOD OF USE

G. *Method of use of selection procedures.* The evidence of both the validity and utility of a selection procedure should support the method the user chooses for operational use of the procedure, if that method of use has a greater adverse impact than another method of use. Evidence which may be sufficient to support the use of a selection procedure on a pass/fail (screening) basis may be insufficient to support the use of the same procedure on a ranking basis under these guidelines. Thus, if a user decides to use a selection procedure on a ranking basis, and that method of use has a greater adverse impact than use on an appropriate pass/fail basis (see section 5H below), the user should have sufficient evidence of validity and utility to support the use on a ranking basis. See sections 3B, 14B (5) and (6), and 14C (8) and (9).

SECTION 5H: CUTOFF SCORES

H. *Cutoff scores.* Where cutoff scores are used, they should normally be set so as to be reasonable and consistent with normal expectations of acceptable proficiency within the work force. Where applicants are ranked on the basis of properly validated selection procedures and those applicants scoring below a higher cutoff score than appropriate in light of such expectations have little or no chance of being selected for employment, the higher cutoff score may be appropriate, but the degree of adverse impact should be considered.

non-linearity, however, selecting higher scoring applicants over lower scoring ones will almost always be the most effective and efficient use of selection procedures, regardless of the validity strategy utilized. This generalization means that ranking of test-takers typically is the most effective method of use, especially where validity evidence is relatively low. Professional practice also suggests that determinations of the method of use of a selection procedure should consider: (a) the validity of the procedure; (b) the utility of selection decisions; (c) the selection ratio (number of persons hired divided by the number of applicants); (d) whether the procedure is the sole selection instrument or one of several selection instruments; and (e) amount of difference in adjacent scores. Variables like these must be considered simultaneously as they interact.

Demonstrations of criterion-related validity almost always constitute statistical evidence that individuals achieving higher scores, in general, will perform better on the job than individuals receiving lower scores on the selection procedure involved, so there is simply no need for additional proof. Given this fact, ranking typically would be an appropriate and readily defensible use. This is true for many content valid procedures as well.

The Guidelines imply that a particular level of validity or utility will support ranking while a lower level will support a pass-fail use. In fact, there is no empirical support for this contention and it is a matter of professional judgment as to what method of use a study or test development effort supports. As already noted, ranking is generally even more desirable when validity is relatively low. Moreover, there is no test score one could take as a passing score and assume that everyone above that passing score is equal, or even "qualified". The agencies' preference for pass-fail interpretations is not supported by scientific evidence.

Use of pass-fail procedures in promotional contexts is often useless, as frequently virtually *all* employees at a lower level could perform the upper level job with *some* degree of competence. Ranking in such a situation is usually the only practical approach.

Pass-fail interpretations may further affirmative action for some groups and there is no professional objection to the concept. The only objection is to the pretense that there is a scientific justification for discouraging ranking in favor of hiring relatively less qualified people through the use of a basic cutoff score. This poses a special problem for employers subject to Civil Service Merit System laws.

5H. Cutoff Scores

LEGAL ANALYSIS

Requiring that cutoff scores be set so as to reflect "normal expectations of acceptable proficiency" hampers employers in effecting improvements in their workforces and is contrary to the language of *Griggs v. Duke Power Co.* to the effect that employers can hire persons on the basis of their *relative* qualifications. This also contradicts the express language in *Furnco* that employers are under no Title VII obligation to maximize the hiring or promotion of minority groups. Again, the agencies appear to confuse desirable affirmative action concepts with the minimum compliance standards which are appropriate in the Uniform Guidelines.

Section 5H also must be read in connection with Section 5G. The clear intent of the agencies is to lower the point of rejection, thus increasing the pool of "selectable" applicants from which proportional or "affirmative action" hiring may be made. Moreover, for employers using cutoff scores and rank ordering (particularly public employers), to inform applicants that they have "passed" when, in fact, their chances of employment are virtually nil is both misleading and unfair. As a voluntary strategy for achieving affirmative action, the setting of lower cutoff scores is legally unobjectionable, but Sections 5G and 5H exceed the proper scope of the Guidelines.

It may be added that some public sector employers under merit selection laws may not consider the "degree of adverse impact" or other non-merit factors in setting cutoff scores.

PROFESSIONAL ANALYSIS

Except under unusual circumstances, a cutoff score should be set as high as feasible after consideration of validity, utility and appropriately defined variables. It is good professional practice to select those who have achieved the better scores on the selection procedures

113

SECTION 5H: CUTOFF SCORES

H. *Cutoff scores.* Where cutoff scores are used, they should normally be set so as to be reasonable and consistent with normal expectations of acceptable proficiency within the work force. Where applicants are ranked on the basis of properly validated selection procedures and those applicants scoring below a higher cutoff score than appropriate in light of such expectations have little or no chance of being selected for employment, the higher cutoff score may be appropriate, but the degree of adverse impact should be considered.

SECTION 5I: HIGHER LEVEL JOBS

I. *Use of selection procedures for higher level jobs.* If job progression structures are so established that employees will probably, within a reasonable period of time and in a majority of cases, progress to a higher level, it may be considered that the applicants are being evaluated for a job or jobs at the higher level. However, where job progression is not so nearly automatic, or the time span is such that higher level jobs or employees' potential may be expected to change in significant ways, it should be considered that applicants are being evaluated for a job at or near the entry level. A "reasonable period of time" will vary for different jobs and employment situations but will seldom be more than 5 years. Use of selection procedures to evaluate applicants for a higher level job would not be appropriate:

(1) If the majority of those remaining employed do not progress to the higher level job;

(2) If there is a reason to doubt that the higher level job will continue to require essentially similar skills during the progression period; or

(3) If the selection procedures measure knowledges, skills, or abilities required for advancement which would be expected to develop principally from the training or experience on the job.

as they will, on the average, perform better than individuals in the lower portions of the score distribution.

The requirement that cutoff scores be set in accordance with "normal" expectations of acceptable proficiency within the workforce presents problems associated with those discussed in Section 5F. An employer initiates selection programs as one means of *raising* the proficiency of the workforce, while the "normal expectations" standard tends to freeze the status quo, or worse. The Section incorrectly presumes that there is a point separating "proficient" from "not proficient" candidates and misses the basic fact that setting a cutoff point is most often a matter of candidate availability. The fact that an employer, because of low candidate availability, chooses to use lower cutoff scores at one point does not transform that score into an effective minimum "acceptable" or "passing" score.

Enforcement agencies have prescribed the "least qualified worker" retained by the employer as the *de facto* cutoff score, using only the score on the selection instrument as the definition of "qualified". This ignores all the other reasons why this individual might have been selected and retained, including legitimate affirmative action considerations.

5I. Use of Selection Procedures for Higher Level Jobs

LEGAL ANALYSIS

The provisions regarding selection for higher level jobs should be interpreted with flexibility when management positions are concerned. The courts have recognized the special problems involved in selection for high level positions. See *Vanguard Justice Society v. Hughes* and cases cited therein.

The agencies' effort to provide a rule of thumb as to the time needed for the progression of a majority to higher level positions is appropriate, so long as it is clear that the Section provides flexible guidelines rather than imposing a rigid rule. Five years, for example, may be more than reasonable as a time span for promotion of many hourly employees (see *Hicks v. Crown Zellerbach Corp.*, 319 F. Supp. 314 (E.D. La. 1970)), but it may be unrealistically short for managerial, professional and other non-exempt employee classes.

Using a "majority" rule also requires flexibility and the standard for comparison should consist only of those who remain in the job category or the line of progression. Those who transfer to other progression lines, those who fail to bid on vacancies and those who refuse offers of promotion should not be counted when the "majority" computations are made.

The concept expressed in this Section first appeared in the 1968 Department of Labor Testing Order. Since that Order specifically exempted management jobs, it is clear that the provisions of that Order from which the Section arises were not initially intended to apply to management positions. The drafters of the 1968 Testing Order were dealing only with progression within non-exempt job classifications.

PROFESSIONAL ANALYSIS

In applying the provisions of this Section, it should be recognized that progression rates are not likely to be stable. For example, in healthy economic times, employees may progress at a rapid rate, yet in a recession employee progression may be non-existent. Thus documenting progression times may be highly problematic, particularly for the small employer; it might take years to obtain a reliable estimate of average progression time. Progression analyses also must take into account employees who *did* progress, but subsequently returned, voluntarily or involuntarily, to a lower level job. Finally, the progression lines involved may change in such a way as to render the data collected meaningless. Thus this Section and its associated documentation requirements (Section 15G) are problematic and should be applied with flexibility.

Particularly in management and often in nonmanagement, progression lines are not well defined. Often an entry level manager will work in a variety of jobs before being promoted. Thus, many companies hire generalists for management and the selection processes appropriately are characterized by broad selection procedures which incorporate the abilities needed to perform at a given level, rather than in a specific job. The application of this Section should not necessarily focus on specific jobs as the agencies apparently prefer.

Furthermore, many times the progression through levels in management may be relatively slow, whereas movement through various career-enhancing jobs at one level may be more rapid. What constitutes progression

SECTION 5I:
HIGHER LEVEL JOBS

I. *Use of selection procedures for higher level jobs.* If job progression structures are so established that employees will probably, within a reasonable period of time and in a majority of cases, progress to a higher level, it may be considered that the applicants are being evaluated for a job or jobs at the higher level. However, where job progression is not so nearly automatic, or the time span is such that higher level jobs or employees' potential may be expected to change in significant ways, it should be considered that applicants are being evaluated for a job at or near the entry level. A "reasonable period of time" will vary for different jobs and employment situations but will seldom be more than 5 years. Use of selection procedures to evaluate applicants for a higher level job would not be appropriate:

(1) If the majority of those remaining employed do not progress to the higher level job;

(2) If there is a reason to doubt that the higher level job will continue to require essentially similar skills during the progression period; or

(3) If the selection procedures measure knowledges, skills, or abilities required for advancement which would be expected to develop principally from the training or experience on the job.

SECTION 5J:
INTERIM USE

J. *Interim use of selection procedures.* Users may continue the use of a selection procedure which is not at the moment fully supported by the required evidence of validity, provided: (1) The user has available substantial evidence of validity, and (2) the user has in progress, when technically feasible, a study which is designed to produce the additional evidence required by these guidelines within a reasonable time. If such a study is not technically feasible, see section 6B. If the study does not demonstrate validity, this provision of these guidelines for interim use shall not constitute a defense in any action, nor shall it relieve the user of any obligations arising under Federal law.

59. Q. Section 5J on interim use requires the user to have available substantial evidence of validity. What does this mean?

A. For purposes of compliance with 5J, "substantial evidence" means evidence which may not meet all the validation requirements of the Guidelines but which raises a strong inference that validity pursuant to these standards will soon be shown. Section 5J is based on the proposition that it would not be an appropriate allocation of Federal resources to bring enforcement proceedings against a user who would soon be able to satisfy fully the standards of the Guidelines. For example, a criterion-related study may have produced evidence which meets almost all of the requirements of the Guidelines with the exception that the gathering of the data of test fairness is still in progress and the fairness study has not yet produced results. If the correlation coefficient for the group as a whole permits the strong inference that the selection procedure is valid, then the selection procedure may be used on an interim basis pending the completion of the fairness study.

60. Q. What are the potential consequences to a user when a selection procedure is used on an interim basis?

A. The fact that the Guidelines permit interim use of a selection procedure under some conditions does not immunize the user from liability for back pay, attorney fees and the like, should use of the selection procedure later be found to be in violation of the Guidelines. Section 5J. For this reason, users should take steps to come into full compliance with the Guidelines as soon as possible. It is also appropriate for users to consider ways of minimizing adverse impact during the period of interim use.

is often a matter of debate and the application of Section 5I must be even more flexible in the case of management than in that of nonmanagement.

In many cases, it may be appropriate to base selection on the requirements of both the entry job or level and a target job or level. This is particularly true in the case of management where a five-year requirement is typically unrealistic and promotion is largely from within. This Section should be interpreted to allow employers a sufficient pool of managers capable of advancement.

It should be noted that subpart (3) indicates that selection procedures to evaluate applicants for higher level jobs would not be appropriate "if the selection procedures measure knowledges, skills or abilities required for advancement which would be expected to develop principally from the training or experience on the job." This provision fails to recognize that applicant populations typically include experienced and less experienced persons. Applicants selected on the basis of possession of those knowledges, skills, or abilities required for advancement are likely to require less training and less supervision, may be more productive earlier and may advance at a faster rate. The Section also places the employer in the position of having to prove a negative, i.e., that the knowledges, skills and abilities measured by the selection procedure are *not* developed principally on the job.

5J. Interim Use of Selection Procedures ————————————————

LEGAL ANALYSIS

The "no defense" provision of this Section undermines its practical utility as it places the user in precisely the same position he or she would be in the absence of "substantial evidence of validity". At most, the provision is an internal instruction to compliance officers to use their subjective judgment in deciding how to allocate the government's enforcement resources. It may be noted that courts have been somewhat more sympathetic to validity studies in progress. In *Vanguard Justice Society v. Hughes,* for example, the court declined to find adverse impact arising out of a 1977 entry level police examination, noting that a validation study was underway and that only 48 appointments had been made on the basis of the examination at the time of trial. Where a selection procedure has very severe adverse impact, however, it would be legally risky and socially unwise to persist in the use of the procedure in the absence of very strong evidence of validity or pressing public policy reasons for exceptional care, such as safety.

PROFESSIONAL ANALYSIS

This Section provides an interesting contrast in terms of Guidelines' consistency. In order to justify interim use of selection procedures, users must have available "substantial evidence of validity". In Section 3B, the agencies provide that users must consider and validate possible suitable alternative procedures with minimal or no evidence to support such effort.

In addition, if the user already has available "substantial" evidence of validity from other sources, it is likely that if the user's study fails to show validity, the failure will be more likely due to deficiencies in study design or to unreliable data which may have failed to reveal the "true" validity of the procedure.

117

SECTION 5K: CURRENCY OF VALIDITY STUDIES

K. *Review of validity studies for currency.* Whenever validity has been shown in accord with these guidelines for the use of a particular selection procedure for a job or group of jobs, additional studies need not be performed until such time as the validity study is subject to review as provided in section 3B above. There are no absolutes in the area of determining the currency of a validity study. All circumstances concerning the study, including the validation strategy used, and changes in the relevant labor market and the job should be considered in the determination of when a validity study is outdated.

49. Q. Do the Guidelines call for a user *continually* to investigate "suitable alternative selection procedures and suitable alternative methods of using the selection procedure which have as little adverse impact as possible"?

A. No. There is no requirement for continual investigation. A reasonable investigation of alternatives is called for by the Guidelines as a part of any validity study. Once the study is complete and validity has been found, however, there is generally no obligation to conduct further investigations, until such time as a new study is called for. See, Sections 3B and 5K. If a government agency, complainant, civil rights organization or other person having a legitimate interest shows such a user an alternative procedure with less adverse impact and with substantial evidence of validity for the same job in similar circumstances, the user is obliged to investigate only the particular procedure which has been presented. Section 3B.

PROFESSIONAL ANALYSIS

It is true that "there are no absolutes in the area of determining the currency of a validity study." *Major* changes in the job are *potentially* relevant to the currency of a validity study, but the other factors suggested by the agencies, namely the validity strategy used and changes in the relevant labor market, if taken literally, are not seen by the profession as relevant to currency, especially if the "changes" in the relevant labor market refer to race or sex make-up. Research findings indicate that valid scoring keys developed on substantial samples do not change as a function of considerable lengths of time and/or changes in the make-up of the labor market. See Brown, Stephen, "Long-Term Validity of A Personal History Item Scoring Procedure", *Journal of Applied Psychology*, 63 No. 6 (1978), 67-676. Thus "currency" is related to the stability of the job functions rather than to changes in the labor market. Professional practice requires job analysis, not labor market analysis.

The changes in the relevant labor market referenced by the agencies appears to reflect their continued adherence to the concept of differential validity, which is generally unsupported by research findings, particularly as it applies to whites and blacks. See Section 14B (8), below.

Finally, the notion that different validation methods produce results with different life spans, irrespective of stability of job duties, has no supporting evidence.

SECTION 6A:
ALTERNATIVE
SELECTION PROCEDURES

Sec. 6. *Use of selection procedures which have not been validated.*—A. *Use of alternate selection procedures to eliminate adverse impact.* A user may choose to utilize alternative selection procedures in order to eliminate adverse impact or as part of an affirmative action program. See section 13 below. Such alternative procedures should eliminate the adverse impact in the total selection process, should be lawful and should be as job related as possible.

30. Q. When may a user be race, sex or ethnic-conscious?

A. The Guidelines recognize that affirmative action programs may be race, sex or ethnic conscious in appropriate circumstances, (See Sections 4E and 13; See also Section 17, Appendix). In addition to obligatory affirmative action programs (See Question 29), the Guidelines encourage the adoption of voluntary affirmative action programs. Users choosing to engage in voluntary affirmative action are referred to EEOC's Guidelines on Affirmative Action (44 F.R. 4422, January 19, 1979). A user may justifiably be race, sex or ethnic-conscious in circumstances where it has reason to believe that qualified persons of specified race, sex or ethnicity have been or may be subject to the exclusionary effects of its selection procedures or other employment practices in its work force or particular jobs therein. In establishing long and short range goals, the employer may use the race, sex, or ethnic classification as the basis for such goals (Section 17(3) (a)).

In establishing a recruiting program, the employer may direct its recruiting activities to locations or institutions which have a high proportion of the race, sex, or ethnic group which has been excluded or underutilized (section 17(3) (b)). In establishing the pool of qualified persons from which final selections are to be made, the employer may take reasonable steps to assure that members of the excluded or underutilized race, sex, or ethnic group are included in the pool (Section 17(3) (e)).

Similarly, the employer may be race, sex or ethnic-conscious in determining what changes should be implemented if the objectives of the programs are not being met (Section 17(3) (g)).

Even apart from affirmative action programs a user may be race, sex or ethnic-conscious in taking appropriate and lawful measures to eliminate adverse impact from selection procedures (Section 6A).

9. Q. Do the Guidelines require that only validated selection procedures be used?

A. No. Although validation of selection procedures is desirable in personnel management, the Uniform Guidelines require users to produce evidence of validity only when the selection procedure adversely affects the opportunities of a race, sex, or ethnic group for hire, transfer, promotion, retention or other employment decision. If there is no adverse impact, there is no validation requirement under the Guidelines. Sections 1B and 3A. See also, Section 6A.

31. Q. Section 6A authorizes the use of alternative selection procedures to eliminate adverse impact, but does not appear to address the issue of validity. Thus, the use of alternative selection procedures without adverse impact seems to be presented as an option in lieu of validation. Is that its intent?

A. Yes. Under Federal equal employment opportunity law the use of any selection procedure which has an adverse impact on any race, sex or ethnic group is discriminatory unless the procedure has been properly validated, or the use of the procedure is otherwise justified under Federal law. *Griggs* v. *Duke Power Co.,* 401 U.S. 424 (1971); Section 3A. If a selection procedure has an adverse impact, therefore, Federal equal employment opportunity law authorizes the user to choose lawful alternative procedures which eliminate the adverse impact rather than demonstrating the validity of the original selection procedure.

Many users, while wishing to validate all of their selection procedures, are not able to conduct the validity studies immediately. Such users have the option of choosing alternative techniques which eliminate adverse impact, with a view to providing a basis for determining subsequently which selection procedures are valid and have as little adverse impact as possible.

Apart from Federal equal employment opportunity law, employers have economic incentives to use properly validated selection procedures. Nothing in Section 6A should be interpreted as discouraging the use of properly validated selection procedures; but Federal equal employment opportunity law does not require validity studies to be conducted unless there is adverse impact. See Section 2C.

Section 6. Use of Selection Procedures Which Have Not Been Validated

6A. Use of Alternate Selection Procedures to Eliminate Adverse Impact

LEGAL ANALYSIS

This discussion supplements the discussion of alternatives in connection with the fifth point in the Overview, found in Part II of the Analysis. See also Section 3B, above.

A word should be said about the history of Section 6 A. In the Overview, the agencies indicate that earlier agency examples of acceptable alternative procedures were eliminated "to avoid the implication that particular procedures are either prescribed or are necessarily appropriate." The examples in the draft Guidelines were variously either plainly illegal, of dubious legality or of questionable practical application. The statement remaining—that elimination of adverse impact is an alternative to validation—appears as a possible invitation to violate the law, even though employers are instructed to do only what is "lawful". The agencies have left to the employer's discretion a choice that they themselves were unable to clarify with practical, lawful suggestions.

Some courts have appeared to sanction employers' modification of selection procedures resulting in fewer successful candidates of a particular race or sex. Dictum in the Supreme Court decision in *County of Los Angeles v. Davis,* 440 U.S. 625 (1979), suggests that five Court members were satisfied to accept quota hiring as a substitute for validation of an examination and the Tenth Circuit in *Navajo Refining* appeared to approve the use of a lower passing score for minority test takers. Similarly, the Second Circuit has spoken with approval of a suggestion that adverse impact be eliminated by lowering the passing grade on a firefighters' examination in *Ass'n. Against Discrimination v. City of Bridgeport,* 594 F.2d 306 (2d Cir., 1979). But none of these cases has actually passed upon the lawfulness of deliberate modification of selection procedures in order to reduce the number of successful whites and/or males outside of a remedial context. Many Second Circuit cases suggest the inappropriateness of such modification where the victims are identifiable.

PROFESSIONAL ANALYSIS

From their inception and until the present document, guidelines have been published with the primary purpose of defining for the user community the method by which they could meet the "professionally developed test" standard established in Section 703 (h) of the Civil Rights Act of 1964. In historical terms, this has translated into guidelines being promulgated for the specific purpose of advising employers concerning the methods by which they could show the job-relatedness of any selection procedure having an adverse impact. This encouragement of validation was entirely consistent with professional standards, which had advocated validation long before the 1964 Civil Rights Act was passed.

Users now appear to be encouraged to use selection procedures of unknown validity in order to produce parity. This is inconsistent with the original purpose of guidelines promulgation in this field, the legitimate need of employers to select according to relative qualifications and contrary to the ethical standards of the profession, which favor consideration of job-relatedness whenever alternatives are explored.

Reilly and Chao (1980) have reviewed the literature on alternatives to paper and pencil tests and have concluded that there is no reasonable alternative other than scored biographical data. If the agencies can suggest other valid alternatives and have data relative to their impact on various racial sex or ethnic groups, the employer should be so informed. Thus far, that evidence has not been forthcoming, despite the agencies having collected validity study reports from the user community for over a decade.

It may be noted that in Federal Personnel Manual System, FPM Publ. No. 331-3 (March 6, 1980), the Office of Personnel Management announced the formation of a task force "to research alternative selection methods and combinations of methods which reduce adverse impact *and retain validity*" (emphasis added). Nine such methods are listed, in addition to the "Behavioral Consistency Approach", and nine separate research reports have been prepared by the Personnel Research and Development Center on these alternatives. While the validity data for some methods are not thus far very impressive, the profession welcomes the effort and will await its results with interest.

SECTION 6B(1)
INFORMAL PROCEDURES:

B. *Where validity studies cannot or need not be performed.* There are circumstances in which a user cannot or need not utilize the validation techniques contemplated by these guidelines. In such circumstances, the user should utilize selection procedures which are as job related as possible and which will minimize or eliminate adverse impact, as set forth below.

(1) *Where informal or unscored procedures are used.* When an informal or unscored selection procedure which has an adverse impact is utilized, the user should eliminate the adverse impact, or modify the procedure to one which is a formal, scored or quantified measure or combination of measures and then validate the procedure in accord with these guidelines, or otherwise justify continued use of the procedure in accord with Federal law.

SECTION 6B(2)
FORMAL PROCEDURES:

(2) *Where formal and scored procedures are used.* When a formal and scored selection procedure is used which has an adverse impact, the validation techniques contemplated by these guidelines usually should be followed if technically feasible. Where the user cannot or need not follow the validation techniques anticipated by these guidelines, the user should either modify the procedure to eliminate adverse impact or otherwise justify continued use of the procedure in accord with Federal law.

2. Q. What is the basic principle of the Guidelines?

A. A selection process which has an adverse impact on the employment opportunities of members of a race, color, religion, sex, or national origin group (referred to as "race, sex, and ethnic group," as defined in Section 16P) and thus disproportionately screens them out is unlawfully discriminatory unless the process or its component procedures have been validated in accord with the Guidelines, or the user otherwise justifies them in accord with Federal law. See Sections 3 and 6.[1] This principle was adopted by the Supreme Court unanimously in *Griggs* v. *Duke Power Co.*, 401 U.S. 424, and was ratified and endorsed by the Congress when it passed the Equal Employment Opportunity Act of 1972, which amended Title VII of the Civil Rights Act of 1964.

36. Q. How can users justify continued use of a procedure on a basis other than validity?

A. Normally, the method of justifying selection procedures with an adverse impact and the method to which the Guidelines are primarily addressed, is validation. The method of justification of a procedure by means other than validity is one to which the Guidelines are not addressed. See Section 6B. In *Griggs* v. *Duke Power Co.*, 401 U.S. 424, the Supreme Court indicated that the burden on the user was a heavy one, but that the selection procedure could be used if there was a "business necessity" for its continued use; therefore, the Federal agencies will consider evidence that a selection procedure is necessary for the safe and efficient operation of a business to justify continued use of a selection procedure.

41. Q. When should a validity study be carried out?

A. When a selection procedure has adverse impact on any race, sex or ethnic group, the Guidelines generally call for a validity study or the elimination of adverse impact. See Sections 3A and 6, and Questions 9, 31, and 36. If a selection procedure has adverse impact, its use in making employment decisions without adequate evidence of validity would be inconsistent with the Guidelines. Users who choose to continue the use of a selection procedure with an adverse impact until the procedure is challenged increase the risk that they will be found to be engaged in discriminatory practices and will be liable for back pay awards, plaintiffs' attorneys' fees, loss of Federal contracts, subcontracts or grants, and the like. Validation studies begun on the eve of litigation have seldom been found to be adequate. Users who choose to validate selection procedures should consider the potential benefit from having a validation study completed or well underway before the procedures are administered for use in employment decisions.

6B. Where Validity Studies Cannot or Need Not Be Performed

LEGAL ANALYSIS

The choice between eliminating adverse impact and shifting to formal, scored procedures is too limiting and advising employers that they may "otherwise justify continued use of the procedure in accord with federal law" provides no guidance. As indicated in the discussion of Section 6A and elsewhere, numerous cases have found job-relatedness despite subjectivity, informality or the lack of formal validation. *EEOC v. E. I. duPont de-Nemours & Co.,* 445 F.Supp. 223 (D.Del. 1978). Indeed, for selection procedures other than formal tests, such showings of job-relatedness appear to be the rule rather than the exception in the courts. The section also ignores "fitness and character" standards necessary for public and many private employers in a wide variety of jobs. Cf. *Guory v. Hampton,* 510 F.2d 1222 (D.C.Cir. 1974). See Part II, "Overview", Point IV, "Where Adverse Impact Exists: The Basic Options" and Section 3A, above.

PROFESSIONAL ANALYSIS

Certainly there are situations in which many private and public employers "cannot . . . utilize the valida-tion techniques contemplated by these Guidelines", and the Section appears to provide at least some flexibility in terms of Guidelines compliance for small employers. In such circumstances, however, small public and private employers would be better advised to form consortia to validate formal, scored selection procedures, not simply to search for procedures which are as "job-related as possible and which minimize or eliminate adverse impact".

The Guidelines recommend that where an informal and unscored procedure is used which has adverse impact, the employer has two options: (a) to eliminate the adverse impact, or (b) to modify the procedure to one which is a formal, scored or quantitative measure. To encourage the employer to prolong the use of informal, unscored procedures by simply eliminating their impact increases the likelihood of selection error and is contrary to professional principles.

The enforcement agencies appear to be instructing the employer community to ignore considerations of competence in favor of eliminating adverse impact against certain groups. The profession, on the other hand, places emphasis on job qualifications and the job-relatedness of selection devices.

6B (2). Where Formal and Scored Procedures are Used

LEGAL ANALYSIS

This section states that validation should usually be followed if technically feasible, but *only if* the procedure cannot be "otherwise justified" in accordance with federal law. As an alternative, modification to "elimi-nate" the adverse impact is suggested. This may be expecting too much—lessening the degree of adverse impact may be all that can or should be expected. It is worth repeating that consortium efforts or use of transported validity evidence may often be the most practical solution.

PROFESSIONAL ANALYSIS

The Guidelines suggest that where a formal, scored selection procedure has an adverse impact, the employer should "usually" follow validation techniques if feasible. The Guidelines go on to suggest that the employer who is unable to validate should "modify the procedure to eliminate adverse impact". No mention is made of transporting validity evidence or that modification of formal, scored selection procedures may be prohibited by copyright laws. Many of the tests used by employers are copyrighted. In addition, modification of a formal, scored selection procedure raises questions as to whether its reliability and validity have been impaired. Sound practice dictates that such questions must be addressed *before any* modified procedure is used.

SECTION 7A
OTHER
VALIDITY
STUDIES

SEC. 7. *Use of other validity studies.*—A. *Validity studies not conducted by the user.* Users may, under certain circumstances, support the use of selection procedures by validity studies conducted by other users or conducted by test publishers or distributors and described in test manuals. While publishers of selection procedures have a professional obligation to provide evidence of validity which meets generally accepted professional standards (see section 5C above), users are cautioned that they are responsible for compliance with these guidelines. Accordingly, users seeking to obtain selection procedures from publishers and distributors should be careful to determine that, in the event the user becomes subject to the validity requirements of these guidelines, the necessary information to support validity has been determined and will be made available to the user.

35. Q. May reports of validity prepared by publishers of commercial tests and printed in test manuals or other literature be helpful in meeting the Guidelines?

A. They may be. However, it is the user's responsibility to determine that the validity evidence is adequate to meet the Guidelines. See Section 7, and Questions 43 and 66. Users should not use selection procedures which are likely to have an adverse impact without reviewing the evidence of validity to make sure that the standards of the Guidelines are met.

44. Q. Is the user of a selection procedure required to develop the procedure?

A. No. A selection procedure developed elsewhere may be used. However, the user has the obligation to show that its use for the particular job is consistent with the Guidelines. See Section 7.

Section 7. Use of Other Validity Studies

7A. Validity Studies Not Conducted by the User

LEGAL ANALYSIS

The transportability of validity evidence from studies performed by other users or test developers often will represent the only practical means by which many smaller employers can obtain validity evidence at all. It is also of use to larger employers, especially for jobs having relatively few incumbents and/or applicants. Accordingly, employers would be very supportive of provisions that make the transportability of validity evidence feasible. Unfortunately, the Guidelines are not helpful in this respect.

It is, of course, true that the courts will not and should not permit transportability of validity evidence without some examination of the claims for validity. In *Vanguard Justice Society v. Hughes,* for example, the court rejected testimony that a number of police departments had validated an examination when no actual validation studies were placed in evidence. At the same time, however, there is a serious question as to whether the courts will apply the government's standards of transportability strictly. In *Friend v. Leidinger,* the Fourth Circuit observed that plaintiffs challenging the use of a fire fighter examination in Richmond, Virginia—an examination that had been validated in studies involving 55 California fire departments—had the burden of showing in what way the Richmond department differed from those in which the test had been validated, despite EEOC guidelines seeking to place on the user the burden of demonstrating the validity of the imported test.

In *Pegues v. Mississippi State Employment Service,* 22 FEP Cases 392 (N.D.Miss. 1980), the court recognized that the tests developed by the United States Employment Service met professional standards. The court also reasoned that since there was no credible evidence that differences between locations, job duties or applicant populations altered validity, the plaintiff's allegation that validity was specific to a particular location, a particular set of tasks and a specific applicant population was unwarranted. The court agreed that the Mississippi State Employment Service in effect could transport the United States Employment Service validity evidence.

PROFESSIONAL ANALYSIS

From a technical point of view, it is imperative that those who interpret these Guidelines understand that, principally for reasons of technical infeasibility, the majority of the country's employers will not be able to conduct the validity research contemplated by the Guidelines. The majority of these employers are smaller employers, with employee numbers of insufficient size for criterion-related validity research efforts and without the technical expertise to conduct content validity research and development when it is appropriate. Further, many companies do not possess the necessary professional competence internally and the professional competence available externally is sometimes too limited to meet the need. Even very large employers will find it difficult, often impossible, to accumulate the very large numbers of persons hired into the same job which are required for validation studies.

Given this background, the federal agencies should not place employers, particularly smaller employers, in a position of having no option to transport validity evidence.

There is no problem with the general intent of this section in the sense that users should be held responsible for the procedures they use regardless of the source. A major problem is raised, however, because Section 7 B refers only to studies using criterion validity methods. Neither content nor construct validity is mentioned, thereby creating the impression that only criterion validity is "transportable". This may not be the agencies' intention, as there is no reason, for example, why a standardized test of typing ability developed by a test publisher using content validity should not be transportable. It makes no sense to require a user either to develop its own typing test from scratch or to validate the transported test using a criterion-related validity method. This would be duplicative, expensive and unnecessary.

Moreover, even for criterion-related studies, publishers almost never have available the type of detailed analysis, particularly investigations of "fairness" or very extensive job analyses, which are required by Section 7. As a practical matter, then, only those very few, very large employers who can do their own studies could fully comply with this section of the Guidelines—and even then, they can comply only for those jobs with very large numbers of incumbents.

SECTION 7B, 1-3
CRITERION-RELATED VALIDITY

B. *Use of criterion-related validity evidence from other sources.* Criterion-related validity studies conducted by one test user, or described in test manuals and the professional literature, will be considered acceptable for use by another user when the following requirements are met:

(1) *Validity evidence.* Evidence from the available studies meeting the standards of section 14B below clearly demonstrates that the selection procedure is valid;

(2) *Job similarity.* The incumbents in the user's job and the incumbents in the job or group of jobs on which the validity study was conducted perform substantially the same major work behaviors, as shown by appropriate job analyses both on the job or group of jobs on which the validity study was performed and on the job for which the selection procedure is to be used; and

(3) *Fairness evidence.* The studies include a study of test fairness for each race, sex, and ethnic group which constitutes a significant factor in the borrowing user's relevant labor market for the job or jobs in question. If the studies under consideration satisfy (1) and (2) above but do not contain an investigation of test fairness, and it is not technically feasible for the borrowing user to conduct an internal study of test fairness, the borrowing user may utilize the study until studies conducted elsewhere meeting the requirements of these guidelines show test unfairness, or until such time as it becomes technically feasible to conduct an internal study of test fairness and the results of that study can be acted upon. Users obtaining selection procedures from publishers should consider, as one factor in the decision to purchase a particular selection procedure, the availability of evidence concerning test fairness.

66. Q. Under what circumstances can a selection procedure be supported (on other than an interim basis) by a criterion-related validity study done elsewhere?

A. A validity study done elsewhere may provide sufficient evidence if four conditions are met (Sec. 7B):

1. The evidence from the other studies clearly demonstrates that the procedure was valid in its use elsewhere.

2. The job(s) for which the selection procedure will be used closely matches the job(s) in the original study as shown by a comparison of major work behaviors as shown by the job analyses in both contexts.

3. Evidence of fairness from the other studies is considered for those groups constituting a significant factor in the user's labor market. Section 7B(3). Where the evidence is not available the user should conduct an internal study of test fairness, if technically feasible. Section 7B(3).

4. Proper account is taken of variables which might affect the applicability of the study in the new setting, such as performance standards, work methods, representativeness of the sample in terms of experience or other relevant factors, and the currency of the study.

7B. Use of Criterion-Related Validity Evidence From Other Sources
(1) Validity Evidence
(2) Job Similarity
(3) Fairness Evidence

LEGAL ANALYSIS

The agencies' thinking regarding transportability of validity evidence is obscured by a conflicting use of the word "study". Section 7B (1), for example, speaks of evidence from available *studies*, suggesting that evidence from more than one study is necessary. Section 7B (2), on the other hand, speaks of a comparison of the user's job or jobs with the job or jobs in the validity *study*. Since Section 7B (2) describes a methodological requirement, however, it appears that the 7B (1) reference to "studies" is an editorial error and that the agencies in fact regard the borrowing of validity evidence from one study as acceptable, providing the other provisions of Section 7 are met. Unfortunately, however, these other provisions are unworkable, as described below.

The reference to evidence that "clearly" demonstrates validity is also questionable. If validity is sufficient to satisfy professional standards, it should be "clear" enough to transport.

PROFESSIONAL ANALYSIS

In Section 7B (1) the agencies indicate that evidence from available studies meeting standards of Section 14 B of the Uniform Guidelines may be used if they clearly demonstrate that the selection procedure involved is valid. The net effect of this statement, if it is an accurate description of the agencies' intent, is to render any validity study conducted *prior* to the issuance of the Uniform Guidelines unusable or at best questionable. In short, the agencies, through oversight perhaps, have neglected to provide a "grandfather" clause dealing with the studies conducted before the issuance of the Uniform Guidelines. If the omission is intentional, then this Section is inconsistent with acceptable professional practice and Section 15A (3) (b).

In Section 7B (2), the agencies present what appears to be a reasonable requirement that the borrowing user must show that the incumbents in the user's job and the incumbents in the job or group of jobs for which the validity study was conducted perform substantially the same major work behaviors "as shown by appropriate job analyses both on the job or group of jobs on which

the validity study was performed and on the job in which the selection procedure is to be used." This requirement is far more difficult than it appears to be. The professional literature dealing with validity work is not sufficient to permit meeting this standard and test publishers' manuals do not contain detailed job analysis data. In short, the small employer, or those wishing generally to pursue the possibility of transporting validity rather than having no validity at all, will usually be unable to demonstrate the job similarity called for.

Furthermore, one need not sample the *whole* job in order to meet professional standards for transportability. The critical distinction here is to see that the two jobs have the same *element(s)* in common. A case in point would be variously titled jobs involving basic, whole number arithmetic computation. In order to transport an arithmetic test validated elsewhere, it would be necessary to show that such arithmetic computation is a critical element in the studied and unstudied jobs. It should *not* be necessary to show that the jobs have ". . . substantially the same major work behaviors . . ."

Finally, in Section 7B (3), the agencies outline test fairness requirements for borrowed validity studies. They take the apparently reasonable position that if it is not technically feasible for the borrowing user to conduct an internal study of test fairness and the borrowed studies do not contain an investigation of test fairness, the borrowing user may utilize the study until studies conducted elsewhere meeting the requirements of these Guidelines show test unfairness. The Guidelines in effect assume that showings of unfairness are necessarily transportable, a point of view that is not supported by the weight of professional research or opinion. The concepts of differential validity and unfairness are discussed more fully in Section 14B (8).

In summary, users should be permitted to transport validity evidence generated elsewhere if they can show that the elements to be predicted in the job in question are the same as elements predicted in the validity research available. This would meet the agencies' legitimate concerns in Section 7 and it is far preferable to abandoning procedures for which external validity evidence is available.

SECTION 7C AND 7D
VARIABLES
AND
TRANSPORTABILITY

C. *Validity evidence from multiunit study.* if validity evidence from a study covering more than one unit within an organization statisfies the requirements of section 14B below, evidence of validity specific to each unit will not be required unless there are variables which are likely to affect validity significantly.

D. *Other significant variables.* If there are variables in the other studies which are likely to affect validity significantly, the user may not rely upon such studies, but will be expected either to conduct an internal validity study or to comply with section 6 above.

LEGAL ANALYSIS

The question whether differences in "variables" between the external validation study population and the user's workforce invalidates use of the study by the user is essentially left to the judgment of the employer or its experts, subject to potential subsequent review. This may require users to engage in proving a negative; that is, that such variables are not present. The burden of proof should be on the agency to show that such variables exist and significantly influence the inference of validity, not on the employer to show their absence. *U.S. v. South Carolina.* See also *Pegues v. Mississippi State Employment Service* and *Friend v. Leidinger.*

PROFESSIONAL ANALYSIS

In Sections 7C and 7D, the transportability of validity data from studies conducted elsewhere is further limited by a stipulation that such studies may not be used if "variables" are present which are likely to affect validity significantly. These variables are described in the response to Question 66 as performance standards, work methods, representativeness of the sample in terms of experience or other relevant factors and the currency of the study. The first factor, performance standards, is an uninterpretable element. If there is to be a requirement related to performance, that requirement should stipulate that the criterion utilized in the borrowed studies should be the same as the criterion the borrowing user is trying to predict. That is, if the borrowing user is trying to predict turnover, the borrowed study should have used as its performance measure the criterion of turnover, not some other type of job success.

As for the remaining variables described, variance in "work methods" is uninterpretable and "representativeness" of the sample in terms of experience is irrelevant. The question to be addressed is the extent to which length of service affects validity and length of service may depress validity where it affects it at all. Since "other relevant factors" are not defined, they cannot be discussed.

The requirement that incumbents in the user's job(s) and the incumbents in the job where the original study was done ". . . perform substantially the same work behaviors . . ." strongly implies that the jobs must be (nearly) identical in total. As indicated in the discussion of Section 7B, this is unduly restrictive.

To comply with Section 7C, so-called contextual variables are incorporated in the research design. This makes Section 7D superfluous. A consortium study, for example, typically involves a research sample across organizational lines, locations, duties and various applicant and incumbent populations. When validity is established for such heterogeneous samples, the degree to which the findings can be generalized is enhanced by the typical showing that job performance is predictable for each such "look" at the data. Under such circumstances, where it is established that the validity findings can be generalized, the requirement of Section 7D becomes moot.

See also the discussion of Section 7B, above.

SECTION 8
COOPERATIVE STUDIES

SEC. 8. *Cooperative studies.*—A. *Encouragement of cooperative studies.* The agencies issuing these guidelines encourage employers, labor organizations, and employment agencies to cooperate in research, development, search for lawful alternatives, and validity studies in order to achieve procedures which are consistent with these guidelines.

B. *Standards for use of cooperative studies.* If validity evidence from a cooperative study satisfies the requirements of section 14 below, evidence of validity specific to each user will not be required unless there are variables in the user's situation which are likely to affect validity significantly.

43. Q. Can a selection procedure be a valid predictor of performance on a job in a certain location and be invalid for predicting success on a different job or the same job in a different location?

A. Yes. Because of differences in work behaviors, criterion measures, study samples or other factors, a selection procedure found to have validity in one situation does not necessarily have validity in different circumstances. Conversely, a selection procedure not found to have validity in one situation may have validity in different circumstances. For these reasons, the Guidelines requires that certain standards be satisfied before a user may rely upon findings of validity in another situation. Section 7 and Section 14D. See also, Question 66. Cooperative and multi-unit studies are however encouraged, and, when those standards of the Guidelines are satisfied, validity evidence specific to each location is not required. See Section 7C and Section 8.

45. Q. Do the Guidelines permit users to engage in cooperative efforts to meet the Guidelines?

A. Yes. The Guidelines not only permit but encourage such efforts. Where users have participated in a cooperative study which meets the validation standards of these Guidelines and proper account has been taken of variables which might affect the applicability of the study to specific users, validity evidence specific to each user will not be required. Section 8.

72. Q. What options does a user have if a criterion-related study is appropriate but is not feasible because there are not enough persons in the job?

A. There are a number of options the user should consider, depending upon the particular facts and circumstances, such as:

1. Change the procedure so as to eliminate adverse impact (see Section 6A);

2. Validate a procedure through a content validity strategy, if appropriate (see Section 14C and Questions 54 and 74);

3. Use a selection procedure validated elsewhere in conformity with the Guidelines (see Sections 7-8 and Question 66);

4. Engage in a cooperative study with other facilities or users (in cooperation with such users either bilaterally or through industry or trade associations or governmental groups), or participate in research studies conducted by the state employment security system. Where different locations are combined, care is needed to insure that the jobs studied are in fact the same and that the study is adequate and in conformity with the Guidelines (see Sections 8 and 14 and Question 45).

5. Combine essentially similar jobs into a single study sample. See Section 14B(1).

54. Q. How does a user choose which validation strategy to use?

A. A user should select a validation strategy or strategies which are (1) appropriate for the type of selection procedure, the job, and the employment situation, and (2) technically and administratively feasible. Whatever method of validation is used, the basic logic is one of prediction; that is, the presumption that level of performance on the selection procedure will, on the average, be indicative of level of performance on the job after selection. Thus, a criterion-related study, particularly a predictive one, is often regarded as the closest to such an ideal. See American Psychological Association *Standards*, pp. 26-27.

Key conditions for a criterion-related study are a substantial number of individuals for inclusion in the study, and a considerable range of performance on the selection and criterion measures. In addition, reliable and valid measures of job performance should be available, or capable of being developed. Section 14B(1). Where such circumstances exist, a user should consider use of the criterion-related strategy.

Content validity is appropriate where it is technically and administratively feasible to develop work samples or measures of operationally defined skills, knowledges, or abilities which are a necessary prerequisite to observable work behaviors. Content validity is not appropriate for demonstrating the validity of tests of mental processes or aptitudes or characteristics; and is not appropriate for knowledges, skills or abilities which an employee will be expected to learn on the job. Section 14C(1)

The application of a construct validity strategy to support employee selection procedures is newer and less developed than criterion-related or content validity strategies. Continuing research may result in construct validity becoming more widely used. Because construct validity represents a generalization of findings, one situation in which construct validity might hold particular promise is that where it is desirable to use the same selection procedures for a variety of jobs. An overriding consideration in whether or not to consider construct validation is the availability of an individual with a high level of expertise in this field.

In some situations only one kind of validation study is likely to be appropriate. More than one strategy may be possible in other circumstances, in which case administrative considerations such as time and expense may be decisive. A combination of approaches may be feasible and desirable.

74. Q. Is the use of a content validity strategy appropriate for a procedure measuring skills or knowledges which are taught in training after initial employment?

A. Usually not. The Guidelines state (Section 14C(1)) that content validity is not appropriate where the selection procedure involves knowledges, skills, or abilities which the employee will be expected to learn "on the job". The phrase "on the job" is intended to apply to training which occurs after hiring, promotion or transfer. However, if an ability, such as speaking and understanding a language, takes a substantial length of time to learn, is required for successful job performance, and is not taught to those initial hires who possess it in advance, a test for that ability may be supported on a content validity basis.

66. Q. Under what circumstances can a selection procedure be supported (on other than an interim basis) by a criterion-related validity study done elsewhere?

A. A validity study done elsewhere may provide sufficient evidence if four conditions are met (Sec. 7B):

1. The evidence from the other studies clearly demonstrates that the procedure was valid in its use elsewhere.

2. The job(s) for which the selection procedure will be used closely matches the job(s) in the original study as shown by a comparison of major work behaviors as shown by the job analyses in both contexts.

3. Evidence of fairness from the other studies is considered for those groups constituting a significant factor in the user's labor market. Section 7B(3). Where the evidence is not available the user should conduct an internal study of test fairness, if technically feasible. Section 7B(3).

4. Proper account is taken of variables which might affect the applicability of the study in the new setting, such as performance standards, work methods, representativeness of the sample in terms of experience or other relevant factors, and the currency of the study.

82. Q. Do the Guidelines have simplified recordkeeping for small users (employers who employ one hundred or fewer employees and other users not required to file EEO-1, *et seq.* reports)?

A. Yes. Although small users are fully covered by Federal equal employment opportunity law, the Guidelines have reduced their record-keeping burden. See option in Section 15A(1). Thus, small users need not make adverse impact determinations nor are they required to keep applicant data on a job-by-job basis. The agencies also recognize that a small user may find that some or all validation strategies are not feasible. See Question 54. If a small user has reason to believe that its selection procedures have adverse impact and validation is not feasible, it should consider other options. See Sections 7A and 8 and Questions 31, 36, 45, 66, and 72.

Section 8. Cooperative Studies

8A. Encouragement of Cooperative Studies
8B. Standards for Use of Cooperative Studies

LEGAL ANALYSIS

As with Section 7, the reference to generally uninterpretable "other significant variables" leaves users in a position of having to show *non*-existence of "possible" effects on validity.

PROFESSIONAL ANALYSIS

Perhaps the most promising language in the Uniform Guidelines is that found in Section 8: "The agencies issuing these Guidelines encourage employers, labor organizations and employment agencies to cooperate in research, development, search for lawful alternatives, and validity studies in order to achieve procedures which are consistent with these Guidelines."

The cooperative, or consortium, study may be the most effective way for both small and large employers alike to meet the Uniform Guideline requirements and to develop the most reliable and valid prediction systems possible. There is, too, an appealing logic to the consortium study. For example, banks in a given community all share the teller job function as well as many of the other functions found in the banking industry. It makes little sense for *each* bank to be validating selection procedures among small samples of tellers when it is a far better strategy for all banks to band together and study the teller job jointly. As another example, the job of supervisor is described in the Dictionary of Occupational Titles as a Master Title, meaning that the Department of Labor recognizes that the critical work and ability elements of the supervisor job are common irrespective of the functional area or the industry in which the supervision takes place. Clerical occupations such as keypunch operators, typists and stenographers also have a commonality across companies and industries. Again, it makes little sense for individual companies to run the validator's risk by independently studying these common jobs. Aside from the economies of scale which employers would enjoy in consortium work, the data which result from such work, being based on larger samples, are much more reliable and the probability of finding validity, if it is present, is extraordinarily heightened.

SECTION 9
NO ASSUMPTION OF VALIDITY

SEC. 9. *No assumption of validity.—*
A. *Unacceptable substitutes for evidence of validity.* Under no circumstances will the general reputation of a test or other selection procedures, its author or its publisher, or casual reports of it's validity be accepted in lieu of evidence of validity. Specifically ruled out are: assumptions of validity based on a procedure's name or descriptive labels; all forms of promotional literature; data bearing on the frequency of a procedure's usage; testimonial statements and credentials of sellers, users, or consultants; and other nonempirical or anecdotal accounts of selection practices or selection outcomes.

B. *Encouragement of professional supervision.* Professional supervision of selection activities is encouraged but is not a substitute for documented evidence of validity. The enforcement agencies will take into account the fact that a thorough job analysis was conducted and that careful development and use of a selection procedure in accordance with professional standards enhance the probability that the selection procedure is valid for the job.

38. Q. Can a user rely upon written or oral assertions of validity instead of evidence of validity?

A. No. If a user's selection procedures have an adverse impact, the user is expected to produce evidence of the validity of the procedures as they are used. Thus, the unsupported assertion by anyone, including representatives of the Federal government or State Employment Services, that a test battery or other selection procedure has been validated is not sufficient to satisfy the Guidelines.

42. Q. Where can a user obtain professional advice concerning validation of selection procedures?

A. Many industrial and personnel psychologists validate selection procedures, review published evidence of validity and make recommendations with respect to the use of selection procedures. Many of these individuals are members or fellows of Division 14 (Industrial and Organizational Psychology) or Division 5 (Evaluation and Measurement) of the American Psychological Association. They can be identified in the membership directory of that organization. A high level of

qualification is represented by a diploma in Industrial Psychology awarded by the American Board of Professional Psychology.

Individuals with the necessary competence may come from a variety of backgrounds. The primary qualification is pertinent training and experience in the conduct of validation research.

Industrial psychologists and other persons competent in the field may be found as faculty members in colleges and universities (normally in the departments of psychology or business administration) or working as individual consultants or as members of a consulting organization.

Not all psychologists have the necessary expertise. States have boards which license and certify psychologists, but not generally in a specialty such as industrial psychology. However, State psychological associations may be a source of information as to individuals qualified to conduct validation studies. Addresses of State psychological associations or other sources of information may be obtained from the American Psychological Association, 1200 Seventeenth Street, NW., Washington, D.C. 20036.

Section 9. No Assumption of Validity

9A. Unacceptable Substitutes for Evidence of Validity

9B. Encouragement of Professional Supervision

LEGAL ANALYSIS

This Section's rule regarding "no assumption of validity" is accurate with respect to tests. As noted previously, however, the courts often have accepted the job-relatedness of other selection procedures without requiring formal validity evidence. The agencies must allow for this large and growing body of law. See Sections 6B and 3A.

PROFESSIONAL ANALYSIS

It is appropriate to disallow the use of "general reputation" and other "casual" reports of validity. Certainly professional supervision should enhance the probability that validity evidence will be properly obtained and interpreted. However, the suggestion that a "thorough job analysis [be] conducted" can be misleading. The results of a job analysis may have no necessary relationship to the probability that the selection procedure is valid for the job. In many instances in a criterion-related study, the performance one is trying to predict will not depend upon or even need a job analysis and the Guidelines in Section 14B expressly acknowledge that a thorough job analysis is not required to support these criteria (e.g., turnover, etc.).

In summary, there is no problem with the intent of this Section. The problem arises from the impression given by the Section, i.e., that formal validity evidence is always needed to justify a selection standard. An example of where such rigor would be impractical and unnecessary is found in the practice of some commercial airlines to require applicants for the position of pilot to be able to reach all necessary controls when strapped into the command pilot's chair. If there is any question as to the applicant's ability in this regard, it is soon resolved by placing the applicant in a flight deck mock up. This requirement results in adverse impact against females and some ethnic groups, but most enforcement agencies have accepted the job-relatedness of the "test" without either a job analysis or a formal validation study. Similarly, the federal government's "fitness" standard disqualifying applicants convicted of crimes having a relationship to the job has been upheld without formal validity evidence.

SECTION 10A
AGENCY-DEVISED
SELECTION
PROCEDURES

SEC. 10. *Employment agencies and employment services.*—A. *Where selection procedures are devised by agency.* An employment agency, including private employment agencies and State employment agencies, which agrees to a request by an employer or labor organization to device and utilize a selection procedure should follow the standards in these guidelines for determining adverse impact. If adverse impact exists the agency should comply with these guidelines. An employment agency is not relieved of its obligation herein because the user did not request such validation or has requested the use of some lesser standard of validation than is provided in these guidelines. The use of an employment agency does not relieve an employer or labor organization or other user of its responsibilities under Federal law to provide equal employment opportunity or its obligations as a user under these guidelines.

63. Q. If selection procedures are administered by an employment agency or a consultant for an employer, is the employer relieved of responsibilities under the Guidelines?

A. No. The employer remains responsible. It is therefore expected that the employer will have sufficient information available to show: (a) What selection procedures are being used on its behalf; (b) the total number of applicants for referral by race, sex and ethnic group; (c) the number of persons, by race, sex and ethnic group, referred to the employer; and (d) the impact of the selection procedures and evidence of the validity of any such procedure having an adverse impact as determined above.

SECTION 10B
PROCEDURES
DEVISED
ELSEWHERE

B. *Where selection procedures are devised elsewhere.* Where an employment agency or service is requested to administer a selection procedure which has been devised elsewhere and to make referrals pursuant to the results, the employment agency or service should maintain and have available evidence of the impact of the selection and referral procedures which it administers. If adverse impact results the agency or service should comply with these guidelines. If the agency or service seeks to comply with these guidelines by reliance upon validity studies or other data in the possession of the employer, it should obtain and have available such information.

Section 10. Employment Agencies and Employment Services

10A. Where Selection Procedures Are Devised by Agency

LEGAL ANALYSIS

The nature of an employer's obligation when an employment agency is used and the employer does not request the employment agency to devise and use a selection procedure is obscure. The agencies say that "[t]he use of an employment agency does not relieve an employer . . . of its responsibilities under Federal law to provide equal employment opportunity or its obligation as a user under these guidelines." Obviously, the employer must monitor its own selection procedures used upon candidates furnished by an employment agency, but the extent to which the employer is responsible for the agency's practices is unclear. It is equally uncertain whether the employer should monitor the employment agency's impact data and/or determine whether validity evidence presented by the employment agency meets the Guidelines' standards. As a practical matter, employers should request employment agencies to provide a statement (a) on procedures used, (b) whether they have adverse impact and, if yes, (c) whether they have been validated. An employer may further wish to require compliance with EEO laws as a matter of contract with any employment agencies it uses and to obtain a "hold harmless" clause from the agency.

PROFESSIONAL ANALYSIS

Other than state and other government employment services, there are relatively few employment agencies which can be categorized as "large". It will be virtually impossible for the small private employment agency to comply even with the recordkeeping and technical requirements of the Guidelines, unless such agencies are treated like small employers for documentation requirement purposes. See Section 15A.

In addition, the inclusion of the sentence on the responsibility of the employment agency and services user is ambiguous. The specification by the employer of job-related selection standards, e.g., education or work experience, for the referral of candidates by the agency should be the employer's responsibility. Other selection procedures used by the agency, however, should be the agency's responsibility.

10B. Where Selection Procedures Are Devised Elsewhere

LEGAL ANALYSIS

As in Section 10A, the employer's obligations, as opposed to those of the employment agency, are obscure.

SECTION 11 DISPARATE TREATMENT

Sec. 11. *Disparate treatment.* The principles of disparate or unequal treatment must be distinguished from the concepts of validation. A selection procedure—even though validated against job performance in accordance with these guidelines—cannot be imposed upon members of a race, sex, or ethnic group where other employees, applicants, or members have not been subjected to that standard. Disparate treatment occurs where members of a race, sex, or ethnic group have been denied the same employment, promotion, membership, or other employment opportunities as have been available to other employees or applicants. Those employees or applicants who have been denied equal treatment, because of prior discriminatory practices or policies, must at least be afforded the same opportunities as had existed for other employees or applicants during the period of discrimination. Thus, the persons who were in the class of persons discriminated against during the period the user followed the discriminatory practices should be allowed the opportunity to qualify under less stringent selection procedures previously followed, unless the user demonstrates that the increased standards are required by business necessity. This section does not prohibit a user who has not previously followed merit standards from adopting merit standards which are in compliance with these guidelines; nor does it preclude a user who has previously used invalid or unvalidated selection procedures from developing and using procedures which are in accord with these guidelines.

SECTION 12 RETESTING

Sec. 12. *Retesting of applicants.* Users should provide a reasonable opportunity for retesting and reconsideration. Where examinations are administered periodically with public notice, such reasonable opportunity exists, unless persons who have previously been tested are precluded from retesting. The user may however take reasonable steps to preserve the security of its procedures.

61. Q. Must provisions for retesting be allowed for job-knowledge tests, where knowledge of the test content would assist in scoring well on it the second time?

A. The primary intent of the provision for retesting is that an applicant who was not selected should be given another chance. Particularly in the case of job-knowledge tests, security precautions may preclude retesting with the same test after a short time. However, the opportunity for retesting should be provided for the same job at a later time, when the applicant may have acquired more of the relevant job knowledges.

Section 11. Disparate Treatment

LEGAL ANALYSIS

The agencies are correct in their view that disparate treatment is a concept distinct from that of adverse impact and validation. Employers are not obligated to use unchanging standards, *Nance v. Union Carbide Corp.,* 540 F. 2d 718, 727–28 (4th Cir. 1976), *vacated and remanded,* 431 U. S. 952 (1977), but in the absence of very clear business necessity, affected class members should be subjected to standards no more stringent than those applied to other groups during the period of discrimination. The agencies' formulation fails to take into account the principles of *Teamsters v. U. S.,* however. Where standards are (nonpretextually) upgraded, disparate treatment occurs only if the discrimination occurred post-Title VII and only if actual victims can be identified.

The agencies offer a single "out"—business necessity—for an employer's use of more stringent standards where there is an alleged history of prior "discrimination". Despite some imprecise language in early cases suggesting that "business necessity" is equivalent to a "plant closing" standard, the Supreme Court has indicated that "job-relatedness" is sufficient to show "business necessity", at least in the context of affected class considerations. *Furnco Construction Co. v. Waters; New York City Transit Authority v. Beazer; Griggs v. Duke Power Co.*

The reference to merit standards is of particular interest to public sector employers. It remains to be seen whether the Title VII "bona fide" merit system standard of Section 703 (h) is a *Griggs* standard subject to adverse impact analyses or a *Teamsters* standard akin to seniority systems or some third, as yet unidentified, standard.

PROFESSIONAL ANALYSIS

While this is primarily a legal issue, it must be noted that employers have a continuing need to develop accurate (that is, job-related) selection standards. When such procedures are applied in place of what may have been apparently random selection decisions, the new procedures may well have an adverse effect on various subgroups. If the new procedures are, in fact, valid, the employer should be encouraged to use them. Moreover, as jobs change, the requirements may well become "higher", i.e., more technical, requiring broader skills, etc. The fact that existing employees were hired without those skills should not prevent the employer from seeking these skills when hiring new people for the evolving jobs.

The assumption that prior procedures were necessarily less stringent is, of course, unwarranted. For example, modern dictation equipment has eliminated the need for shorthand in many secretarial jobs.

Section 12. Retesting of Applicants

PROFESSIONAL ANALYSIS

The following quotation from the Division 14 Principles on the Validation and Use of Personnel Selection Procedures (1980) expresses an appropriate professional position on retesting:

Employers should provide reasonable opportunities for reconsidering candidates whenever alternative forms exist and reconsideration is technically feasible. Under at least some circumstances, employers should allow candidates to reapply. There might be any of several reasons for questioning the validity of prior assessment for any given person. Where there has been opportunity for new learning, retesting or re-evaluation is usually a desirable practice.

It must be noted, however, that in many employment situations alternate forms are not available and therefore retesting will not be technically feasible. Moreover, almost never are more than two alternate forms available to any employer. Retesting without alternate forms destroys the security of the test items and can result in a very inaccurate interpretation of a candidate's test score.

Unless it is recognized that retesting is frequently infeasible, this Section could be interpreted to require widespread retesting, which could in turn render tests invalid and therefore virtually useless.

SECTION 13
AFFIRMATIVE ACTION

Sec. 13. *Affirmative action.*—A. *Affirmative action obligations.* The use of selection procedures which have been validated pursuant to these guidelines does not relieve users of any obligations they may have to undertake affirmative action to assure equal employment opportunity. Nothing in these guidelines is intended to preclude the use of lawful selection procedures which assist in remedying the effects of prior discriminatory practices, or the achievement of affirmative action objectives.

B. *Encouragement of voluntary affirmative action programs.* These guidelines are also intended to encourage the adoption and implementation of voluntary affirmative action programs by users who have no obligation under Federal law to adopt them; but are not intended to impose any new obligations in that regard. The agencies issuing and endorsing these guidelines endorse for all private employers and reaffirm for all governmental employers the Equal Employment Opportunity Coordinating Council's "Policy Statement on Affirmative Action Programs for State and Local Government Agencies" (41 FR 38814, September 13, 1976). That policy statement is attached hereto as appendix, section 17.

29. Q. What is the relationship between affirmative action and the requirements of the Uniform Guidelines?

A. The two subjects are different, although related. Compliance with the Guidelines does not relieve users of their affirmative action obligations, including those of Federal contractors and subcontractors under Executive Order 11246. Section 13.

The Guidelines encourage the development and effective implementation of affirmative action plans or programs in two ways. First, in determining whether to institute action against a user on the basis of a selection procedure which has adverse impact and which has not been validated, the enforcement agency will take into account the general equal employment opportunity posture of the user with respect to the job classifications for which the procedure is used and the progress which has been made in carrying out any affirmative action program. Section 4E. If the user has demonstrated over a substantial period of time that it is in fact appropriately utilizing in the job or group of jobs in question the available race, sex or ethnic groups in the relevant labor force, the enforcement agency will generally exercise its discretion by not initiating enforcement proceedings based on adverse impact in relation to the applicant flow. Second, nothing in the Guidelines is intended to preclude the use of selection procedures, consistent with Federal law, which assist in the achievement of affirmative action objectives. Section 13A. See also, Questions 30 and 31.

30. Q. When may a user be race, sex or ethnic-conscious?

A. The Guidelines recognize that affirmative action programs may be race, sex or ethnic conscious in appropriate circumstances, (See Sections 4E and 13; See also Section 17, Appendix). In addition to obligatory affirmative action programs (See Question 29), the Guidelines encourage the adoption of voluntary affirmative action programs. Users choosing to engage in voluntary affirmative action are referred to EEOC's Guidelines on Affirmative Action (44 F.R. 4422, January 19, 1979). A user may justifiably be race, sex or ethnic-conscious in circumstances where it has reason to believe that qualified persons of specified race, sex or ethnicity have been or may be subject to the exclusionary effects of its selection procedures or other employment practices in its work force or particular jobs therein. In establishing long and short range goals, the employer may use the race, sex, or ethnic classification as the basis for such goals (Section 17(3) (a)).

In establishing a recruiting program, the employer may direct its recruiting activities to locations or institutions which have a high proportion of the race, sex, or ethnic group which has been excluded or underutilized (section 17(3) (b)). In establishing the pool of qualified persons from which final selections are to be made, the employer may take reasonable steps to assure that members of the excluded or underutilized race, sex, or ethnic group are included in the pool (Section 17(3) (e)).

Similarly, the employer may be race, sex or ethnic-conscious in determining what changes should be implemented if the objectives of the programs are not being met (Section 17(3) (g)).

Even apart from affirmative action programs a user may be race, sex or ethnic-conscious in taking appropriate and lawful measures to eliminate adverse impact from selection procedures (Section 6A).

31. Q. Section 6A authorizes the use of alternative selection procedures to eliminate adverse impact, but does not appear to address the issue of validity. Thus, the use of alternative selection procedures without adverse impact seems to be presented as an option in lieu of validation. Is that its intent?

A. Yes. Under Federal equal employment opportunity law the use of any selection procedure which has an adverse impact on any race, sex or ethnic group is discriminatory unless the procedure has been properly validated, or the use of the procedure is otherwise justified under Federal law. *Griggs* v. *Duke Power Co.,* 401 U.S. 424 (1971); Section 3A. If a selection procedure has an adverse impact, therefore, Federal equal employment opportunity law authorizes the user to choose lawful alternative procedures which eliminate the adverse impact rather than demonstrating the validity of the original selection procedure.

Many users, while wishing to validate all of their selection procedures, are not able to conduct the validity studies immediately. Such users have the option of choosing alternative techniques which eliminate adverse impact, with a view to providing a basis for determining subsequently which selection procedures are valid and have as little adverse impact as possible.

Apart from Federal equal employment opportunity law, employers have economic incentives to use properly validated selection procedures. Nothing in Section 6A should be interpreted as discouraging the use of properly validated selection procedures; but Federal equal employment opportunity law does not require validity studies to be conducted unless there is adverse impact. See Section 2C.

Section 13. Affirmative Action

13A. Affirmative Action Obligations
13B. Encouragement of Voluntary Affirmative Action Programs

LEGAL ANALYSIS

As already indicated, encouragement of affirmative action is irrelevant to the function of the Guidelines. The agencies are correct, however, in stating that compliance with the Guidelines is not necessarily equivalent to meeting affirmative action obligations, so long as it is understood that those obligations do not stem from Title VII.

Apart from the question of whether it is appropriate to include the EEOCC's Policy Statement on Affirmative Action in Guidelines having as their discrete purpose the definition of minimum standards of compliance with Title VII, the Affirmative Action Statement is inconsistent in some respects with other sections of the Guidelines. For example, the method for inferring disparities or adverse impact summarized in the Policy Statement involves an examination of workforce data relative to group representation in the relevant labor market. This method conflicts with the standard for determining evidence of adverse impact proposed in Section 4, a standard concerned with differences in selection rates. It also contradicts Section 703 (j) of the statute.

As another example, the Policy Statement advises that when adverse impact is found, *each* element of the overall selection process should be examined for its validity. This provision goes beyond Sections 4C and 3A of the Guidelines which, taken together, indicate that if the total selection process has an adverse impact, the individual components must be examined for such impact and only those components found to have adverse impact must be validated or otherwise justified in accordance with Section 6 of the Guidelines. Components of the process which do not have adverse impact need not be validated.

SECTION 14
TECHNICAL
STANDARDS

SEC. 14. *Technical standards for validity studies.* The following minimum standards, as applicable, should be met in conducting a validity study. Nothing in these guidelines is intended to preclude the development and use of other professionally acceptable techniques with respect to validation of selection procedures. Where it is not technically feasible for a user to conduct a validity study, the user has the obligation otherwise to comply with these guidelines. See sections 6 and 7 above.

39. Q. Are there any formal requirements imposed by these Guidelines as to who is allowed to perform a validity study?

A. No. A validity study is judged on its own merits, and may be performed by any person competent to apply the principles of validity research, including a member of the user's staff or a consultant. However, it is the user's responsibility to see that the study meets validity provisions of the Guidelines, which are based upon professionally accepted standards. See Question 42.

40. Q. What is the relationship between the validation provisions of the Guidelines and other statements of psychological principles, such as the *Standards for Educational and Psychological Tests*, published by the American Psychological Association (Wash., D.C., 1974) (hereinafter "American Psychological Association *Standards*")?

A. The validation provisions of the Guidelines are designed to be consistent with the generally accepted standards of the psychological profession. These Guidelines also interpret Federal equal employment opportunity law, and embody some policy determinations of an administrative nature. To the extent that there may be differences between particular provisions of the Guidelines and expressions of validation principles found elsewhere, the Guidelines will be given precedence by the enforcement agencies.

SECTION 14A
REVIEW OF
JOB INFORMATION

A. *Validity studies should be based on review of information about the job.* Any validity study should be based upon a review of information about the job for which the selection procedure is to be used. The review should include a job analysis except as provided in section 14B(3) below with respect to criterion-related validity. Any method of job analysis may be used if it provides the information required for the specific validation strategy used.

58. Q. Is a full job analysis necessary for all validity studies?

A. It is required for all content and construct studies, but not for all criterion-related studies. See Sections 14A and 14B(2). Measures of the results or outcomes of work behaviors such as production rate or error rate may be used without a full job analysis where a review of information about the job shows that these criteria are important to the employment situation of the user. Similarly, measures such as absenteeism, tardiness or turnover may be used without a full job analysis if these behaviors are shown by a review of information about the job to be important in the specific situation. A rating of overall job performance may be used without a full job analysis only if the user can demonstrate its appropriateness for the specific job and employment situation through a study of the job. The Supreme Court held in *Albemarle Paper Co.* v. *Moody*, 422 U.S. 405 (1975), that measures of overall job performance should be carefully developed and their use should be standardized and controlled.

Technical Standards

Section 14. Technical Standards for Validity Studies

LEGAL ANALYSIS

This section, as written, is very positive in the acknowledgement of the use of other professionally acceptable validation techniques. However, there is a conflict in phraseology between this section and Section 5. Section 5 and Qs and As 39 and 40 suggest that the enforcement agencies will determine what is professionally acceptable, while the language in Section 14 is more liberal and is also legally preferable in its greater deference to professional standards. See *Vulcan Society of the New York City Fire Department, Inc. v. Civil Service Commission*, 490 F. 2d 387 (2d Cir. 1973).

14A. Validity Studies Should Be Based on Review of Information About the Job

LEGAL ANALYSIS

As this is largely a matter governed by professional expertise, the legal significance of Section 14A depends upon the degree to which courts have endorsed job analysis as a requirement for validation. In general, courts have readily endorsed this requirement. *Albemarle Paper Co. v. Moody; United States v. State of New York; Guardians Association v. Civil Service Commission.*

PROFESSIONAL ANALYSIS

Section 14A provides that any validity study should be based upon a review of information about the job for which the selection procedure is to be used. It provides further that a full job analysis is not required in all situations. The Answer to Question 58 provides fuller detail concerning performance measures not requiring a full job analysis.

The measures listed in the Answer to Question 58, namely, production rate, error rate, absenteeism, tardiness and turnover, do not represent an all-inclusive list, however. Other elements which would not require a full job analysis could include progression rate, job responsibility level and other criteria.

Unfortunately, the Answer to Question 58 also stipulates with respect to measures not requiring a full job analysis that a review of information about the job, nevertheless, should show that these measures are important in the specific situation. It is difficult to imagine when production rate, error rate, absenteeism, tardiness, turnover or the other elements named are not important and a review of information about the job to confirm the importance of these elements is professionally unnecessary.

Finally, the Answer to Question 58 stating that "a rating of overall job performance may be used without a full job analysis only if the user can demonstrate its appropriateness for the specific job and employment situation through a study of the job" is not helpful. A more appropriate statement would have been that a standardized rating of overall work performance may be utilized without a full job analysis if it can be demonstrated that instructions to the raters and the actual ratings were based on a specific, focused and stable set of work behaviors or outcome factors and that all raters were instructed to consider the same set of factors in arriving at their overall rating.

SECTION 14B (1) CRITERION-RELATED STUDIES: TECHNICAL FEASIBILITY

B. *Technical standards for criterion-related validity studies.*—(1) *Technical feasibility.* Users choosing to validate a selection procedure by a criterion-related validity strategy should determine whether it is technically feasible (as defined in section 16) to conduct such a study in the particular employment context. The determination of the number of persons necessary to permit the conduct of a meaningful criterion-related study should be made by the user on the basis of all relevant information concerning the selection procedure, the potential sample and the employment situation. Where appropriate, jobs with substantially the same major work behaviors may be grouped together for validity studies, in order to obtain an adequate sample. These guidelines do not require a user to hire or promote persons for the purpose of making it possible to conduct a criterion-related study.

93. Q. Can the use of a selection procedure which has been shown to be significantly related to only one or two job duties be justified under the Guidelines?

A. Yes. For example, where one or two work behaviors are the only critical or important ones, the sole use of a selection procedure which is related only to these behaviors may be appropriate. For example, a truck driver has the major duty of driving; and in addition handles customer accounts. Use of a selection procedure related only to truck driving might be acceptable, even if it showed no relationship to the handling of customer accounts. However, one or two significant relationships may occur by chance when many relationships are examined. In addition, in most practical situations, there are many critical and/or important work behaviors or work outcomes. For these reasons, reliance upon one or two significant relationships will be subject to close review, particularly where they are not the only important or critical ones.

14B. Technical Standards for Criterion-Related Validity Studies

14B (1). Technical Feasibility

Legal Analysis

The last sentence of Section 14B (1) explicitly provides that persons need not be hired in order to create a large enough group to permit a criterion-related study. This provision may be useful if compliance agencies seek to challenge an employer's decision to use appropriate strategies other than criterion-related validation.

Professional Analysis

This section correctly points out that criterion-related validation is not always technically feasible, but incorrectly implies that technical feasibility is based solely on sample size problems. Definition U in Section 16 is referenced and, although there are professional problems with this definition, it does add the important consideration of whether or not adequate criterion measures will be available.

The next to last sentence in this Section seriously violates sound professional principles by limiting the grouping of jobs to those situations where the jobs have "substantially the same major work behaviors". This limitation implies that job grouping is only appropriate with jobs such as typist and keypunch operator where the skill requirements for performing the *entire* job are very similar. The profession, however, recognizes that a validity study may deal with only a segment of the overall requirements of several jobs. If a given segment or a given requirement of two jobs is similar, and the validation study is aimed at this segment, it would be professionally sound to combine the jobs in the study. This means that jobs might be combined differently in different validation studies (or in the same study).

According to professional standards, a determination of technical feasibility should be based upon all relevant considerations, such as the availability of appropriate samples of adequate size, having or being able to obtain appropriate criterion measures, or having or being able to obtain predictor and criterion scores with an adequate range. It also should permit the user to group jobs, where appropriate, for validity studies, provided that the reasons for determining the similarity of the jobs, or relevant segments of the jobs, are explained.

Finally, the Answer to Question 93 adds new substance and is in serious error in its statement that the sole use of a selection procedure which has been shown to be significantly related to only one or two job duties is acceptable only if the one or two elements are the *only* critical or important ones. Previous Guidelines have permitted this practice without such a condition and professional standards would find the sole use of a selection procedure to predict one or two critical job elements to be perfectly acceptable. In addition, the Answer's apparent limitation of such a practice to prediction of *duty* performance only is contrary to professional practice.

SECTION 14B (2)
ANALYSIS OF
THE JOB

(2) *Analysis of the job.* There should be a review of job information to determine measures of work behavior(s) or performance that are relevant to the job or group of jobs in question. These measures or criteria are relevant to the extent that they represent critical or important job duties, work behaviors or work outcomes as developed from the review of job information. The possibility of bias should be considered both in selection of the criterion measures and their application. In view of the possibility of bias in subjective evaluations, supervisory rating techniques and instructions to raters should be carefully developed. All criterion measures and the methods for gathering data need to be examined for freedom from factors which would unfairly alter scores of members of any group. The relevance of criteria and their freedom from bias are of particular concern when there are significant differences in measures of job performance for different groups.

SECTION 14B (3)
CRITERION MEASURES

(3) *Criterion measures.* Proper safeguards should be taken to insure that scores on selection procedures do not enter into any judgments of employee adequacy that are to be used as criterion measures. Whatever criteria are used should represent important or critical work behavior(s) or work outcomes. Certain criteria may be used without a full job analysis if the user can show the importance of the criteria to the particular employment context. These criteria include but are not limited to production rate, error rate, tardiness, absenteeism, and length of service. A standardized rating of overall work performance may be used where a study of the job shows that it is an appropriate criterion. Where performance in training is used as a criterion, success in training should be properly measured and the relevance of the training should be shown either through a comparsion of the content of the training program with the critical or important work behavior(s) of the job(s), or through a demonstration of the relationship between measures of performance in training and measures of job performance. Measures of relative success in training include but are not limited to instructor evaluations, performance samples, or tests. Criterion measures consisting of paper and pencil tests will be closely reviewed for job relevance.

64. Q. Under what circumstances may success in training be used as a criterion in criterion-related validity studies?

A. Success in training is an appropriate criterion when it is (1) necessary for successful job performance or has been shown to be related to degree of proficiency on the job and (2) properly measured. Section 14B(3). The measure of success in training should be carefully developed to ensure that factors which are not job related do not influence the measure of training success. Section 14B(3).

92. Q. Do significant differences between races, sexes, or ethnic groups on criterion measures mean that the criterion measures are biased?

A. Not necessarily. However, criterion instruments should be carefully constructed and data collection procedures should be carefully controlled to minimize the possibility of bias. See Section 14B(2). All steps taken to ensure that criterion measures are free from factors which would unfairly alter the scores of members of any group should be described in the validation report, as required by Section 15B(5) of the Guidelines

LEGAL ANALYSIS

The enforcement agencies' implication in the last sentence of this section is that *any* difference in criterion measures between race or sex groups constitutes bias. *Julian v. United Air Lines* (Illinois F.E.P.C. 1975), *rev'd.* 19 EPD ¶9185 (Ill. App. Ct. 1979), illustrates the absurdity to which this approach may lead. A black flight attendant was dismissed for theft, an act to which she admitted. However, her defense was that more blacks were dismissed for theft than were whites, a fact that was also true. The defendant was able eventually to show that more blacks committed theft than whites, but it took four years, several appeals and costly litigation to show that this was a fair and unbiased criterion. The point is that the mere presence of group differences does not necessarily constitute bias.

PROFESSIONAL ANALYSIS

This section leaves the impression that evidence of rating bias can be (1) identified, (2) quantified and (3) eliminated, when none of these objectives is truly possible to achieve. It must be recognized that when there are significant differences in rating measures of job performance for different groups, the amount of difference, if any, which is attributable to the various types of criterion contamination as opposed to true performance differences is impossible to measure.

While the absence of bias cannot be assured, supervisory ratings should be focused or based on specific critical or important job duties, work behaviors, work requirements or work outcomes, and instructions to the raters should be detailed and carefully developed in order to maximize the objectivity of the procedure and to sensitize them to factors that can contribute to rating error.

Jobs may differ markedly in work behaviors (tasks) and yet require the same underlying abilities and aptitudes. This is convincingly demonstrated in the American Petroleum Institute Validity Generalization Project (Schmidt, 1980), in which validity for very broad categories of jobs is generalized. For example, in the petroleum industry the maintenance category includes mechanics, electricians, pipefitters, machinists, welders, riggers, pipe coverers, sheet metal workers, etc. The Institute's study, as well as others in various stages of publication, provide substantial evidence that even though many jobs differ markedly in terms of specific task behaviors, they are quite similar in terms of the underlying abilities and aptitudes needed to learn and carry out these behaviors.

14B (3). Criterion Measures

LEGAL ANALYSIS

Apparently in the context of measurement of success in training, the agencies remark that "measures consisting of paper and pencil tests will be closely reviewed for job relevance". This appears contrary to *Washington v. Davis,* where the court accepted the relevance of a paper and pencil test to training, not to the job. The relevance of the training to the job must, of course, also be demonstrated. See, *U.S. v. South Carolina.*

PROFESSIONAL ANALYSIS

The answer to Question 64 indicates "success in training is an appropriate criterion when it is . . . necessary for successful job performance or has been shown to be related to degree of proficiency on the job." This answer suggests that only criterion-related studies of the relationship of training success to job success are acceptable. The Guidelines, however, may be satisfied with a showing of the relevance of training through a comparison of the *content* of the training program with critical or important work behaviors of the job.

The last sentence in this section ("Criterion measures consisting of paper and pencil tests will be closely reviewed for job relevance") is unnecessary in light of the rest of this section. The implication from this sentence is that criterion measures consisting of paper and pencil tests are highly suspect to the enforcement agencies. This is an especially vexing problem to companies that engage in a large amount of apprenticeship or similarly expensive and lengthy training. Often, paper and pencil tests are the only efficient means of assessing trainee performance.

An additional point is that trainees in industrial training programs are typically paid during training. "Trainee" or apprentice job titles are common. Therefore, performance in training is in effect performance on the job and should not be singled out for special treatment by the Guidelines.

SECTION 14B (4)
REPRESENTATIVENESS OF SAMPLE

(4) *Representativeness of the sample.* Whether the study is predictive or concurrent, the sample subjects should insofar as feasible be representative of the candidates normally available in the relevant labor market for the job or group of jobs in question, and should insofar as feasible include the races, sexes, and ethnic groups normally available in the relevant job market. In determining the representativeness of the sample in a concurrent validity study, the user should take into account the extent to which the specific knowledges or skills which are the primary focus of the test are those which employees learn on the job.

Where samples are combined or compared, attention should be given to see that such samples are comparable in terms of the actual job they perform, the length of time on the job where time on the job is likely to affect performance, and other relevant factors likely to affect validity differences; or that these factors are included in the design of the study and their effects identified.

65. Q. When may concurrent validity be used?

A. A concurrent validity strategy assumes that the findings from a criterion-related validity study of current employees can be applied to applicants for the same job. Therefore, if concurrent validity is to be used, differences between the applicant and employee groups which might affect validity should be taken into account. The user should be particularly concerned with those differences between the applicant group and current employees used in the research sample which are caused by work experience or other work related events or by prior selection of employees and selection of the sample. See Section 14B(4).

78. Q. What is required to show the content validity of a paper-and-pencil test that is intended to approximate work behaviors?

A. Where a test is intended to replicate a work behavior, content validity is established by a demonstration of the similarities between the test and the job with respect to behaviors, products, and the surrounding environmental conditions. Section 14B(4).

Paper-and-pencil tests which are intended to replicate a work behavior are most likely to be appropriate where work behaviors are performed in paper and pencil form (e.g., editing and bookkeeping). Paper-and-pencil tests of effectiveness in interpersonal relations (*e.g.*, sales or supervision), or of physical activities (*e.g.*, automobile repair) or ability to function properly under danger (*e.g.*, firefighters) generally are not close enough approximations of work behaviors to show content validity.

The appropriateness of tests of job knowledge, whether or not in pencil and paper form, is addressed in Question 79.

79. Q. What is required to show the content validity of a test of a job knowledge?

A. There must be a defined, well recognized body of information, and knowledge of the information must be prerequisite to performance of the required work behaviors. The work behavior(s) to which each knowledge is related should be identified on an item by item basis. The test should fairly sample the information that is actually used by the employee on the job, so that the level of difficulty of the test items should correspond to the level of difficulty of the knowledge as used in the work behavior. See Section 14C(1) and (4).

LEGAL ANALYSIS

The statements in Section 14B (4) that the validation sample should resemble the "relevant labor market" or the "relevant job market" are vague as to what constitutes a labor market. The Supreme Court has indicated that when labor market comparisons are to be made for jobs requiring qualifications, the comparison is not to the labor market in general but to those in the market who possess the necessary qualifications (*Hazelwood, Teamsters, EEOC v. United Virginia Bank*, 555 F.2d 403 (4th Cir. 1977). See also *Hill v. Western Electric* regarding comparisons of higher level jobs to internal "applicant pools" of qualified candidates.)

There may be some tension between this section and Section 14B (1), as the latter indicates that a user need not hire applicants of a particular race, sex or ethnic group in order to make possible a criterion-related study. Section 14B (4) inappropriately raises a question concerning the adequacy of study samples which are not representative of such groups, even if the overall sample size is otherwise sufficient.

PROFESSIONAL ANALYSIS

The advisory in Section 14B (4) concerning the representativeness of study samples in terms of their race, sex and ethnic group makeup has its origins in the differential validity-fairness concept. The section reflects the continuing insistence on the part of the agencies that differential validity is a viable hypothesis. If one were to express the general consensus of professional opinion at this point, however, it would be that showings of validity should not be called into question or discredited because of the race, sex or ethnic group composition of the samples within which that validity was demonstrated. (See the discussion of "fairness" in Section 14B (8).)

On the other hand, the importance of having a representative sample is well established in the profession and is articulated to ensure that the results obtained from the sample reflect the relationships between variables which are found in the applicable population. This is obscured by Section 14B (4), especially when one considers that enforcement agencies may seek to define the "relevant labor market" in terms of crude population statistics in given geographical areas. If the employer achieves representation of candidates normally available in the relevant labor market, it is unlikely that any agency investigation of the validity of selection procedures would be conducted at all.

The section's assumption that a key factor in determining sample representativeness is the ethnic and sex mix of the sample is therefore incorrect. In the opinion of many professionals, questions of sample representativeness are most appropriately addressed in terms of score distributions rather than any other characteristic. This section is, therefore, misleading and can cause employers to eschew necessary and appropriate validity research or to use strategies more complicated and costly than needed.

A practical problem with the concept of "sample representativeness" is the determination of the qualified or available applicant pool. For example, a significant proportion of females, though perhaps basically qualified for a specific job, may not be active participants in the labor market. Also, the qualified pool for jobs requiring specialized skills and/or knowledge may be greatly different from SMSA statistics. Given the enforcement agencies' broad definitions of labor market and the realities of labor market conditions, it is likely that many disagreements will occur between users and enforcement agencies as to what constitutes a representative sample.

In noting that "the user should take into account the extent to which the specific knowledges and skills (tested) are those which employees learn on the job", the Guidelines seem to imply that the researcher should choose predictors designed to determine if an applicant is qualifiable for a job in preference to predictors which measure relative qualifications currently possessed. This is quite different from ensuring that predictors do not focus on knowledges or skills which many or all of those selected are generally expected to acquire on the job in a short period of time.

Finally, the last paragraph of Section 14B (4) notes that "where samples are combined or compared, attention should be given to see that such samples are comparable in terms of the actual job they perform." This fiat is not professionally accurate because, for example, a study may focus on the comparability of segments of various jobs, even though the jobs may appear on the whole to be dissimilar.

SECTION 14B (5)
STATISTICAL
RELATIONSHIPS

(5) *Statistical relationships.* The degree of relationship between selection procedure scores and criterion measures should be examined and computed, using professionally acceptable statistical procedures. Generally, a selection procedure is considered related to the criterion, for the purposes of these guidelines, when the relationship between performance on the procedure and performance on the criterion measure is statistically significant at the 0.05 level of significance, which means that it is sufficiently high as to have a probability of no more than one (1) in twenty (20) to have occurred by chance. Absence of a statistically significant relationship between a selection procedure and job performance should not necessarily discourage other investigations of the validity of that selection procedure.

SECTION 14B (6)
OPERATIONAL
USE

(6) *Operational use of selection procedures.* Users should evaluate each selection procedure to assure that it is appropriate for operational use, including establishment of cutoff scores or rank ordering. Generally, if other factors reman the same, the greater the magnitude of the relationship (e.g., coorelation coefficient) between performance on a selection procedure and one or more criteria of performance on the job, and the greater the importance and number of aspects of job performance covered by the criteria, the more likely it is that the procedure will be appropriate for use. Reliance upon a selection procedure which is significantly related to a criterion measure, but which is based upon a study involving a large number of subjects and has a low correlation coefficient will be subject to close review if it has a large adverse impact. Sole reliance upon a single selection instrument which is related to only one of many job duties or aspects of job performance will also be subject to close review. The appropriateness of a selection procedure is best evaluated in each particular situation and there are no minimum correlation coefficients applicable to all employment situations. In determining whether a selection procedure is appropriate for operational use the following considerations should also be taken into account: The degree of adverse impact of the procedure, the availability of other selection procedures of greater or substantially equal validity.

73. Q. Must a selection procedure supported by content validity be an actual "on the job" sample of work behaviors?

A. No. The Guidelines emphasize the importance of a close approximation between the content of the selection procedure and the observable behaviors or products of the job, so as to minimize the inferential leap between performance on the selection procedure and job performance. However, the Guidelines also permit justification on the basis of content validity of selection procedures measuring knowledges, skills, or abilities which are not necessarily samples of work behaviors if: (1) The knowledge, skill, or ability being measured is operationally defined in accord with Section 14C(4); and (2) that knowledge, skill, or ability is a prerequisite for critical or important work behaviors. In addition users may justify a requirement for training, or for experience obtained from prior employment or volunteer work, on the basis of content validity, even though the prior training or experience does not duplicate the job. See Section 14B(6).

14B (5). Statistical Relationships

LEGAL ANALYSIS

It is inconsistent that the agencies recognize the need for statistical significance in validation studies but reject statistical significance in making adverse impact calculations.

See also comments on Section 14B (6).

PROFESSIONAL ANALYSIS

Although perhaps simplistic, this section is professionally unobjectionable. The last sentence, however, permitting a second attempt at validation using a different strategy if the first study fails, should not be used to prolong the search for "equally valid, less adverse alternatives" as provided in the debatable provisions of Sections 3B and 6A, discussed above.

The profession would concur in the statement that the .05 level of significance is "generally" proper. Where a very few are to be selected from among a very large number of applicants, however, procedures with validities which do not reach the .05 significance level would be professionally acceptable. It is assumed that the agencies have recognized this acceptability with their use of the word "generally" in introducing the significance level requirement.

14B (6). Operational Use of Selection Procedures

LEGAL ANALYSIS

To consider the *degree* of adverse impact in order to assess the appropriateness of a selection procedure appears inconsistent with *Griggs* (which requires only job-relatedness), as well as with *Furnco* and *Keene State College* (which respectively show that an employer need not seek methods of maximizing minority participation and that any showing of job-relatedness is sufficient to dispel the inference of discrimination arising from a prima facie case). As for the availability of less adverse procedures having "substantially equal" validity, this, too, is an incorrect measure of appropriateness, unless it can be shown that the user knew or should have known about such alternatives but ignored them. In that case, evidence of pretextual use of the validated procedure might be established, the burden of proof being, of course, on the enforcement agency. *Albemarle Paper Co. v. Moody.*

The concept of "appropriateness" more properly belongs in a manual treating fulfillment of affirmative action obligations than in Guidelines treating minimum compliance with legal requirements.

PROFESSIONAL ANALYSIS

The statement that "the appropriateness of a selection procedure is best evaluated in each particular situation and there are no minimum correlation coefficients applicable to all employment situations" is an excellent description of decision theory. The balance of the section, however, appears to give priority to the agencies' social objectives rather than to critical elements of utility determinations, such as: the selection ratio, that is, the number of openings available as compared to the number of applicants; the consequences of misclassification, that is, the extent of damage that can be brought upon the individual, co-workers, the public or the organization by mistakes in selection; and the extent to which variability in performance is possible in a given job classification.

The assumption that low (yet significant) validity is not acceptable is erroneous. Reference to the Taylor-Russell tables found in nearly every elementary industrial psychology textbook shows conclusively that selection instruments with low validity can serve a legitimate business function depending on the number of hires and the ratio of persons selected as compared to applicants.

149

SECTION 14B (7)
OVERSTATEMENT OF FINDINGS

(7) *Overstatement of validity findings.* Users should avoid reliance upon techniques which tend to overestimate validity findings as a result of capitalization on chance unless an appropriate safeguard is taken. Reliance upon a few selection procedures or criteria of successful job performance when many selection procedures or criteria of performance have been studied, or the use of optimal statistical weights for selection procedures computed in one sample, are techniques which tend to inflate validity estimates as a result of chance. Use of a large sample is one safeguard: cross-validation is another.

SECTION 14B (8)(a)(b)(c)
FAIRNESS

(8) *Fairness.* This section generally calls for studies of unfairness where technically feasible. The concept of fairness or unfairness of selection procedures is a developing concept. In addition, fairness studies generally require substantial numbers of employees in the job or group of jobs being studied. For these reasons, the Federal enforcement agencies recognize that the obligation to conduct studies of fairness imposed by the guidelines generally will be upon users or groups of users with a large number of persons in a a job class, or test developers; and that small users utilizing their own selection procedures will generally not be obligated to conduct such studies because it will be technically infeasible for them to do so.

(a) *Unfairness defined.* When members of one race, sex, or ethnic group characteristically obtain lower scores on a selection procedure than members of another group; and the differences in scores are not reflected in differences in a measure of job performance, use of the selection procedure may unfairly deny opportunities to members of the group that obtains the lower scores.

(b) *Investigation of fairness.* Where a selection procedure results in an adverse impact on a race, sex, or ethnic group identified in accordance with the classifications set forth in section 4 above and that group is a significant factor in the relevant labor market, the user generally should investigate the possible existence of unfairness for that group if it is technically feasible to do so. The greater the severity of the adverse impact on a group, the greater the need to investigate the possible existence of unfairness. Where the weight of evidence from other studies shows that the selection procedure predicts fairly for the group in question and for the same or similar jobs, such evidence may be relied on in connection with the selection procedure at issue.

(c) *General considerations in fairness investigations.* Users conducting a study of fairness should review the A.P.A. Standards regarding investigation of possible bias in testing. An investigation of fairness of a selection procedure depends on both evidence of validity and the manner in which the selection procedure is to be used in a particular employment context. Fairness of a selection procedure cannot necessarily be specified in advance without investigating these factors. Investigation of fairness of a selection procedure in samples where the range of scores on selection procedures or criterion measures is severely restricted for any subgroup sample (as compared to other subgroup samples) may produce misleading evidence of unfairness. That factor should accordingly be taken into account in conducting such studies and before reliance is placed on the results.

150

PROFESSIONAL ANALYSIS

This Section anticipates a situation in which an excessive number of criteria are used and validity at the .05 level of significance is found only for one or a few of the criteria. In such a case, validity even of those criteria would be subject to review. Techniques which tend to inflate validity estimates also are open to challenge, but it should be noted that commonly accepted statistical adjustments (e.g., for criterion unreliability or for restriction in range) are not viewed by the profession as techniques which overstate validity. If this is understood, the Section comports with commonly accepted standards of professional practice.

14B (8). Fairness

(a) Unfairness Defined
(b) Investigation of Fairness
(c) General Considerations in Fairness Investigations

LEGAL ANALYSIS

There is no statutory, judicial, or professional basis for including the concept of "fairness" in the Guidelines. In some ways, it attempts to permit the agencies to avoid the rule in *Teamsters, Evans* and *Hazelwood* against liability for pre-Act conduct or for historical factors beyond the employer's control.

The implication of Section 14B (8) is that if a selection procedure does not result in equal employment, that is, comparable proportions of jobs for members of each class of applicants, there is unfairness. This is a false premise. The Clark-Case Memorandum of Understanding from the legislative history of Title VII indicates that Congress recognized that legitimate tests do not necessarily produce "parity" results. As indicated in the discussion of Section 5G, the statement of Senators Clark and Case was quoted by the Supreme Court in its unanimous opinion in *Griggs:*

> There is no requirement in Title VII that employers abandon *bona fide* qualification tests where, because of differences in background and education, members of some groups are able to perform better on these tests than members of other groups.

One unusual feature of this Section is its apparent effort to preclude employers who have previously discriminated from using criterion-related studies. The technical inability of such an employer to conduct a fairness study is held not to be an excuse for failure to conduct one. See Section 14B (8) (f).

The notion of item fairness introduced in this Section has not found favor in the courts. See *Friend v. Leidin-ger; Smith v. Troyan,* 520 F.2d 492 (6th Cir. 1975), *cert. denied,* 426 U.S. 934 (1976).

PROFESSIONAL ANALYSIS

The rationale for inclusion of Section 14B (8) in the Guidelines is stated quite clearly in its subsection (a): "When members of one ethnic, racial, or sex group characteristically obtain lower scores on a selection procedure than members of another group, and the differences are not reflected in differences in measures of job performance, use of the selection procedure may unfairly deny opportunities to members of the group that obtains the lower scores." One sentence thus describes the theory of differential prediction—that tests valid for whites might be less valid or invalid for blacks and other affected subgroups.

However, the concept of "fairness" as it appears in Section 14B (8)* and elsewhere in the Guidelines is professionally objectionable for at least four reasons:
1) The concept of fairness reflected in the Guidelines is oversimplistic and obsolescent from a professional standpoint.
2) There is no generally accepted professional definition of fairness and proposed definitions and models conflict with one another. Some are plainly erroneous.
3) However "unfairness" is defined, the weight of

---

*In addition to Section 14B (8), this discussion touches on material from Part II, "Overview," Point 7, Sections 15B (8) and 16V of the Guidelines, and Questions and Answers 67–71.

(8) *Fairness.* This section generally calls for studies of unfairness where technically feasible. The concept of fairness or unfairness of selection procedures is a developing concept. In addition, fairness studies generally require substantial numbers of employees in the job or group of jobs being studied. For these reasons, the Federal enforcement agencies recognize that the obligation to conduct studies of fairness imposed by the guidelines generally will be upon users or groups of users with a large number of persons in a a job class, or test developers; and that small users utilizing their own selection procedures will generally not be obligated to conduct such studies because it will be technically infeasible for them to do so.

(a) *Unfairness defined.* When members of one race, sex, or ethnic group characteristically obtain lower scores on a selection procedure than members of another group, and the differences in scores are not reflected in differences in a measure of job performance, use of the selection procedure may unfairly deny opportunities to members of the group that obtains the lower scores.

(b) *Investigation of fairness.* Where a selection procedure results in an adverse impact on a race, sex, or ethnic group identified in accordance with the classifications set forth in section 4 above and that group is a significant factor in the relevant labor market, the user generally should investigate the possible existence of unfairness for that group if it is technically feasible to do so. The greater the severity of the adverse impact on a group, the greater the need to investigate the possible existence of unfairness. Where the weight of evidence from other studies shows that the selection procedure predicts fairly for the group in question and for the same or similar jobs, such evidence may be relied on in connection with the selection procedure at issue.

(c) *General considerations in fairness investigations.* Users conducting a study of fairness should review the A.P.A. Standards regarding investigation of possible bias in testing. An investigation of fairness of a selection procedure depends on both evidence of validity and the manner in which the selection procedure is to be used in a particular employment context. Fairness of a selection procedure cannot necessarily be specified in advance without investigating these factors. Investigation of fairness of a selection procedure in samples where the range of scores on selection procedures or criterion measures is severely restricted for any subgroup sample (as compared to other subgroup samples) may produce misleading evidence of unfairness. That factor should accordingly be taken into account in conducting such studies and before reliance is placed on the results.

---

67. Q. What does "unfairness of a selection procedure" mean?

A. When a specific score on a selection procedure has a different meaning in terms of expected job performance for members of one race, sex or ethnic group than the same score does for members of another group, the use of that selection procedure may be unfair for members of one of the groups. See section 16V. For example, if members of one group have an average score of 40 on the selection procedure, but perform on the job as well as another group which has an average score of 50, then some uses of the selection procedure would be unfair to the members of the lower scoring group. See Question 70.

68. Q. When should the user investigate the question of fairness?

A. Fairness should be investigated generally at the same time that a criterion-related validity study is conducted, or as soon thereafter as feasible. Section 14B(8).

69. Q. Why do the Guidelines require that users look for evidence of unfairness?

A. The consequences of using unfair selection procedures are severe in terms of discriminating against applicants on the basis of race, sex or ethnic group membership. Accordingly, these studies should be performed routinely where technically feasible and appropriate, whether or not the probability of finding unfairness is small. Thus, the Supreme Court indicated in *Albemarle Paper Co.* v. *Moody*, 422 U.S. 405, that a validation study was "materially deficient" because, among other reasons, it failed to investigate fairness where it was not shown to be unfeasible to do so. Moreover, the American Psychological Association *Standards* published in 1974 call for the investigation of test fairness in criterion-related studies wherever feasible (pp. 43–44).

71. Q. How is test unfairness related to differential validity and to differential prediction?

A. Test unfairness refers to use of selection procedures based on scores when members of one group characteristically obtain lower scores than members of another group, and the differences are not reflected in measures of job performance. See Sections 16V and 14B(8)(a), and Question 67.

Differential validity and test unfairness are conceptually distinct. Differential validity is defined as a situation in which a given instrument has significantly different validity coefficients for different race, sex or ethnic groups. Use of a test may be unfair to some groups even when differential validity is not found.

Differential prediction is a central concept for one definition of test unfairness. Differential prediction occurs when the use of the same set of scores systematically overpredicts or underpredicts job performance for members of one group as compared to members of another group.

Other definitions of test unfairness which do not relate to differential prediction may, however, also be appropriately applied to employment decisions. Thus these Guidelines are not intended to choose between fairness models as long as the model selected is appropriate to the manner in which the selection procedure is used.

empirical evidence clearly indicates that it does not occur very often; when it does occur as a statistical phenomenon, it is highly likely to be a chance finding.

4) In those few instances when "unfairness" is found, the results of such studies would usually, if implemented by organizations, operate to *undercut* affirmative action undertakings.

At the time of its espousal in the mid-1960s, the differential validity hypothesis generated an instant and hopeful reaction, particularly as it applied to blacks. It held that because of cultural differences and deprivations, test scores achieved by blacks could have a different meaning from test scores achieved by whites; that given the chance, blacks would perform better on the job than their test scores would indicate and at a higher level than whites with similar test scores would perform. If pursued to its logical conclusion through a major program of basic research, the prediction error the theory assumed to exist for blacks and other subgroups could be corrected.

As a consequence of its extremely positive appeal, differential prediction was incorporated into the 1968 OFCC Testing Order, although there was little research evidence to support its inclusion. The requirement later was incorporated in the 1970 EEOC Guidelines, again without adequate supporting evidence to warrant its inclusion.

In the early 1970s, however, substantial professional research was conducted regarding the differential prediction theory and the data produced by such investigations permitted the tentative conclusions that:

(1) Tests which were valid predictors for the majority group are usually valid predictors for the minority group also (Boehm, 1972; Schmidt et al., 1973).

(2) In those unusual instances where tests differentially predict job performance for minorities and whites, they more often *over*predict the performance of minorities—in other words, they are "unfair" to whites (Cleary, 1968; Campbell et al., 1973; Linn, 1973; Ruch, 1972).

(3) Findings that seemed to indicate different relationships between test scores and job performance might well be due to methodological inadequacies in the research (Bray and Moses, 1972; Wallace, 1972).

At a conference held to discuss a series of key studies in this area (Campbell et al., 1973), the following statement by the late S. Rains Wallace expressed the emerging stance of the profession:

It appears to me to be about time for us to accept the proposition that written aptitude tests, administered correctly and evaluated against reasonable, reliable, unbiased, and relevant criteria, do about the same job in one ethnic group as in another. It seems clear that people like me who expected race to act as a moderator variable for validity relationships were wrong. . . . In short, differential or single group validity is an artifact of small samples, inequalities in restrictions or their correction, or biases in criteria.

While the Uniform Guidelines were being drafted and redrafted, two professional developments occurred which make the treatment of the topic in the Uniform Guidelines inadequate.

1) Test fairness models were clearly recognized as themselves incorporating some value system into their assumptions (Fincher, 1975; Gross and Su, 1975; Hunter and Schmidt, 1976). Not only do various fairness models yield conflicting results, but the *choice* of which fairness model to use is in and of itself a policy decision as well as a scientific one, based on considerations of perceived utility of outcome.

While the Guidelines recognize that "there is serious debate in the psychological profession on the question of test fairness", they do not mention the sources of this debate, i.e., conflicting results produced by the various fairness models and the underlying philosophic controversy. Treatment of fairness in the Guidelines is thus extremely simplistic and obsolescent, based as it appears to be on the notion that there is a commonly agreed upon model for evaluating fairness.

2) There were numerous empirical studies of differences in test validities (for example, Cascio, 1976; Gael, Grant and Ritchie, 1975a, 1975b; Fox and Lefkowitz, 1974; Huck and Bray, 1976). As the volume of such studies grew, it became increasingly clear that in the portion of the fairness controversy which dealt with the examination of the differences between validity coefficients, i.e., differential validity, a consensus was emerging: "The track record for differential validity is not impressive" (Fincher, 1975, p. 483); "Differential prediction as a research hypothesis has been repeatedly investigated and repeatedly found wanting" (Boehm, 1977, p. 153); "Differential validity may well be labeled a *pseudo problem* . . ." (Linn, 1978, p. 511).

While the Questions and Answers make the

WHEN ARE FAIRNESS INVESTIGATIONS REQUIRED BY THE UNIFORM GUIDELINES?

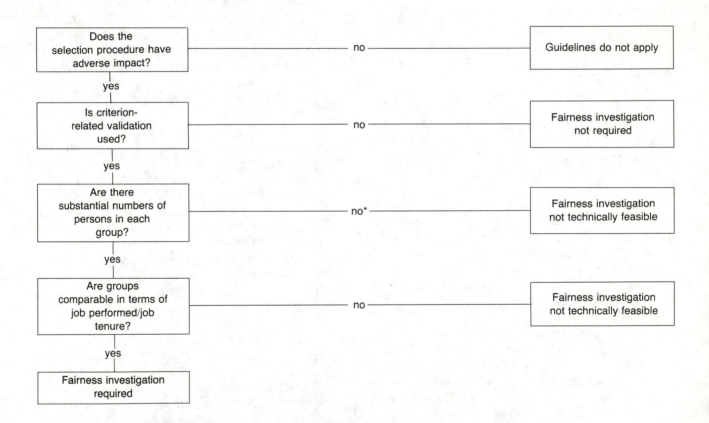

*The Guidelines appear to require a fairness study even if not technically feasible if the lack of adequate samples from certain groups is caused by the employer's prior discriminatory acts. See Section 14B (8) (f).

conceptual distinction between the statistical concept of differential validity and the broader fairness issue, which also incorporates policy and test usage concepts, the Guidelines themselves do not do so. The language of Section 14B (8) uses the concepts interchangeably and without even indirect recognition that the simpler issue of differential validity has virtually been resolved and that very few psychologists now grant it credence. (A rare exception to this growing consensus is taken by Katzell and Dyer (1977, 1978).)

Given these findings, the weight of the evidence strongly indicates that fairness studies should not be required by the Guidelines.

In addition, since the evidence suggests that tests *over*-predict performance of blacks rather than the reverse, the Guidelines' fairness requirements could lead to results that would not enhance job opportunities for minorities.

This can be illustrated by examining the example in Question 67. The more typical outcome would be that if the members of the group which had an average score of 40 on the selection procedure were black and the group which had an average score of 50 on the procedure were white, the blacks with a score of 40 would typically be found to be performing *less* well on the job than whites with a score of 40. To respond to the agencies' direction in Section 14B (8), therefore, would require setting a higher cutoff score for blacks if it were known that their scores of 40 predict that they will not perform as well as whites having a score of 40.

The reference in Question 69 to the *Standards* published by the American Psychological Association in 1974 also requires clarification. The *Standards* state that: "It is important to recognize that there are different definitions of fairness and whether a given procedure is or is not fair may depend upon the definition accepted. Moreover, there are statistical and psychometric uncertainties about some of the sources of apparent differences in validity or regression. Unless a difference is observed on samples of substantial size, and unless there is a reasonably sound psychological/sociological theory upon which to explain an observed difference, the difference should be viewed with caution." This is far from constituting an endorsement of the fairness doctrine.

The response to Question 70 introduces new substance not covered in the Guidelines, specifically, the concept of *item* unfairness. In the answer to Question 70, the agencies indicate that " . . . certain items may be found to be the only ones which cause the unfairness to a particular group, and these items may be deleted or replaced by others." The agencies do not indicate how item fairness is to be determined. Item fairness is not determined merely by examining differences in performance by each group on each item or by examining results of interview questions for members of different groups and then comparing the proportion in each group which gets an answer "right", under the assumption that any significant difference between proportions constitutes bias. There is no agreed upon method for determining item bias or as the agencies describe it, item fairness.

Some researchers believe that item fairness is determined in the same way as test fairness and, to the extent this is true, all of the objections to test fairness discussed above also apply. In any event, requiring studies of item fairness increases exponentially the employer's burden and expense of showing job-relatedness.

In practice, fairness studies are seldom actually required under the Guidelines. The Guidelines require a fairness study only if four conditions are met. These circumstances seldom occur—especially technical feasibility. Consequently, the fact that fairness studies are mentioned in the Guidelines creates a misleading impression that they can or should be a routine aspect of criterion-related validity studies. The four conditions are outlined in the flow chart on the facing page.

SECTION 14B (8)(d)
WHEN UNFAIRNESS
SHOWN

(d) *When unfairness is shown.* If unfairness is demonstrated through a showing that members of a particular group perform better or poorer on the job than their scores on the selection procedure would indicate through comparison with how members of other groups perform, the user may either revise or replace the selection instrument in accordance with these guidelines, or may continue to use the selection instrument operationally with appropriate revisions in its use to assure compatibility between the probability of successful job performance and the probability of being selected.

70. Q. What should be done if a selection procedure is unfair for one or more groups in the relevant labor market?

A. The Guidelines discuss three options. See Section 14B(8)(d). First, the selection instrument may be replaced by another validated instrument which is fair to all groups. Second, the selection instrument may be revised to eliminate the sources of unfairness. For example, certain items may be found to be the only ones which cause the unfairness to a particular group, and these items may be deleted or replaced by others. Finally, revisions may be made in the method of use of the selection procedure to ensure that the probability of being selected is compatible with the probability of successful job performance.

The Federal enforcement agencies recognize that there is serious debate in the psychological profession on the question of test fairness, and that information on that concept is developing. Accordingly, the enforcement agencies will consider developments in this field in evaluating actions occasioned by a finding of test unfairness.

SECTION 14B (8)(e)
TECHNICAL
FEASIBILITY

(e) *Technical feasibility of fairness studies.* In addition to the general conditions needed for technical feasibility for the conduct of a criterion-related study (see section 16, below) an investigation of fairness requires the following:

(i) An adequate sample of persons in each group available for the study to achieve findings of statistical significance. Guidelines do not require a user to hire or promote persons on the basis of group classifications for the purpose of making it possible to conduct a study of fairness; but the user has the obligation otherwise to comply with these guidelines.

(ii) The samples for each group should be comparable in terms of the actual job they perform, length of time on the job where time on the job is likely to affect performance, and other relevant factors likely to affect validity differences; or such factors should be included in the design of the study and their effects identified.

SECTION 14B (8)(f)
CONTINUED USE

(f) *Continued use of selection procedures when fairness studies not feasible.* If a study of fairness should otherwise be performed, but is not technically feasible, a selection procedure may be used which has otherwise met the validity standards of these guidelines, unless the technical infeasibility resulted from discriminatory employment practices which are demonstrated by facts other than past failure to conform with requirements for validation of selection procedures. However, when it becomes technically feasible for the user to perform a study of fairness and such a study is otherwise called for, the user should conduct the study of fairness.

14B (8) (d). When "Unfairness" Is Shown

PROFESSIONAL ANALYSIS

The Guidelines discuss three ways of dealing with unfairness. One is to change "the method of use of the selection procedure to ensure that the probability of being selected is compatible with the probability of successful job performance." However, as pointed out above, where there are differences in the prediction of job performance for majority and minority group members, the performance of minority group members is usually *over*predicted. (See e.g., Hunter and Schmidt, 1976; Linn, 1978.) Thus, maximizing the outcome " . . . to insure that the probability of being selected is compatible with the probability of successful job per-

formance" would usually, in those few instances where there is differential prediction, lead to the establishment of a cut-off point on the predictor at a *higher* level for minority group members than for whites.

The Guidelines suggest two other ways of dealing with unfairness: replacing the selection instrument with another validated instrument and deleting those portions of the procedure which are the sources of the unfairness. In practice, both options require additional validation efforts. Deleting portions of a validated procedure will, of course, impact on the validity of the procedure and require further validation research. At that point, the issue ceases to be a fairness question.

14B (8) (e). Technical Feasibility of Fairness Studies

LEGAL ANALYSIS

See discussion under Section 14B (8) (a).

PROFESSIONAL ANALYSIS

Section 14B (8) (e) indicates that fairness studies will rarely be technically feasible, especially for smaller

employers. With modern data processing capabilities, the required statistical manipulations may not be unduly burdensome for a few large employers, but the studies will most likely not be technically feasible for other reasons.

14B (8) (f). Continued Use of Selection Procedures When Fairness Studies Not Feasible

LEGAL ANALYSIS

The agencies permit use of a validated selection procedure without conducting a fairness study if such a study is technically infeasible, unless the technical infeasibility resulted from prior discriminatory practices "other than past failure to conform with requirements for validation of selection procedures". First, failure to validate even a procedure that has severe adverse impact is not a "discriminatory practice", so the exception to the ban on use of procedures where the infeasibility of fairness studies stems from prior discrimination is meaningless. More important, the ban makes no sense: the remedies for prior discrimination are the province of the courts; a ban on a selection procedure because a fairness study is not feasible, where the infeasibility results from alleged prior discrimination, is an inappropriate remedy for such discrimination. If the procedure is otherwise validated (i.e., if formally shown to be job-related), this is as much as the courts require. As the Supreme Court made clear in *United Air Lines, Inc. v. Evans,* present effects of past discrimination do not in themselves constitute discrimination under Title VII. Thus, penalizing an employer for alleged past discrim-

ination by prohibiting use of a job-related test is unlawful, especially as the only present effect is the lack of sufficient numbers of minority group individuals to permit a fairness study.

See also Q and A 69 and comments at Section 14B (8) (a).

PROFESSIONAL ANALYSIS

Not mentioned in this section but an issue which would be of serious concern to users is the potential liability employers would incur from using a validated selection procedure when fairness was not originally technically feasible to assess but subsequently became feasible and statistical evidence of unfairness was found, assuming for the sake of argument that such evidence could have any professional significance in light of the professional literature questioning the fairness concept, discussed above in Section 14B (8) (a). As implied in Section 7B (3), evidence of unfairness from a study not conducted by the user will be taken as evidence of unfairness (implying that unfairness is transportable but validity is not, when actually the converse is more likely to be true).

157

C. *Technical standards for content validity studies.*—(1) *Appropriateness of content validity studies.* Users choosing to validate a selection procedure by a content validity strategy should determine whether it is appropriate to conduct such a study in the particular employment context. A selection procedure can be supported by a content validity strategy to the extent that it is a representative sample of the content of the job. Selection procedures which purport to measure knowledges, skills, or abilities may in certain circumstances be justified by content validity, although they may not be representative samples, if the knowledge, skill, or ability measured by the selection procedure can be operationally defined as provided in section 14C(4) below, and if that knowledge, skill, or ability is a necessary prerequisite to successful job performance.

A selection procedure based upon inferences about mental processes cannot be supported solely or primarily on the basis of content validity.

Thus, a content strategy is not appropriate for demonstrating the validity of selection procedures which purport to measure traits or constructs, such as intelligence, aptitude, personality, commonsense, judgment, leadership, and spatial ability. Content validity is also not an appropriate strategy when the selection procedure involves knowledges, skills, or abilities which an employee will be expected to learn on the job.

54. Q. How does a user choose which validation strategy to use?

A. A user should select a validation strategy or strategies which are (1) appropriate for the type of selection procedure, the job, and the employment situation, and (2) technically and administratively feasible. Whatever method of validation is used, the basic logic is one of prediction; that is, the presumption that level of performance on the selection procedure will, on the average, be indicative of level of performance on the job after selection. Thus, a criterion-related study, particularly a predictive one, is often regarded as the closest to such an ideal. See American Psychological Association *Standards,* pp. 26-27.

Key conditions for a criterion-related study are a substantial number of individuals for inclusion in the study, and a considerable range of performance on the selection and criterion measures. In addition, reliable and valid measures of job performance should be available, or capable of being developed. Section 14B(1). Where such circumstances exist, a user should consider use of the criterion-related strategy.

Content validity is appropriate where it is technically and administratively feasible to develop work samples or measures of operationally defined skills, knowledges, or abilities which are a necessary prerequisite to observable work behaviors. Content validity is not appropriate for demonstrating the validity of tests of mental processes or aptitudes or characteristics; and is not appropriate for knowledges, skills or abilities which an employee will be expected to learn on the job. Section 14C(1)

The application of a construct validity strategy to support employee selection procedures is newer and less developed than criterion-related or content validity strategies. Continuing research may result in construct validity becoming more widely used. Because construct validity represents a generalization of findings, one situation in which construct validity might hold particular promise is that where it is desirable to use the same selection procedures for a variety of jobs. An overriding consideration in whether or not to consider construct validation is the availability of an individual with a high level of expertise in this field.

In some situations only one kind of validation study is likely to be appropriate. More than one strategy may be possible in other circumstances, in which case administrative considerations such as time and expense may be decisive. A combination of approaches may be feasible and desirable.

72. Q. What options does a user have if a criterion-related study is appropriate but is not feasible because there are not enough persons in the job?

A. There are a number of options the user should consider, depending upon the particular facts and circumstances, such as:

1. Change the procedure so as to eliminate adverse impact (see Section 6A);

2. Validate a procedure through a content validity strategy, if appropriate (see Section 14C and Questions 54 and 74);

3. Use a selection procedure validated elsewhere in conformity with the Guidelines (see Sections 7-8 and Question 66);

4. Engage in a cooperative study with other facilities or users (in cooperation with such users either bilaterally or through industry or trade associations or governmental groups), or participate in research studies conducted by the state employment security system. Where different locations are combined, care is needed to insure that the jobs studied are in fact the same and that the study is adequate and in conformity with the Guidelines (see Sections 8 and 14 and Question 45).

5. Combine essentially similar jobs into a single study sample. See Section 14B(1).

74. Q. Is the use of a content validity strategy appropriate for a procedure measuring skills or knowledges which are taught in training after initial employment?

A. Usually not. The Guidelines state (Section 14C(1)) that content validity is not appropriate where the selection procedure involves knowledges, skills, or abilities which the employee will be expected to learn "on the job". The phrase "on the job" is intended to apply to training which occurs after hiring, promotion or transfer. However, if an ability, such as speaking and understanding a language, takes a substantial length of time to learn, is required for successful job performance, and is not taught to those initial hires who possess it in advance, a test for that ability may be supported on a content validity basis.

75. Q. Can a measure of a trait or construct be validated on the basis of content validity?

A. No. Traits or constructs are by definition underlying characteristics which are intangible and are not directly observable. They are therefore not appropriate for the sampling approach of content validity. Some selection procedures, while labeled as construct measures, may actually be samples of observable work behaviors. Whatever the label, if the operational definitions are in fact based upon observable work behaviors, a selection procedure measuring those behaviors may be appropriately supported by a content validity strategy. For example, while a measure of the construct "dependability" should not be supported on the basis of content validity, promptness and regularity of attendance in a prior work record are frequently inquired into as a part of a selection procedure, and such measures may be supported on the basis of content validity.

76. Q. May a test which measures what the employee has learned in a training program be justified for use in employment decisions on the basis of content validity?

A. Yes. While the Guidelines (Section 14C(1)) note that content validity is not an appropriate strategy for knowledges, skills or abilities which an employee "will be expected to learn on the job", nothing in the Guidelines suggests that a test supported by content validity is not appropriate for determining what the employee has learned on the job, or in a training program. If the content of the test is relevant to the job, it may be used for employment decisions such as retention or assignment. See Section 14C(7).

79. Q. What is required to show the content validity of a test of a job knowledge?

A. There must be a defined, well recognized body of information, and knowledge of the information must be prerequisite to performance of the required work behaviors. The work behavior(s) to which each knowledge is related should be identified on an item by item basis. The test should fairly sample the information that is actually used by the employee on the job, so that the level of difficulty of the test items should correspond to the level of difficulty of the knowledge as used in the work behavior. See Section 14C(1) and (4).

14C. Technical Standards for Content Validity Studies

14C (1). Appropriateness of Content Validity Studies

LEGAL ANALYSIS

This Section was relied upon to invalidate the content validity study of a state police test in *U.S. v State of New York,* 474 F. Supp. 1103 (N.D.N.Y. 1979). Other courts have sanctioned content valid tests in the police context. *Guardians Association v. Civil Service Commission,* 23 FEP Cases 909 (2d Cir. 1980).

PROFESSIONAL ANALYSIS

It should be established at the outset that a selection procedure can be supported by a content validity strategy to the extent that it is a representative sample of the content of one or more critical work behaviors in a job. In order to be supported by a content validity strategy, it is *not* necessary under professional standards or practice that the selection procedure be a representative sample of the content of the entire job.

It also should be noted that the statement in Section 14C (1) that "content validity is also not an appropriate strategy when the selection procedure involves knowledges, skills, or abilities which an employee will be expected to learn on the job" is inconsistent with professional opinion. Literally interpreted, the statement articulates the professionally and practically untenable position that no employer may defend a selection procedure on the basis of its content validity if the procedure measures knowledges, skills or abilities which employees can be expected to learn on the job no matter how long it takes. The statement also is inconsistent with the requirements of the 1970 EEOC Guidelines which indicated that the only knowledges, skills or abilities which were not acceptable under the content validity strategy were those which could be acquired *in a brief orientation to the job,* as provided generally in Section 5F, above. This latter stipulation is much more realistic in terms of the realities of employee performance. The statement in this Section does not recognize the fact that candidates possessing higher levels of knowledge, skill or ability required on the job will typically learn faster, require less supervision and be more productive sooner and more likely to progress faster. In short, there is no basis in professional principles or opinion or in previous Guideline requirements for the agencies to have extended what was originally a reasonable interpretation.

An example would be the job of reservations agent for an airline. Although labor market conditions frequently require that airlines hire inexperienced persons as agents and train them (a very expensive process), such costs are decreased proportionately for every person hired who is experienced. Justification of the use of prior reservations experience on the basis of its content validity is professionally acceptable, as is a preference for people who have it, even though the majority of those hired will be trained.

There are also problems with the provision that content validation cannot be used to support tests or other procedures purporting to measure traits or constructs. Not all "constructs" are broad, abstract traits. Many constructs, particularly those in the ability area, can be defined quite narrowly and may lend themselves to measurement by procedures developed through content validation (Tenopyr, 1977). Question and Answer 75 seems to provide support for these contentions in its statement: "Some selection procedures, while labeled as construct measures, may actually be samples of observable work behaviors. Whatever the label, if the operational definitions are in fact based upon observable work behaviors, a selection procedure measuring those behaviors may be appropriately supported by a content validity strategy." See *Guardians Association v. Civil Service Commission, supra,* where the court criticized the Guidelines' excessively narrow interpretation of the concept of "ability" and endorsed a practical view of abilities as existing on a continuum with constructs and as frequently permitting validation under a content strategy. Thus where a construct is operationally defined in terms of work behaviors and the selection procedure is an objective measure of these behaviors, the construct may be seen as a convenient label for an aggregate of work behaviors and may properly be validated by a content strategy.

159

SECTION 14C (2)
JOB ANALYSIS

(2) *Job analysis for content validity.* There should be a job analysis which includes an analysis of the important work behavior(s) required for successful performance and their relative importance and, if the behavior results in work product(s), an analysis of the work product(s). Any job analysis should focus on the work behavior(s) and the tasks associated with them. If work behavior(s) are not observable, the job analysis should identify and analyze those aspects of the behavior(s) that can be observed and the observed work products. The work behavior(s) selected for measurement should be critical work behavior(s) and/or important work behavior(s) constituting most of the job.

75. Q. Can a measure of a trait or construct be validated on the basis of content validity?

A. No. Traits or constructs are by definition underlying characteristics which are intangible and are not directly observable. They are therefore not appropriate for the sampling approach of content validity. Some selection procedures, while labeled as construct measures, may actually be samples of observable work behaviors. Whatever the label, if the operational definitions are in fact based upon observable work behaviors, a selection procedure measuring those behaviors may be appropriately supported by a content validity strategy. For example, while a measure of the construct "dependability" should not be supported on the basis of content validity, promptness and regularity of attendance in a prior work record are frequently inquired into as a part of a selection procedure, and such measures may be supported on the basis of content validity.

77. Q. Is a task analysis necessary to support a selection procedure based on content validity?

A. A description of all tasks is not required by the Guidelines. However, the job analysis should describe all important work behaviors and their relative importance and their level of difficulty. Sections 14C(2) and 15C(3). The job analysis should focus on observable work behaviors and, to the extent appropriate, observable work products, and the tasks associated with the important observable work behaviors and/or work products. The job analysis should identify how the critical or important work behaviors are used in the job, and should support the content of the selection procedure.

SECTION 14C (3)
SELECTION
PROCEDURES

(3) *Development of selection procedures.* A selection procedure designed to measure the work behavior may be developed specifically from the job and job analysis in question, or may have been previously developed by the user, or by other users or by a test publisher.

14C (2). Job Analysis for Content Validity

LEGAL ANALYSIS

The adequacy of job analysis in content-oriented test construction has been an issue in *U.S. v. State of New York, Fire Fighters Institute for Racial Equality v. City of St. Louis, Louisville Black Police Officers Organization v. City of Louisville* and *Guardians Association v. Civil Service Commission*. The courts have been receptive to job analysis requirements, but flexible in their implementation of such requirements.

PROFESSIONAL ANALYSIS

The Uniform Guidelines suggest a preference for the task-oriented methodology of job analysis. Task-oriented procedures focus on the identification of work behaviors and their related tasks and products. The Section 16 definition of "work behavior" includes the identification of both observable (physical) and unobservable (mental) components of work behavior, but Section 14C (2) appears to stress the observable.

In contrast, professional standards permit and even in some circumstances urge job analysts to go beyond the identification of work behaviors by using *worker*-oriented job analysis methodologies to identify knowledges, skills and abilities where this is appropriate to the researcher's purpose. Specifically, the Division 14 *Principles* state that the content domains "may be restricted to critical or frequent activities or to prerequisite knowledges, skills or abilities". (*Principles,* p. 12 (1980).) Lawshe (1975) suggested that job performance domains would include a vast array of behaviors. "Behaviors constituting job performance domains range all the way from behavior which is directly observable, through that which is reportable to behavior that is highly abstract. The continuum extends from the exercise of simple proficiencies (arithmetic and typing) to the use of high mental processes . . ." (p. 565).

Section 14C (2) also suggests that work behaviors selected for measurement be "critical work behaviors and/or important work behaviors constituting *most* of the job". This only partly agrees with Lawshe (1975), who has stressed the need to attend to the criticality of the job requirements sampled by the final selection procedure. He states: "[I]f a job truly requires a specific skill or certain job knowledge, and the candidate cannot demonstrate the possession of that skill or knowledge, defensible grounds for rejection certainly exist. . . . It is irrelevant that other aspects of the job (other job performance domains) may not involve this ability." It can thus be sufficient to screen applicants for *one* critical ability and to make an employment decision based on the results *without* assessing other important work behaviors. The job performance domain sampled is usually not the total job performance universe, but rather a segment of it which has been identified and operationally defined. The recognition in Question and Answer 77 that a description of all tasks is not required is, therefore, appropriate. This is not inconsistent with the *Principles'* position (p. 6) that a thorough, systematic examination of the job and the context in which it is performed is essential.

Question and Answer 77 requires the employer to supply in the job analysis information pertaining to the "level of difficulty" of the work behaviors. The purpose of this requirement is unclear, it exceeds professional requirements and is virtually impossible to meet.

The issue of training is overlooked. For example, the most difficult task in a job may be taught to each employee after selection. However, it may be necessary to assess some prerequisite qualifications at the outset of the selection process. Also, the identification of "level of difficulty" of the work behaviors is further confused by the hiring of experienced and inexperienced workers (as discussed earlier).

14C (3). Development of Selection Procedures

LEGAL ANALYSIS

The options given here for test development will be helpful for employers with limited resources.

PROFESSIONAL ANALYSIS

If, as is suggested by the Guidelines, content-valid selection procedures are developed on the basis of the job analysis and the job analysis is focused on the observable, then only a work sample test would be deemed "safe". A literal interpretation of this section would virtually preclude paper-and-pencil tests and limit severely training and experience requirements.

The subsection also should note that a selection procedure may be developed as part of a cooperative or consortium study in addition to the sources listed. See Section 8.

SECTION 14C (4) STANDARDS FOR CONTENT VALIDITY

(4) *Standards for demonstrating content validity.* To demonstrate the content validity of a selection procedure, a user should show that the behavior(s) demonstrated in the selection procedure are a representative sample of the behavior(s) of the job in question or that the selection procedure provides a representative sample of the work product of the job. In the case of a selection procedure measuring a knowledge, skill, or ability, the knowledge, skill, or ability being measured should be operationally defined. In the case of a selection procedure measuring a knowledge, the knowledge being measured should be operationally defined as that body of learned information which is used in and is a necessary prerequisite for observable aspects of work behavior of the job. In the case of skills or abilities, the skill or ability being measured should be operationally defined in terms of observable aspects of work behavior of the job. For any selection procedure measuring a knowledge, skill, or ability the user should show that (a) the selection procedure measures and is a representative sample of that knowledge, skill, or ability; and (b) that knowledge, skill, or ability is used in and is a necessary prerequisite to performance of critical or important work behavior(s). In addition, to be content valid, a selection procedure measuring a skill or ability should either closely approximate an observable work behavior, or its product should closely approximate an observable work product. If a test purports to sample a work behavior or to provide a sample of a work product, the manner and setting of the selection procedure and its level and complexity should closely approximate the work situation. The closer the content and the context of the selection procedure are to work samples or work behaviors, the stronger is the basis for showing content validity. As the content of the selection procedure less resembles a work behavior, or the setting and manner of the administration of the selection procedure less resemble the work situation, or the result less resembles a work product, the less likely the selection procedure is to be content valid, and the greater the need for other evidence of validity.

32. Q. What is "validation" according to the Uniform Guidelines?

A. Validation is the demonstration of the job relatedness of a selection procedure. The Uniform Guidelines recognize the same three validity strategies recognized by the American Psychological Association:

(1) Criterion-related validity—a statistical demonstration of a relationship between scores on a selection procedure and job performance of a sample of workers.

(2) Content validity—a demonstration that the content of a selection procedure is representative of important aspects of performance on the job.

(3) Construct validity—a demonstration that (a) a selection procedure measures a construct (something believed to be an underlying human trait or characteristic, such as honesty) and (b) the construct is important for successful job performance.

73. Q. Must a selection procedure supported by content validity be an actual "on the job" sample of work behaviors?

A. No. The Guidelines emphasize the importance of a close approximation between the content of the selection procedure and the observable behaviors or products of the job, so as to minimize the inferential leap between performance on the selection procedure and job performance. However, the Guidelines also permit justification on the basis of content validity of selection procedures measuring knowledges, skills, or abilities which are not necessarily samples of work behaviors if: (1) The knowledge, skill, or ability being measured is operationally defined in accord with Section 14C(4); and (2) that knowledge, skill, or ability is a prerequisite for critical or important work behaviors. In addition users may justify a requirement for training, or for experience obtained from prior employment or volunteer work, on the basis of content validity, even though the prior training or experience does not duplicate the job. See Section 14B(6).

79. Q. What is required to show the content validity of a test of a job knowledge?

A. There must be a defined, well recognized body of information, and knowledge of the information must be prerequisite to performance of the required work behaviors. The work behavior(s) to which each knowledge is related should be identified on an item by item basis. The test should fairly sample the information that is actually used by the employee on the job, so that the level of difficulty of the test items should correspond to the level of difficulty of the knowledge as used in the work behavior. See Section 14C(1) and (4).

14C (4). Standards for Demonstrating Content Validity

LEGAL ANALYSIS

The "representativeness" requirement may be interpreted in a way that is inconsistent with Section 14C (8). It is likely that courts will be sympathetic to tests that screen on the basis of "critical" rather than "representative" or total aspects of job behavior, as is the case in *Guardians Association v. Civil Service Commission*.

PROFESSIONAL ANALYSIS

The definition provided in the Uniform Guidelines in Question and Answer 32 which states "content validity (is) a demonstration that the content of a selection procedure is representative of important aspects of performance on the job" is inconsistent with professional definitions of "content validity". While content validity is given a parity with criterion-related validity and construct validity in earlier sections of the Guidelines, the apparent insistence on job fidelity and the emphasis on the observable makes content validity quite difficult to use in accordance with the Guidelines. See also Sections 5G and 14C (2).

Guion (1978b) supports the idea that "content validity", depending upon test construction, is a form of job-relatedness that does not depend on a classical psychometric understanding of validity. Certainly, professional standards view the content strategy as a means of demonstrating job-relatedness. They emphasize the matching of the content of the test to one or more content domains of the job. The Division 14 *Principles* (1980) state: "Appropriate development of a selection procedure on the basis of content requires developing the procedure to be an appropriate sample of a specified content domain. If a selection procedure is to be used for employment decisions, the content domain is performance (or the knowledge, skill or ability necessary for performance) on the job, in relevant job training, or on specified aspects of either" (p. 12). The APA *Standards* (1974) suggest that "evidence of content validity is required when the test user wishes to estimate how an individual performs in the universe of situations the test is intended to represent." Similarly, Lawshe (1975) concluded that content validity "is the extent to which communality or overlap exists between (a) performance on the test under investigation and (b) ability to function in the defined job performance domain . . ." (p. 566).

In this context, then, and aside from exceeding responsible professional standards, the requirement that the manner and setting of the selection procedure should closely approximate the work situation presents at least five serious practical problems:

1. Strict adherence to the Section would require decentralized testing which raises a serious practical question for psychologists—whether to institute a job knowledge test or similar device which can be administered centrally under controlled conditions, but possibly cannot be defended because of the "work situation" requirement, or to opt for decentralized, equipment-oriented testing which cannot be controlled properly and, thus, in the long run also cannot be defended.

2. If applied literally, the requirement for standardization virtually assures that even work samples cannot meet the Section 14C (4) standards. For example, equipment may function variably on the job and dealing with such equipment may be a major job function. Yet in the testing situation, to ensure *complete* standardization, equipment must be kept in perfect working order. The only way to ensure this is to set equipment aside just for the purpose of giving tests. The expense involved may be prohibitive.

3. A practical consideration is the need to select employees when work requirements are variable or subject to change. A typing test, as used by most companies, does not fit the government's model of a content-valid test. This test represents an abstraction when compared with the typing requirements in any one job. In order to comply absolutely with the Guidelines, an employer might have to have a dozen or more typing tests to reflect different job demands and/or types of equipment.

4. It is axiomatic that the closer a test is to an actual work sample, the more it has to be changed to reflect small changes in the job. The apparent requirement for fidelity of a selection procedure to the exact job could require constant changes in selection procedures.

5. In some cases, it is more appropriate to use a selection procedure which is *not* a reproduction of the actual job situation. Consider the selection of a Fire Service Supervisor, where items constructed to ask candidates to demonstrate their knowledge of fire combat procedures provide useful information for selection decisions without placing the candidate in a hazardous situation. If

SECTION 14C (4) STANDARDS FOR CONTENT VALIDITY

(4) *Standards for demonstrating content validity.* To demonstrate the content validity of a selection procedure, a user should show that the behavior(s) demonstrated in the selection procedure are a representative sample of the behavior(s) of the job in question or that the selection procedure provides a representative sample of the work product of the job. In the case of a selection procedure measuring a knowledge, skill, or ability, the knowledge, skill, or ability being measured should be operationally defined. In the case of a selection procedure measuring a knowledge, the knowledge being measured should be operationally defined as that body of learned information which is used in and is a necessary prerequisite for observable aspects of work behavior of the job. In the case of skills or abilities, the skill or ability being measured should be operationally defined in terms of observable aspects of work behavior of the job. For any selection procedure measuring a knowledge, skill, or ability the user should show that (a) the selection procedure measures and is a representative sample of that knowledge, skill, or ability; and (b) that knowledge, skill, or ability is used in and is a necessary prerequisite to performance of critical or important work behavior(s). In addition, to be content valid, a selection procedure measuring a skill or ability should either closely approximate an observable work behavior, or its product should closely approximate an observable work product. If a test purports to sample a work behavior or to provide a sample of a work product, the manner and setting of the selection procedure and its level and complexity should closely approximate the work situation. The closer the content and the context of the selection procedure are to work samples or work behaviors, the stronger is the basis for showing content validity. As the content of the selection procedure less resembles a work behavior, or the setting and manner of the administration of the selection procedure less resemble the work situation, or the result less resembles a work product, the less likely the selection procedure is to be content valid, and the greater the need for other evidence of validity.

SECTION 14C (5) RELIABILITY

(5) *Reliability.* The reliability of selection procedures justified on the basis of content validity should be a matter of concern to the user. Whenever it is feasible, appropriate statistical estimates should be made of the reliability of the selection procedure.

SECTION 14C (6) PRIOR TRAINING

(6) *Prior training or experience.* A requirement for or evaluation of specific prior training or experience based on content validity, including a specification of level or amount of training or experience, should be justified on the basis of the relationship between the content of the training or experience and the content of the job for which the training or experience is to be required or evaluated. The critical consideration is the resemblance between the specific behaviors, products, knowledges, skills, or abilities in the experience or training and the specific behaviors, products, knowledges, skills, or abilities required on the job, whether or not there is close resemblance between the experience or training as a whole and the job as a whole.

a candidate demonstrates the theoretical knowledge, then a second selection device—a work replication measure—may be warranted to see the knowledge in practice. It is appropriate that the candidate not be immediately placed directly in the work sample where a lack of knowledge could result in injuries to self or to others.

14C (5). Reliability of Content-Valid Selection Procedures

LEGAL ANALYSIS

The courts typically have focused their attention on questions of validity, rather than reliability. The court in *Guardians Association v. Civil Service Commission*, however, relied upon professional standards (rather than upon the Guidelines) to introduce the issue of reliability as an important consideration in examining the method of use to which the scores in a selection instrument were put.

PROFESSIONAL ANALYSIS

The suggestion that reliability be a matter of concern for the user is appropriate and it is not incorrect to suggest the use of "appropriate statistical estimates of reliability". This may not be easy, however. Measures of internal consistency may or may not be "appropriate" depending upon the diversity of the factors tapped by the selection procedure. Test-retest reliability coefficients would be useful if candidates were not given feedback as to the correct and incorrect responses and if the period of time between test administrations was too short to permit additional study time or practice, but long enough to reduce memory effects. In practice, however, it is often very difficult to obtain "appropriate reliability estimates".

14C (6). Prior Training or Experience

PROFESSIONAL ANALYSIS

While a demonstration of the job-relatedness of prior training or experience requirements is professionally desirable, and the Divison 14 *Principles* (1980) recognize the appropriateness of training and experience requirements (p. 13), most employers will find it nearly impossible to comply literally with the provisions in this Section demanding that all prior training or experience requirements and "evaluations", including a specification of levels or amounts, be related to specific job behavior (etc.). In the extreme, it would be necessary for employers to develop application blanks listing all observable activities of every job and to ask each applicant to furnish proof that he or she has performed these activities or has been trained to do so.

Guion (1974) provides an example in which the resemblance between training requirements and job behavior is not very close, but the training is undoubtedly needed for effective performance on the job. Guion's example involves a mechanical engineering degree requirement for employees who design heavy equipment. Guion agrees that the content validity for the mechanical engineering degree requirement is probably low for a *specific* job content domain, noting that the degree "includes performance in nonengineering subjects, many of the engineering subjects studied may be irrelevant to the particular job, and many aspects of the job may not have been reflected in the work toward the degree." In short, the knowledge and skill required to obtain the degree is a sample of a different domain from that of the job (p. 292). He goes on to state, however, as would a majority of professionals, that he "would consider a degree in engineering related to the job of designing heavy equipment. When I say this, I am implying a hypothesis that people with a degree are more likely to be able to perform the required tasks than are people without the degree. This is a testable hypothesis, but the interests of society are not well served by hiring a lot of nonengineers to design heavy equipment just to do a criterion-related validity study . . ." (p. 292).

As to justifying specifications of levels or amount of training or experience, users will find it very difficult to show that a specific prior experience or training requirement is more effective than some lesser standard without empirical evidence, i.e., criterion-related validity.

SECTION 14C (7)
CONTENT VALIDITY OF TRAINING SUCCESS

(7) *Content validity of training success.* Where a measure of success in a training program is used as a selection procedure and the content of a training program is justified on the basis of content validity, the use should be justified on the relationship between the content of the training program and the content of the job.

76. Q. May a test which measures what the employee has learned in a training program be justified for use in employment decisions on the basis of content validity?

A. Yes. While the Guidelines (Section 14C(1)) note that content validity is not an appropriate strategy for knowledges, skills or abilities which an employee "will be expected to learn on the job", nothing in the Guidelines suggests that a test supported by content validity is not appropriate for determining what the employee has learned on the job, or in a training program. If the content of the test is relevant to the job, it may be used for employment decisions such as retention or assignment. See Section 14C(7).

80. Q. Under content validity, may a selection procedure for entry into a job be justified on the grounds that the knowledges, skills or abilities measured by the selection procedure are prerequisites to successful performance in a training program?

A. Yes, but only if the training material and the training program closely approximate the content and level of difficulty of the job and if the knowledges, skills or abilities are not those taught in the training program. For example, if training materials are at a level of reading difficulty substantially in excess of the reading difficulty of materials used on the job, the Guidelines would not permit justification on a content validity basis of a reading test based on those training materials for entry into the job.

Under the Guidelines a training program itself is a selection procedure if passing it is a prerequisite to retention or advancement. See Section 2C and 14C(17). As such, the content of the training program may only be justified by the relationship between the program and critical or important behaviors of the job itself, or through a demonstration of the relationship between measures of performance in training and measures of job performance.

Under the example given above, therefore, where the requirements in the training materials exceed those on the job, the training program itself could not be validated on a content validity basis if passing it is a basis for retention or promotion.

LEGAL ANALYSIS

This Section correctly requires that training program content generally be validated. See *Fisher v. Procter & Gamble Mfg. Co.*, 613 F.2d 527 (5th Cir. 1980). For a pragmatic approach to Guidelines' requirements in this area, see *Guardians Association v. Civil Service Commission.*

PROFESSIONAL ANALYSIS

The Answer to Question 76 states that if the content of a test which measures what the employee has learned in a training program is "relevant" to the job, then that test may be used for employment decisions, such as retention or assignment.

A literal application of the Guidelines' emphasis on the observable, the demands for replication of duties and for fidelity in setting could, in effect, reduce all training to "hands on" only. If the Guidelines' emphasis on actual behavior were carried to an extreme, it would be impossible to teach an automobile mechanic how an automobile engine works. Even if it were possible to teach using pencil and paper course work, every time a required behavior changed, there would have to be corresponding changes in training, for apparently the teaching of principles is excluded by the Guidelines' literal emphasis on behavior. Without teaching of principles, learning will not transfer when there are minor job changes.

Finally, the requirement that the measure of training success should be related to the job is in error. Users should show the relationship of training content to one or more domains of job content. Measures of training success should be shown to be related to *training* content.

SECTION 14C (8)
OPERATIONAL USE

(8) *Operational use.* A selection procedure which is supported on the basis of content validity may be used for a job if it represents a critical work behavior (i.e., a behavior which is necessary for performance of the job) or work behaviors which constitute most of the important parts of the job.

SECTION 14C (9)
RANKING

(9) *Ranking based on content validity studies.* If a user can show, by a job analysis or otherwise, that a higher score on a content valid selection procedure is likely to result in better job performance, the results may be used to rank persons who score above minimum levels. Where a selection procedure supported solely or primarily by content validity is used to rank job candidates, the selection procedure should measure those aspects of performance which differentiate among levels of job performance.

62 Q. Under what circumstances may a selection procedure be used for ranking?

A. Criterion-related and construct validity strategies are essentially empirical, statistical processes showing a relationship between performance on the selection procedure and performance on the job. To justify ranking under such validity strategies, therefore, the user need show mathematical support for the proposition that persons who receive higher scores on the procedure are likely to perform better on the job.

Content validity, on the other hand, is primarily a judgmental process concerned with the adequacy of the selection procedure as a sample of the work behaviors. Use of a selection procedure on a ranking basis may be supported by content validity if there is evidence from job analysis or other empirical data that what is measured by the selection procedure is associated with differences in levels of job performance. Section 14C(9); see also Section 5G.

Any conclusion that a content validated procedure is appropriate for ranking must rest on an inference that higher scores on the procedure are related to better job performance. The more closely and completely the selection procedure approximates the important work behaviors, the easier it is to make such an inference. Evidence that better performance on the procedure is related to greater productivity or to performance of behaviors of greater difficulty may also support such an inference.

Where the content and context of the selection procedure are unlike those of the job, as, for example, in many paper-and-pencil job knowledge tests, it is difficult to infer an association between levels of performance on the procedure and on the job. To support a test of job knowledge on a content validity basis, there must be evidence of a specific tie-in between each item of knowledge tested and one or more work behaviors. See Question 79. To justify use of such a test for ranking, it would also have to be demonstrated from empirical evidence either that mastery of more difficult work behaviors, or that mastery of a greater scope of knowledge corresponds to a greater scope of important work behaviors.

For example, for a particular warehouse worker job, the job analysis may show that lifting a 50-pound object is essential, but the job analysis does not show that lifting heavier objects is essential or would result in significantly better job performance. In this case a test of ability to lift 50 pounds could be justified on a content validity basis for a pass/fail determination. However, ranking of candidates based on relative amount of weight that can be lifted would be inappropriate.

In another instance, a job analysis may reflect that, for the job of machine operator, reading of simple instructions is not a major part of the job but is essential. Thus, reading would be a critical behavior under the Guidelines. See Section 14C(8). since the job analysis in this example did not also show that the ability to read such instructions more quickly or to understand more complex materials would be likely to result in better job performance, a reading test suported by content validity alone should be used on a pass/fail rather than a ranking basis. In such circumstances, use of the test for ranking would have to be supported by evidence from a criterion-related (or construct) validity study.

On the other hand, in the case of a person to be hired for a typing pool, the job analysis may show that the job consists almost entirely of typing from manuscript, and that productivity can be measured directly in terms of finished typed copy. For such a job, typing constitutes not only a critical behavior, but it constitutes most of the job. A higher score on a test which measured words per minute typed, with adjustments for errors, would therefore be likely to predict better job performance than a significantly lower score. Ranking or grouping based on such a typing test would therefore be appropriate under the Guidelines.

79. Q. What is required to show the content validity of a test of a job knowledge?

A. There must be a defined, well recognized body of information, and knowledge of the information must be prerequisite to performance of the required work behaviors. The work behavior(s) to which each knowledge is related should be identified on an item by item basis. The test should fairly sample the information that is actually used by the employee on the job, so that the level of difficulty of the test items should correspond to the level of difficulty of the knowledge as used in the work behavior. See Section 14C(1) and (4).

168

14C (8). Operational Use

LEGAL ANALYSIS

See comments on Section 14C (4).

PROFESSIONAL ANALYSIS

See comments under Section 14C (2) pertaining to the measurement of "critical" aspects of a job.

14C (9). Ranking Based on Content Validity Studies

LEGAL ANALYSIS

As indicated in the discussion of Section 5G, the agencies' requirement that method of use always be supported by additional evidence if there is a difference in degree of adverse impact is inconsistent with professional opinion. Under facts showing substantial adverse impact from ranking candidates on the basis of close scores on tests for which validity evidence was weak, however, the courts have followed the Guidelines. *Louisville Black Police Officers Organization v. City of Louisville; Guardians Association v. Civil Service Commission*.

PROFESSIONAL ANALYSIS

As stated in the Division 14 *Principles* (1980), interpretation of content-oriented selection procedures may reflect the measurement properties of the given procedure (pp. 12–15). If a selection instrument yields reliable results and provides adequate differentiation in the score ranges involved, persons may be ranked on the basis of its results. However, if an instrument is constructed more in the manner of a training mastery test in which the examinee is expected to get all or nearly all the items correct, a critical score may be appropri-

ate. A critical score is also appropriate in situations in which the greater speed at which a typist can type cannot be reflected in production because of equipment or process limitations. In this case, the selection procedure should be utilized with the limiting conditions considered.

An example of how the prohibition against ranking can be a problem for employers is the traditional content-valid example of the typing test for selection of clerk-typists. All other things being equal, any organization would prefer the applicant who types 70 wpm to the one who types 50 wpm even though the minimum "standard" is 40 wpm. If ranking on the basis of wpm performance results in increased adverse impact, this section would require the user to show empirically that poorer typing test performance is related to poor typing performance on the job, an exercise that is unnecessary. In summary, the Guidelines' suggestion that criterion-related proof is required to show that those who perform less well on content valid knowledge, skill, or ability tests will also perform less well on jobs requiring those knowledges, skills, or abilities is without professional foundation and is inconsistent with professional opinion

See also Section 5G.

SECTION 14D (1)
APPROPRIATENESS

D. *Technical standards for construct validity studies.*— (1) *Appropriateness of construct validity studies.* Construct validity is a more complex strategy than either criterion-related or content validity. Construct validation is a relatively new and developing procedure in the employment field, and there is at present a lack of substantial literature extending the concept to employment practices. The user should be aware that the effort to obtain sufficient empirical support for construct validity is both an extensive and arduous effort involving a series of research studies, which include criterion related validity studies and which may include content validity studies. Users choosing to justify use of a selection procedure by this strategy should therefore take particular care to assure that the validity study meets the standards set forth below.

43. Q. Can a selection procedure be a valid predictor of performance on a job in a certain location and be invalid for predicting success on a different job or the same job in a different location?

A. Yes. Because of differences in work behaviors, criterion measures, study samples or other factors, a selection procedure found to have validity in one situation does not necessarily have validity in different circumstances. Conversely, a selection procedure not found to have validity in one situation may have validity in different circumstances. For these reasons, the Guidelines requires that certain standards be satisfied before a user may rely upon findings of validity in another situation. Section 7 and Section 14D. See also, Question 66. Cooperative and multi-unit studies are however encouraged, and, when those standards of the Guidelines are satisfied, validity evidence specific to each location is not required. See Section 7C and Section 8.

66. Q. Under what circumstances can a selection procedure be supported (on other than an interim basis) by a criterion-related validity study done elsewhere?

A. A validity study done elsewhere may provide sufficient evidence if four conditions are met (Sec. 7B):

1. The evidence from the other studies clearly demonstrates that the procedure was valid in its use elsewhere.

2. The job(s) for which the selection procedure will be used closely matches the job(s) in the original study as shown by a comparison of major work behaviors as shown by the job analyses in both contexts.

3. Evidence of fairness from the other studies is considered for those groups constituting a significant factor in the user's labor market. Section 7B(3). Where the evidence is not available the user should conduct an internal study of test fairness, if technically feasible. Section 7B(3).

4. Proper account is taken of variables which might affect the applicability of the study in the new setting, such as performance standards, work methods, representativeness of the sample in terms of experience or other relevant factors, and the currency of the study.

81. Q. In Section 5, "General Standards for Validity Studies," construct validity is identified as no less acceptable than criterion-related and content validity. However, the specific requirements for construct validity, in Section 14D, seem to limit the generalizability of construct validity to the rules governing criterion-related validity. Can this apparent inconsistency be reconciled?

A. Yes. In view of the developing nature of construct validation for employment selection procedures, the approach taken concerning the generalizability of construct validity (section 14D) is intended to be a cautious one. However, construct validity may be generalized in circumstances where transportability of tests supported on the basis of criterion-related validity would not be appropriate. In establishing transportability of criterion-related validity, the jobs should have substantially the same major work behaviors. Section 7B(2). Construct validity, on the other hand, allows for situations where only some of the important work behaviors are the same. Thus, well-established measures of the construct which underlie particular work behaviors and which have been shown to be valid for some jobs may be generalized to other jobs which have some of the same work behaviors but which are different with respect to other work behaviors. Section 14D(4).

As further research and professional guidance on construct validity in employment situations emerge, additional extensions of construct validity for employee selection may become generally accepted in the profession. The agencies encourage further research and professional guidance with respect to the appropriate use of construct validity.

14D. Technical Standards for Construct Validity Studies

14D (1). Appropriateness of Construct Validity Studies

LEGAL ANALYSIS

As described below, the Guidelines virtually negate use of construct validity. As construct validity is professionally recognized, the preference accorded professional standards over EEOC pronouncements in various cases permits prediction that professionally acceptable construct studies will prevail in the courts.

PROFESSIONAL ANALYSIS

The 1974 version of the American Psychological Association *Standards for Educational and Psychological Tests* defined a "construct" as:

> . . . an idea developed or 'constructed' as a work of informed, scientific imagination; that is, it is a theoretical idea developed to explain and to organize some aspect of existing knowledge. Terms such as "anxiety" or "clerical aptitude", or "reading readiness" refer to such constructs, but the construct is more than a label; it is a dimension understood or inferred from its network or interrelationship.

The term *construct validity* has been a part of the official vocabulary of psychologists since at least 1954 when it appeared in the *Technical Recommendations for Psychological Tests and Diagnostic Techniques* (the first edition of the APA *Standards*). The concept has been discussed in the profession for nearly three decades and over the years has played a highly influential role in the theory of test construction.

Construct validity is treated in many of the standard texts on psychological testing, including Cronbach and Meehl (1955) and Anastasi (1976). Anastasi, in particular, describes a number of uses for construct validation and also provides a wide range of specific techniques suitable to the process. Among the techniques listed are correlations with other tests, factor or cluster analysis and internal consistency analysis. A detailed coverage of the Campbell-Fiske multi-trait, multi-method method of establishing construct validity is also included.*

---

*Campbell (1960) points out that in order to demonstrate construct validity, a test must not only be shown to correlate highly with other variables with which it should theoretically correlate, but also that it does not correlate significantly with variables from which it should differ. The Campbell-Fiske convergent and discriminate validity process is one means of demonstrating satisfactory construct validity.

Anastasi declares that "observations about content validity are relevant to construct validity. In fact, there is no information provided by any validation procedure that is *not* relevant to construct validation" (p. 159). Specifically, Anastasi explains that "construct validation is suitable for investigating the validity of criterion measures used in traditional criterion-related test validation" (p. 160) and adds that construct validation can be used to evaluate tests "in situations that do not permit acceptable criterion-related validation studies" (p. 160).

Anastasi is not alone in recognizing the rich potential of construct validity. For example, in 1960 Campbell provided a probing analysis of construct validity, clarifying the relationship between the concept and the Campbell-Fiske multi-trait, multi-method procedures. Both Anastasi and D. T. Campbell underline the care and professional rigor that must support the construct research strategy.

Most psychologists would disagree with the statement in Section 14D (1) that "construct validation is a relatively new and developing procedure in the employment field, and there is at present a lack of substantial literature extending the concept to employment practices." This is simply inaccurate. Even so, professional optimism is encouraged by the statement in the Overview to the Guidelines that "the Guidelines leave open the possibility that different evidence of construct validity may be accepted in the future, as new methodologies develop and become incorporated in professional standards and professional literature." Question and Answer 54 appears to sustain this rational approach by endorsing the possible superiority of construct validation to other strategies in some situations and Question and Answer 81 apparently suggests a similar superiority in some circumstances with respect to generalizability and transportability. Unfortunately, a reading of Section 14D dispels the impression that the Guidelines' treatment of construct validity is either rational or flexible. The inevitable conclusion is that construct validity is virtually eliminated by Section 14D.

Section 14D (1) claims that in obtaining support for a construct validation study, the user must engage in "a series of research studies, which include criterion-related validity studies." Most professionals would agree that it is sometimes desirable and appropriate to move from construct to criterion-related research strategies, but nowhere in the professional literature is there

D. *Technical standards for construct validity studies.*— (1) *Appropriateness of construct validity studies.* Construct validity is a more complex strategy than either criterion-related or content validity. Construct validation is a relatively new and developing procedure in the employment field, and there is at present a lack of substantial literature extending the concept to employment practices. The user should be aware that the effort to obtain sufficient empirical support for construct validity is both an extensive and arduous effort involving a series of research studies, which include criterion related validity studies and which may include content validity studies. Users choosing to justify use of a selection procedure by this strategy should therefore take particular care to assure that the validity study meets the standards set forth below.

54. Q. How does a user choose which validation strategy to use?

A. A user should select a validation strategy or strategies which are (1) appropriate for the type of selection procedure, the job, and the employment situation, and (2) technically and administratively feasible. Whatever method of validation is used, the basic logic is one of prediction; that is, the presumption that level of performance on the selection procedure will, on the average, be indicative of level of performance on the job after selection. Thus, a criterion-related study, particularly a predictive one, is often regarded as the closest to such an ideal. See American Psychological Association *Standards*, pp. 26–27.

Key conditions for a criterion-related study are a substantial number of individuals for inclusion in the study, and a considerable range of performance on the selection and criterion measures. In addition, reliable and valid measures of job performance should be available, or capable of being developed. Section 14B(1). Where such circumstances exist, a user should consider use of the criterion-related strategy.

Content validity is appropriate where it is technically and administratively feasible to develop work samples or measures of operationally defined skills, knowledges, or abilities which are a necessary prerequisite to observable work behaviors. Content validity is not appropriate for demonstrating the validity of tests of mental processes or aptitudes or characteristics; and is not appropriate for knowledges, skills or abilities which an employee will be expected to learn on the job. Section 14C(1)

The application of a construct validity strategy to support employee selection procedures is newer and less developed than criterion-related or content validity strategies. Continuing research may result in construct validity becoming more widely used. Because construct validity represents a generalization of findings, one situation in which construct validity might hold particular promise is that where it is desirable to use the same selection procedures for a variety of jobs. An overriding consideration in whether or not to consider construct validation is the availability of an individual with a high level of expertise in this field.

In some situations only one kind of validation study is likely to be appropriate. More than one strategy may be possible in other circumstances, in which case administrative considerations such as time and expense may be decisive. A combination of approaches may be feasible and desirable.

a statement that such a step is necessary. In contrast, this Section unequivocally states that construct validity cannot be used as an independent research strategy, but is acceptable only when incorporated as a part of another validation strategy. That "construct validity" can be no more than a part of other research procedures is again emphasized in Section 14D (3) *(Relationship to the Job)* where the link to criterion-related validity is made an explicit requirement: "the relationship between the construct as measured by the selection procedure and the related work behavior(s) should be supported by empirical evidence from one or more criterion-related studies involving the job or jobs in question which satisfy the provisions of Section 14B above." The exception to this rule in Section 14D (4) (permitting limited transportation of criterion-related validity studies) is too limiting to be of practical value.

SECTION 14D (2)
JOB ANALYSIS

(2) *Job analysis for construct validity studies.* There should be a job analysis. This job analysis should show the work behavior(s) required for successful performance of the job, or the groups of jobs being studied, the critical or important work behavior(s) in the job or group of jobs being studied, and an identification of the construct(s) believed to underlie successful performance of these critical or important work behaviors in the job or jobs in question. Each construct should be named and defined, so as to distinguish it from other constructs. If a group of jobs is being studied the jobs should have in common one or more critical or important work behaviors at a comparable level of complexity.

SECTION 14D (3)
RELATIONSHIP

(3) *Relationship to the job.* A selection procedure should then be identified or developed which measures the construct identified in accord with subparagraph (2) above. The user should show by empirical evidence that the selection procedure is validly related to the construct and that the construct is validly related to the performance of critical or important work behavior(s). The relationship between the construct as measured by the selection procedure and the related work behavior(s) should be supported by empirical evidence from one or more criterion-related studies involving the job or jobs in question which satisfy the provisions of section 14B above.

SECTION 14D (4) USE OF STUDY

(4) *Use of construct validity study without new criterion-related evidence.*—(a) *Standards for use.* Until such time as professional literature provides more guidance on the use of construct validity in employment situations, the Federal agencies will accept a claim of construct validity without a criterion-related study which satisfies section 14B above only when the selection procedure has been used elsewhere in a situation in which a criterion-related study has been conducted and the use of a criterion-related validity study in this context meets the standards for transportability of criterion-related validity studies as set forth above in section 7. However, if a study pertains to a number of jobs having common critical or important work behaviors at a comparable level of complexity, and the evidence satisfies subparagraphs 14B (2) and (3) above for those jobs with criterion-related validity evidence for those jobs, the selection procedure may be used for all the jobs to which the study pertains. If construct validity is to be generalized to other jobs or groups of jobs not in the group studied, the Federal enforcement agencies will expect at a minimum additional empirical research evidence meeting the standards of subparagraphs section 14B (2) and (3) above for the additional jobs or groups of jobs.

(b) *Determination of common work behaviors.* In determining whether two or more jobs have one or more work behavior(s) in common, the user should compare the observed work behavior(s) in each of the jobs and should compare the observed work product(s) in each of the jobs. If neither the observed work behavior(s) in each of the jobs nor the observed work product(s) in each of the jobs are the same, the Federal enforcement agencies will presume that the work behavior(s) in each job are different. If the work behaviors are not observable, then evidence of similarity of work products and any other relevant research evidence will be considered in determining whether the work behavior(s) in the two jobs are the same.

---

51. Q. What are the factors to be considered in determining whether the validity for one procedure is substantially the same as or greater than that of another procedure?

A. In the case of a criterion-related validity study, the factors include the importance of the criteria for which significant relationships are found, the magnitude of the relationship between selection procedure scores and criterion measures, and the size and composition of the samples used. For content validity, the strength of validity evidence would depend upon the proportion of critical and/or important job behaviors measured, and the extent to which the selection procedure resembles actual work samples or work behaviors. Where selection procedures have been validated by different strategies, or by construct validity, the determination should be made on a case by case basis.

81. Q. In Section 5, "General Standards for Validity Studies," construct validity is identified as no less acceptable than criterion-related and content validity. However, the specific requirements for construct validity, in Section 14D, seem to limit the generalizability of construct validity to the rules governing criterion-related validity. Can this apparent inconsistency be reconciled?

A. Yes. In view of the developing nature of construct validation for employment selection procedures, the approach taken concerning the generalizability of construct validity (section 14D) is intended to be a cautious one. However, construct validity may be generalized in circumstances where transportability of tests supported on the basis of criterion-related validity would not be appropriate. In establishing transportability of criterion-related validity, the jobs should have substantially the same major work behaviors. Section 7B(2). Construct validity, on the other hand, allows for situations where only some of the important work behaviors are the same. Thus, well-established measures of the construct which underlie particular work behaviors and which have been shown to be valid for some jobs may be generalized to other jobs which have some of the same work behaviors but which are different with respect to other work behaviors. Section 14D(4).

As further research and professional guidance on construct validity in employment situations emerge, additional extensions of construct validity for employee selection may become generally accepted in the profession. The agencies encourage further research and professional guidance with respect to the appropriate use of construct validity.

14D (2). Job Analysis for Construct Validity Studies

See comments under Section 14D (1).

14D (3). Relationship to the Job

See comments under Section 14D (1).

14D (4). Use of Construct Validity Study Without New Criterion-Related Evidence

See comments under Section 14D (1).

PROFESSIONAL ANALYSIS

(Sections 14D (3) and (4))

As already indicated in the discussion of Section 14 D (1), above, the Guidelines' linkage of construct validity to criterion-related validity is unwarranted. In Question and Answer 51, the agencies appear to retreat from this rigid viewpoint, but Question and Answer 51 is merely inconsistent with Section 14D. Section 14D states that construct validity is acceptable only when supported by a criterion-related study. While the Answer to Question 51 *appears* not to require the criterion-related strategy, it leaves the issue of construct validity further confused. Similarly puzzling is Question and Answer 81 which suggests the possibility that "construct validity may be generalized in circumstances where tests supported on the basis of criterion-related validity would not be appropriate." It is difficult to understand why (given the appropriateness of the criterion) criterion-related validity apparently could not be equally well generalized.

This section should make transportability of construct validity a relatively easy matter. Instead, it makes transportability nearly impossible.

In summary, the impression is given that construct validity is so difficult and so little understood that it has no place in employee selection. The truth is that many selection procedures, especially for higher level or complex jobs, are based on construct validity. This Section is misleading and confusing to potential users and serves to block a potentially fruitful line of research.

SEC. 15. *Documentation of impact and validity evidence.*—A. *Required information.* Users of selection procedures other than those users complying with section 15A(1) below should maintain and have available for each job information on adverse impact of the selection process for that job and, where it is determined a selection process has an adverse impact, evidence of validity as set forth below.

13. Q. Is adverse impact determined on the basis of the overall selection process or for the components in that process?

A. Adverse impact is determined first for the overall selection process for each job. If the overall selection process has an adverse impact, the adverse impact of the individual selection procedure should be analyzed. For any selection procedures in the process having an adverse impact which the user continues to use in the same manner, the user is expected to have evidence of validity satisfying the Guidelines. Sections 4C and 5D. If there is no adverse impact for the overall selection process, in most circumstances there is no obligation under the Guidelines to investigate adverse impact for the components, or to validate the selection procedures, used for that job. Section 4C. But see Question 25.

27. Q. An employer uses one test or other selection procedure to select persons for a number of different jobs. Applicants are given the test, and the successful applicants are then referred to different departments and positions on the basis of openings available and their interests. The Guidelines appear to require assessment of adverse impact on a job-by-job basis (Section 15A(2)(a)). Is there some way to show that the test as a whole does not have adverse impact even though the proportions of members of each race, sex or ethnic group assigned to different jobs may vary?

A. Yes, in some circumstances. The Guidelines require evidence of validity only for those selection procedures which have an adverse impact, and which are part of a selection process which has an adverse impact. If the test is administered and used in the same fashion for a variety of jobs, the impact of that test can be assessed in the aggregate. The records showing the results of the test, and the total number of persons selected, generally would be sufficient to show the impact of the test. If the test has no adverse impact, it need not be validated.

But the absence of adverse impact of the test in the aggregate does not end the inquiry. For there may be discrimination or adverse impact in the assignment of individuals to, or in the selection of persons for, particular jobs. The Guidelines call for records to be kept and determinations of adverse impact to be made of the overall selection process on a job by job basis. Thus, if there is adverse impact in the assignment or selection procedures for a job even though there is no adverse impact from the test, the user should eliminate the adverse impact from the assignment procedure or justify the assignment procedure.

34. Q. Can a user send its validity evidence to an enforcement agency before a review, so as to assure its validity?

A. No. Enforcement agencies will not review validity reports except in the context of investigations or reviews. Even in those circumstances, validity evidence will not be reviewed without evidence of how the selection procedure is used and what impact its use has on various race, sex, and ethnic groups.

89. Q. What information should be included in documenting a validity study for purposes of these Guidelines?

A. Generally, reports of validity studies should contain all the information necessary to permit an enforcement agency to conclude whether a selection procedure has been validated. Information that is critical to this determination is denoted in Section 15 of the Guidelines by the word "(essential)".

Any reports completed after September 25, 1978, (the effective date of the Guidelines) which do not contain this information will be considered incomplete by the agencies unless there is good reason for not including the information. Users should therefore prepare validation reports according to the format of Section 15 of the Guidelines, and should carefully document the reasons if any of the information labeled "(essential)" is missing.

The major elements for all types of validation studies include the following:

When and where the study was conducted.

A description of the selection procedure, how it is used, and the results by race, sex, and ethnic group.

How the job was analyzed or reviewed and what information was obtained from this job analysis or review.

The evidence demonstrating that the selection procedure is related to the job. The nature of this evidence varies, depending upon the strategy used.

What alternative selection procedures and alternative methods of using the selection procedure were studied and the results of this study.

The name, address and telephone number of a contact person who can provide further information about the study.

The documentation requirements for each validation strategy are set forth in detail in Section 15 B. C. D. E. F. and G. Among the requirements for each validity strategy are the following:

1. *Criterion-Related Validity*

A description of the criterion measures of job performance, how and why they were selected, and how they were used to evaluate employees.

A description of the sample used in the study, how it was selected, and the size of each race, sex, or ethnic group in it.

A description of the statistical methods used to determine whether scores on the selection procedure are related to scores on the criterion measures of job performance, and the results of these statistical calculations.

2. *Content Validity*

The content of the job, as identified from the job analysis.

The content of the selection procedure.

The evidence demonstrating that the content of the selection procedure is a representative sample of the content of the job.

3. *Construct Validity*

A definition of the construct and how it relates to other constructs in the psychological literature.

The evidence that the selection procedure measures the construct.

The evidence showing that the measure of the construct is related to work behaviors which involve the construct.

Documentation of Impact and Validity Evidence

Section 15. Documentation of Impact and Validity Evidence

15A. Required Information

LEGAL ANALYSIS

The requirement in the second part of Q & A 27 that employers maintain adverse impact data for every job appears to exceed minimum requirements for Title VII compliance. While it is both risky and inadvisable, an employer has the legal right to await a prima facie statistical challenge to its employment practices before undertaking to determine whether those practices are job-related. An impact audit may be an appropriate requirement for compliance with the voluntary affirmative action obligation under Executive Order 11246, but the Guidelines do not address affirmative action obligations. (Of course, employers concerned about the impact of their selection procedures may already have available the information listed in Section 15A; moreover, OFCCP requires that federal contractors maintain such data.) See discussion of Sections 4A, 4B, 15A (1) and 15A (2).

The statement that whenever a selection procedure has adverse impact validity evidence must be demonstrated is inaccurate. As shown in Section 6, Q & A 13 and elsewhere, a user has various options when a selection procedure has adverse impact. Moreover, adverse impact for the overall selection process for a particular job triggers an examination of the components for adverse impact, rather than validation of the overall process. See Section 3.

Requiring that data be maintained on a job by job basis reflects a concern that a user may be selecting on the basis of validated procedures but will be discriminating in assigning those hired to the various jobs for which the selection procedure is used. On the surface, this has some appeal. In practical terms, however, it reflects a lack of understanding of hiring and assignment realities. For example, a user, after meeting requirements on job comparability, may use one selection battery for hiring into a group of clerical jobs. Some of these jobs may have entry level pay higher than others and some may have progression opportunities greater than others. Assignments into these jobs, however, is very much a function of (1) availability of openings coinciding with availability of individuals, (2) the varying experiences of candidates for the positions and (3) the desires of the applicants in terms of the work they wish to do. All of these elements may enter into the assignment process. In any event, discrimination in job assignments says absolutely nothing about the impact of the *selection* instrument used, and validation of the selection "process", if that were possible, would not provide a relevant defense to a charge of assignment discrimination.

It may be added that even very large employers find it necessary to treat applicants for groups of jobs having common skill and ability components interchangeably for recordkeeping and impact purposes. Impact data should be maintained according to whatever job groupings the employer maintains for selection purposes. Frequently the procedure will also be validated for the same group of jobs. Q & A 27 permits this kind of aggregate recordkeeping and correctly cautions employers that even in the absence of aggregate adverse impact they must be alert for possible adverse impact in resulting job assignment procedures. But, as noted above, the second part of Q & A 27 reflects an excessive recordkeeping requirement.

PROFESSIONAL ANALYSIS

It should be stated at the outset that the *Standards* published by the American Psychological Association and the *Principles* published by the Division of Industrial and Organizational Psychology of that Association recite that they are statements of ideals toward which every professional should strive. There is the fullest possible recognition within the profession that research efforts are unlikely to meet all of the standards enunciated and the test of competence is not whether all standards are achieved, but whether all standards were recognized and attempts made to achieve them to the fullest extent reasonably possible. Thus adequacy is measured by an evaluation of the total effort, not by a rigid application of an item by item checklist.

The Guidelines on the other hand adopt the word "essential" as used in the *Standards,* but express an intent to use it in a significantly different way. Those things described in the Guidelines documentation section as "essential" are mandatory. The absence of any "essential" element or an "inadequate" response to some federal employee's idea of what is required may mean that a study will be deemed incomplete or inadequate for Guideline purposes. Further, the Guidelines adopt many of the ideals of the *Standards* but adopt

SECTION 15A
REQUIRED INFORMATION

SEC. 15. *Documentation of impact and validity evidence.—A. Required information.* Users of selection procedures other than those users complying with section 15A(1) below should maintain and have available for each job information on adverse impact of the selection process for that job and, where it is determined a selection process has an adverse impact, evidence of validity as set forth below.

SECTION 15A (1) RECORDKEEPING

(1) *Simplified recordkeeping for users with less than 100 employees.* In order to minimize recordkeeping burdens on employers who employ one hundred (100) or fewer employees, and other users not required to file EEO-1, et seq., reports, such users may satisfy the requirements of this section 15 if they maintain and have available records showing, for each year:

(a) The number of persons hired, promoted, and terminated for each job, by sex, and where appropriate by race and national origin;

(b) The number of applicants for hire and promotion by sex and where appropriate by race and national origin; and

(c) The selection procedures utilized (either standardized or not standardized).

These records should be maintained for each race or national origin group (see section 4 above) constituting more than two percent (2%) of the labor force in the relevant labor area. However, it is not necessary to maintain records by race and/or national origin (see § 4 above) if one race or national origin group in the relevant labor area constitutes more than ninety-eight percent (98%) of the labor force in the area. If the user has reason to believe that a selection procedure has an adverse impact, the user should maintain any available evidence of validity for that procedure (see sections 7A and 8).

---

82. Q. Do the Guidelines have simplified recordkeeping for small users (employers who employ one hundred or fewer employees and other users not required to file EEO-1, et seq. reports)?

A. Yes. Although small users are fully covered by Federal equal employment opportunity law, the Guidelines have reduced their record-keeping burden. See option in Section 15A(1). Thus, small users need not make adverse impact determinations nor are they required to keep applicant data on a job-by-job basis. The agencies also recognize that a small user may find that some or all validation strategies are not feasible. See Question 54. If a small user has reason to believe that its selection procedures have adverse impact and validation is not feasible, it should consider other options. See Sections 7A and 8 and Questions 31, 36, 45, 66, and 72.

54. Q. How does a user choose which validation strategy to use?

A. A user should select a validation strategy or strategies which are (1) appropriate for the type of selection procedure, the job, and the employment situation, and (2) technically and administratively feasible. Whatever method of validation is used, the basic logic is one of prediction; that is, the presumption that level of performance on the selection procedure will, on the average, be indicative of level of performance on the job after selection. Thus, a criterion-related study, particularly a predictive one, is often regarded as the closest to such an ideal. See **American Psychological Association** *Standards*, pp. 26-27.

Key conditions for a criterion-related study are a substantial number of individuals for inclusion in the study, and a considerable range of performance on the selection and criterion measures. In addition, reliable and valid measures of job performance should be available, or capable of being developed. Section 14B(1). Where such circumstances exist, a user should consider use of the criterion-related strategy.

Content validity is appropriate where it is technically and administratively feasible to develop work samples or measures of operationally defined skills, knowledges, or abilities which are a necessary prerequisite to observable work behaviors. Content validity is not appropriate for demonstrating the validity of tests of mental processes or aptitudes or characteristics; and is not appropriate for knowledges, skills or abilities which an employee will be expected to learn on the job. Section 14C(1)

The application of a construct validity strategy to support employee selection procedures is newer and less developed than criterion-related or content validity strategies. Continuing research may result in construct validity becoming more widely used. Because construct validity represents a generalization of findings, one situation in which construct validity might hold particular promise is that where it is desirable to use the same selection procedures for a variety of jobs. An overriding consideration in whether or not to consider construct validation is the availability of an individual with a high level of expertise in this field.

In some situations only one kind of validation study is likely to be appropriate. More than one strategy may be possible in other circumstances, in which case administrative considerations such as time and expense may be decisive. A combination of approaches may be feasible and desirable.

15. Q. What is meant by the terms "applicant" and "candidate" as they are used in the Uniform Guidelines?

A. The precise definition of the term "applicant" depends upon the user's recruitment and selection procedures. The concept of an applicant is that of a person who has indicated an interest in being considered for hiring, promotion, or other employment opportunities. This interest might be expressed by completing an application form, or might be expressed orally, depending upon the employer's practice.

The term "candidate" has been included to cover those situations where the initial step by the user involves consideration of current employees for promotion, or training, or other employment opportunities, without inviting applications. The procedure by which persons are identified as candidates is itself a selection procedure under the Guidelines.

A person who voluntarily withdraws formally or informally at any stage of the selection process is no longer an applicant or candidate for purposes of computing adverse impact. Employment standards imposed by the user which discourage disproportionately applicants of a race, sex or ethnic group may, however, require justification. Records should be kept for persons who were applicants or candidates at any stage of the process.

See also Q & A 86 page 180.

them as *legal minima*. The documentation requirements thus exceed professional standards in their rigidity.

It also should be noted that these requirements were *not* subjected to full public comment. The documentation section of the December 30, 1977 draft, which was the subject of comment and the subject of hearings held in April 1978, was eliminated in June of 1978 in favor of a totally revised section that was not based on comments received.

15A (1). Simplified Recordkeeping for Users ———————— with Less Than 100 Employees

PROFESSIONAL ANALYSIS

This subsection is appropriately intended to "minimize recordkeeping burdens" on small employers. But even among large employers, most selections are made by individual divisions or locations, although there are exceptions where a central personnel office makes the selection and assigns those selected. Since the individual plant typically makes the selection, the simplified recordkeeping procedure should be made available to the small *establishment,* regardless of the number of employees in the employer's total organization. This is particularly true in situations where a small unit may have no counterpart in the rest of the organization. Further, unless turnover is severe, a few individual establishments are unlikely to make enough selection decisions for most jobs to determine meaningful adverse impact, so combining data from one unit with that of the entire organization on a national basis is simply unwarranted unless there is a centralized personnel office doing the selection or centralized selection standards.

The 100 number is thus purely arbitrary. The critical factor should be the size of the job group. It is entirely possible for a larger employer with two or three or four hundred employees to have no single job group with more than 30 or 40 incumbents. Given normal turnover, this larger employer may hire only three or four persons into each job group in a given year and yet this employer is not eligible for the "small employer" recordkeeping rules.

This is not to say that the "small employer" recordkeeping provisions are without fault. It should be pointed out that these requirements are not so simple as they may seem. The most serious difficulty is presented because the Questions and Answers apparently define an applicant as anyone who merely expresses interest orally in a job. For recordkeeping purposes, a reasonable definition of "applicant" would require (1) that a formal application was made in such a way as to permit race/ethnic/sex identification, (2) that the application was directed to a specific job available in the employer's organization for which the employer was accepting applications at the time of filing and (3) that the application was pursued to a conclusion.

Q & A 15 appears to be more realistic than the Guidelines by recognizing that a flexible approach to a definition of "applicant" is required, "depending upon the employer's practice". The agencies' position, expressed in the Overview and elsewhere, that any person who expresses interest in a job is an "applicant" is erroneous. An employer is entitled to consider as applicants only those who formally apply for a particular position, if that is the employer's usual practice. Employers should follow the precepts of Q & A 15, which also are consistent with sound professional practice.

For further discussion of "applicant" see comments at Sections 15A (2) (b), below, and 4C, above, and in the discussions of adverse impact in Part II.

(2) *Information on impact.*—(a) *Collection of information on impact.* Users of selection procedures other than those complying with section 15A(1) above should maintain and have available for each job records or other information showing whether the total selection process for that job has an adverse impact on any of the groups for which records are called for by sections 4B above. Adverse impact determinations should be made at least annually for each such group which constitutes at least 2 percent of the labor force in the relevant labor area or 2 percent of the applicable workforce. Where a total selection process for a job has an adverse impact, the user should maintain and have available records or other information showing which components have an adverse impact. Where the total selection process for a job does not have an adverse impact, information need not be maintained for individual components except in circumstances set forth in subsection 15A(2)(b) below. If the determination of adverse impact is made using a procedure other than the "four-fifths rule," as defined in the first sentence of section 4D above, a justification, consistent with section 4D above, for the procedure used to determine adverse impact should be available.

16. Q. Should adverse impact determinations be made for all groups regardless of their size?

A. No. Section 15A(2) calls for annual adverse impact determinations to be made for each group which constitutes either 2% or more of the total labor force in the relevant labor area, or 2% or more of the applicable workforce. Thus, impact determinations should be made for any employment decision for each group which constitutes 2% or more of the labor force in the relevant labor area. For hiring, such determination should also be made for groups, which constitute more than 2% of the applicants; and for promotions, determinations should also be made for those groups which constitute at least 2% of the user's workforce. There are record keeping obligations for all groups, even those which are less than 2%. See Question 86.

27. Q. An employer uses one test or other selection procedure to select persons for a number of different jobs. Applicants are given the test, and the successful applicants are then referred to different departments and positions on the basis of openings available and their interests. The Guidelines appear to require assessment of adverse impact on a job-by-job basis (Section 15A(2)(a)). Is there some way to show that the test as a whole does not have adverse impact even though the proportions of members of each race, sex or ethnic group assigned to different jobs may vary?

A. Yes, in some circumstances. The Guidelines require evidence of validity only for those selection procedures which have an adverse impact, and which are part of a selection process which has an adverse impact. If the test is administered and used in the same fashion for a variety of jobs, the impact of that test can be assessed in the aggregate. The records showing the results of the test, and the total number of persons selected, generally would be sufficient to show the impact of the test. If the test has no adverse impact, it need not be validated.

But the absence of adverse impact of the test in the aggregate does not end the inquiry. For there may be discrimination or adverse impact in the assignment of individuals to, or in the selection of persons for, particular jobs. The Guidelines call for records to be kept and determinations of adverse impact to be made of the overall selection process on a job by job basis. Thus, if there is adverse impact in the assignment or selection procedures for a job even though there is no adverse impact from the test, the user should eliminate the adverse impact from the assignment procedure or justify the assignment procedure.

84. Q. Is the user obliged to keep records which show whether its selection processes have an adverse impact on race, sex, or ethnic groups?

A. Yes. Under the Guidelines users are obliged to maintain evidence indicating the impact which their selection processes have on identifiable race, sex or ethnic groups. Sections 4 A and B. If the selection process for a job does have an adverse impact on one or more such groups, the user is expected to maintain records showing the impact for the individual procedures. Section 15A(2).

86. Q. Should applicant and selection information be maintained for race or ethnic groups constituting less than 2% of the labor force and the applicants?

A. Small employers and other small users are not obliged to keep such records. Section 15A(1). Employers with more than 100 employees and other users required to file EEO-1 *et seq.* reports should maintain records and other information upon which impact determinations could be made, because section 15A2 requires the maintenance of such information for "any of the groups for which records are called for by section 4B above." See also, Section 4A.

No user, regardless of size, is required to make adverse impact determinations for race or ethnic groups constituting less than 2% of the labor force and the applicants. See Question 16.

LEGAL ANALYSIS

The requirement that data be maintained for all groups regardless of whether they constitute at least two percent of the appropriate labor force population is unjustified. It is very doubtful whether significant statistics could ever be accumulated for such groups, even assuming that cumulative statistics over a long period could properly be used to demonstrate adverse impact. See Q & A 16.

PROFESSIONAL ANALYSIS

This section provides that users are not required to make adverse impact determinations for race or ethnic groups which constitute less than two percent of the labor force in the relevant labor area, or two percent of the applicable workforce. Two percent of the applicable workforce appears to apply to progression, while two percent of the labor force applies to applicant hiring. This latter percentage is inappropriate. The two percent applicant exclusion should be for groups constituting less than two percent of the *relevant labor market,* not the labor force. In addition, the Answer to Question 86 extends the Guidelines provision by stipulating that users are not required to make adverse impact determination for race or ethnic groups which constitute less than two percent of the labor force *and* less than two percent of the applicants. The Answer to Question 86, therefore, confuses the issue. It cannot be clearly deter-

mined whether by "applicants" the agencies mean employees eligible for progression or outside applicants.

This subsection is confounded further by the continued reference to "each job". The employer is expected to determine annually the extent of adverse impact for each group (race, sex or ethnic) which "constitutes at least two percent of the applicable workforce." In addition to objections noted in connection with Section 15 A, above, the data on "each job" will frequently be meaningless because of the small number of selections. See Section 4D. In addition, application of the "four-fifths rule" is to be based on applicant flow data, which in many if not most instances are very unlikely to represent even the minimally qualified, available labor force. As noted in connection with Sections 15A (2) and 4C, major problems are also raised by the meaning of "applicant" and a consistent definition that permits identification of applicants by race and sex has proved elusive. Finally, the recordkeeping will be onerous even for moderate-sized employers with relatively few job categories; for most employers, indeed, computer tracking will be necessary, at a staggering cost. Again, the emphasis should be on the overall impact of the selection process when looking at the entire job.

No provision is even attempted for dealing with procedures that are used for unrelated groups of jobs (e.g., medical examinations), or for procedures that are used for related jobs, yet both practices are very common. See comments at Section 15A, above, and Q and A 27.

SECTION 15A (2)(b)
ADVERSE IMPACT
ELIMINATED

(b) *When adverse impact has been eliminated in the total selection process.* Whenever the total selection process for a particular job has had an adverse impact, as defined in section 4 above, in any year, but no longer has an adverse impact, the user should maintain and have available the information on individual components of the selection process required in the preceding paragraph for the period in which there was adverse impact. In addition, the user should continue to collect such information for at least two (2) years after the adverse impact has been eliminated.

SECTION 15A (2)(c)
INSUFFICIENT
DATA

(c) *When data insufficient to determine impact.* Where there has been an insufficient number of selections to determine whether there is an adverse impact of the total selection process for a particular job, the user should continue to collect, maintain and have available the information on individual components of the selection process required in section 15(A)(2)(a) above until the information is sufficient to determine that the overall selection process does not have an adverse impact as defined in section 4 above, or until the job has changed substantially.

19. Q. Does the ⅘ths rule of thumb mean that the Guidelines will tolerate up to 20% discrimination?

A. No. The ⅘ths rule of thumb speaks only to the question of adverse impact, and is not intended to resolve the ultimate question of unlawful discrimination. Regardless of the amount of difference in selection rates, unlawful discrimination may be present, and may be demonstrated through appropriate evidence. The ⅘ths rule merely establishes a numerical basis for drawing an initial inference and for requiring additional information.

With respect to adverse impact, the Guidelines expressly state (section 4D) that differences in selection rates of less than 20% may still amount to adverse impact where the differences are significant in both statistical and practical terms. See Question 20. In the absence of differences which are large enough to meet the ⅘ths rule of thumb or a test of statistical significance, there is no reason to assume that the differences are reliable, or that they are based upon anything other than chance.

20. Q. Why is the ⅘ths rule called a rule of thumb?

A. Because it is not intended to be controlling in all circumstances. If, for the sake of illustration, we assume that nationwide statistics show that use of an arrest record would disqualify 10% of all Hispanic persons but only 4% of all whites other than His-

panic (hereafter non-Hispanic), the selection rate for that selection procedure is 90% for Hispanics and 96% for non-Hispanics. Therefore, the ⅘ rule of thumb would not indicate the presence of adverse impact (90% is approximately 94% of 96%). But in this example, the information is based upon nationwide statistics, and the sample is large enough to yield statistically significant results, and the difference (Hispanics are 2½ times as likely to be disqualified as non-Hispanics) is large enough to be practically significant. Thus, in this example the enforcement agencies would consider a disqualification based on an arrest record alone as having an adverse impact. Likewise, in *Gregory* v. *Litton Industries*, 472 F. 2d 631 (9th Cir., 1972), the court held that the employer violated Title VII by disqualifying persons from employment solely on the basis of an arrest record, where that disqualification had an adverse impact on blacks and was not shown to be justified by business necessity.

On the other hand, a difference of more than 20% in rates of selection may not provide a basis for finding adverse impact if the number of persons selected is very small. For example, if the employer selected three males and one female from an applicant pool of 20 males and 10 females, the ⅘ths rule would indicate adverse impact (selection rate for women is 10%; for men 15%; ¹⁰⁄₁₅ or 66⅔% is less than 80%), yet the number of selections is too small to warrant a determination of

adverse impact. In these circumstances, the enforcement agency would not require validity evidence in the absence of additional information (such as selection rates for a longer period of time) indicating adverse impact. For recordkeeping requirements, see Section 15A(2)(c) and Questions 84 and 85.

84. Q. Is the user obliged to keep records which show whether its selection processes have an adverse impact on race, sex, or ethnic groups?

A. Yes. Under the Guidelines users are obliged to maintain evidence indicating the impact which their selection processes have on identifiable race, sex or ethnic groups. Sections 4 A and B. If the selection process for a job does have an adverse impact on one or more such groups, the user is expected to maintain records showing the impact for the individual procedures. Section 15A(2).

85. Q. What are the recordkeeping obligations of a user who cannot determine whether a selection process for a job has adverse impact because it makes an insufficient number of selections for that job in a year?

A. In such circumstances the user should collect, maintain, and have available information on the impact of the selection process and the component procedures until it can determine that adverse impact does not exist for the overall process or until the job has changed substantially. Section 15A(2)(c).

15A (2) (b). When Adverse Impact Has Been Eliminated in the Total Selection Process

LEGAL ANALYSIS

This subsection provides that when an employer has successfully eliminated adverse impact ("as defined in Section 4") he or she should still *maintain* information covering the period of adverse impact on individual components of the selection process indefinitely. Given the legislative history of the Act, particularly that related to the 1972 Amendments, there is serious question as to whether EEOC can participate in such a requirement. Also, the reference again is to a particular job and is subject to the criticism stated at Section 15A, above. In addition, the subsection requires the user to continue to collect such information "for at least two years after the adverse impact has been eliminated", a requirement that also appears to exceed EEOC's authority.

The provision for stopping data collection on a component basis is appropriate, but elsewhere in the Guidelines (e.g., Q & A 19) there appears to be pressure to maintain excessive data for defense purposes in the event of an allegation of discrimination.

PROFESSIONAL ANALYSIS

As noted above, the impact of this subsection may be to require detailed recordkeeping at all times. This can be extremely cumbersome and expensive for the employer. Moreover, the requirement that information on individual components be collected may imply that the employer may be expected to validate those components. It must be noted that if the reason the total selection process no longer has adverse impact is that the components were changed to achieve that effect (see Section 6), it would be impossible to validate those components without reintroducing them into the process once again. This does not seem desirable from any viewpoint.

15A (2) (c). When Data Insufficient to Determine Impact

LEGAL ANALYSIS

Accumulation of impact data over many years is of doubtful probative value. The courts have not been inclined to credit this sort of data, except where defensively it could be shown that "snapshot" data was unreliable as compared to employment practices over a period of time. *See Movement for Opportunity and Equality v. General Motors*, 622 F. 2d 1235 (7th Cir. 1980); *Vanguard Justice Society v. Hughes*. Also the agencies do not indicate the amount of data considered "sufficient". It would seem that the courts will require data of sufficient size to be statistically significant. *Friend v. Leidinger; Vanguard Justice Society v. Hughes; Williams v. Tallahassee Motors, Inc.*

An odd twist is the requirement that data be maintained on components where numbers are very small. This seems to exceed the requirements of Section 4D and to increase employers' burdens regarding jobs about which the agencies are unlikely to take an interest.

PROFESSIONAL ANALYSIS

This subsection attempts to remedy the problem of small numbers mentioned above. It provides that the employer will continue collecting data until a sufficient number of selections have been made, or until the job has changed substantially. Emphasis on "each job" and on components of selection processes will make this a never-ending process for many jobs. See comments at Section 15A.

183

SECTION 15A (3)(a)
EVIDENCE

(3) *Documentation of validity evidence.*—(a) *Types of evidence.* Where a total selection process has an adverse impact (see section 4 above) the user should maintain and have available for each component of that process which has an adverse impact, one or more of the following types of documentation evidence:

(i) Documentation evidence showing criterion-related validity of the selection procedure (see section 15B, below).

(ii) Documentation evidence showing content validity of the selection procedure (see section 15C, below).

(iii) Documentation evidence showing construct validity of the selection procedure (see section 15D, below).

(iv) Documentation evidence from other studies showing validity of the selection procedure in the user's facility (see section 15E, below).

(v) Documentation evidence showing why a validity study cannot or need not be performed and why continued use of the procedure is consistent with Federal law.

SECTION 15A (3)(b)
FORM OF REPORT

(b) *Form of report.* This evidence should be compiled in a reasonably complete and organized manner to permit direct evaluation of the validity of the selection procedure. Previously written employer or consultant reports of validity, or reports describing validity studies completed before the issuance of these guidelines are acceptable if they are complete in regard to the documentation requirements contained in this section, or if they satisfied requirements of guidelines which were in effect when the validity study was completed. If they are not complete, the required additional documentation should be appended. If necessary information is not available the report of the validity study may still be used as documentation, but its adequacy will be evaluated in terms of compliance with the requirements of these guidelines.

33. Q. What is the typical process by which validity studies are reviewed by an enforcement agency?

A. The validity study is normally requested by an enforcement officer during the course of a review. The officer will first determine whether the user's data show that the overall selection process has an adverse impact, and if so, which component selection procedures have an adverse impact. See Section 15A(3). The officer will then ask for the evidence of validity for each procedure which has an adverse impact. See Sections 15B, C, and D. This validity evidence will be referred to appropriate personnel for review. Agency findings will then be communicated to the user.

36. Q. How can users justify continued use of a procedure on a basis other than validity?

A. Normally, the method of justifying selection procedures with an adverse impact and the method to which the Guidelines are primarily addressed, is validation. The method of justification of a procedure by means other than validity is one to which the Guidelines are not addressed. See Section 6B. In *Griggs* v. *Duke Power Co.,* 401 U.S. 424, the Supreme Court indicated that the burden on the user was a heavy one, but that the selection procedure could be used if there was a "business necessity" for its continued use; therefore, the Federal agencies will consider evidence that a selection procedure is necessary for the safe and efficient operation of a business to justify continued use of a selection procedure.

89. Q. What information should be included in documenting a validity study for purposes of these Guidelines?

A. Generally, reports of validity studies should contain all the information necessary to permit an enforcement agency to conclude whether a selection procedure has been validated. Information that is critical to this determination is denoted in Section 15 of the Guidelines by the word "(essential)".

Any reports completed after September 25, 1978, (the effective date of the Guidelines) which do not contain this information will be considered incomplete by the agencies unless there is good reason for not including the information. Users should therefore prepare validation reports according to the format of Section 15 of the Guidelines, and should carefully document the reasons if any of the information labeled "(essential)" is missing.

The major elements for all types of validation studies include the following:

When and where the study was conducted.

A description of the selection procedure, how it is used, and the results by race, sex, and ethnic group.

How the job was analyzed or reviewed and what information was obtained from this job analysis or review.

The evidence demonstrating that the selection procedure is related to the job. The nature of this evidence varies, depending upon the strategy used.

What alternative selection procedures and alternative methods of using the selection procedure were studied and the results of this study.

The name, address and telephone number of a contact person who can provide further information about the study.

The documentation requirements for each validation strategy are set forth in detail in Section 15 B, C, D, E, F, and G. Among the requirements for each validity strategy are the following:

1. *Criterion-Related Validity*

A description of the criterion measures of job performance, how and why they were selected, and how they were used to evaluate employees.

A description of the sample used in the study, how it was selected, and the size of each race, sex, or ethnic group in it.

A description of the statistical methods used to determine whether scores on the selection procedure are related to scores on the criterion measures of job performance, and the results of these statistical calculations.

2. *Content Validity*

The content of the job, as identified from the job analysis.

The content of the selection procedure.

The evidence demonstrating that the content of the selection procedure is a representative sample of the content of the job.

3. *Construct Validity*

A definition of the construct and how it relates to other constructs in the psychological literature.

The evidence that the selection procedure measures the construct.

The evidence showing that the measure of the construct is related to work behaviors which involve the construct.

15A (3). Documentation of Validity Evidence

15A (3)(a). Types of Evidence

PROFESSIONAL ANALYSIS

This section merely describes what is to follow and notes that separate requirements are promulgated for a showing of (1) criterion-related validity, (2) content validity, (3) construct validity, (4) evidence of validity from other studies and (5) evidence to show why a validity study cannot or need not be performed. Perhaps reference should be made to other kinds of documentation evidence, such as that from cooperative studies (see Section 8) or evidence of business necessity (see Q & A 36).

15A (3) (b). Form of Report

PROFESSIONAL ANALYSIS

Section 15A (3) (b) describes the form that validity reports should take. There is in this section a "grandfather" clause which indicates that reports describing validity studies completed before the issuance of these Guidelines are acceptable, either if they satisfy these Guidelines or if they satisfied requirements of Guidelines which were in effect when the validity study was completed. As noted under Section 7B, there is no such grandfather clause provided for work completed before *any* Guidelines were in place, or for those users wishing to transport validity studies conducted elsewhere. Further, the response to Question 89 is inconsistent even with these provisions. The Guidelines provide the "grandfather" protection on the basis of *study* comple-

tion dates. The Answer to Question 89 inappropriately provides the protection based upon *report* completion dates.

Q & A 89 is inaccurate in other respects, as well. For example, it refers to a description of the selection "procedure" rather than "process". The latter is a much more meaningful description.

This subsection is permissive to the extent that it does provide for use of at least some reports completed before issuance of the Uniform Guidelines. However, it does ask for additional documentation if such reports do not meet the requirements of these Guidelines and, given the excessive reporting requirements of the document, it may be questioned whether *any* reports will be able to be deemed complete.

SECTION 15A (3)(c)
COMPLETENESS

(c) *Completeness.* In the event that evidence of validity is reviewed by an enforcement agency, the validation reports completed after the effective date of these guidelines are expected to contain the information set forth below. Evidence denoted by use of the word "(Essential)" is considered critical. If information denoted essential is not included, the report will be considered incomplete unless the user affirmatively demonstrates either its unavailability due to circumstances beyond the user's control or special circumstances of the user's study which make the information irrelevant. Evidence not so denoted is desirable but its absence will not be a basis for considering a report incomplete. The user should maintain and have available the information called for under the heading "Source Data" in sections 15B(11) and 15D(11). While it is a necessary part of the study, it need not be submitted with the report. All statistical results should be organized and presented in tabular or graphic form to the extent feasible.

SECTION 15B
CRITERION-RELATED
VALIDITY STUDIES

B. *Criterion-related validity studies.* Reports of criterion-related validity for a selection procedure should include the following information:

SECTION 15B (1)
USER, LOCATION
AND DATE

(1) *User(s), location(s), and date(s) of study.* Dates and location(s) of the job analysis or review of job information, the date(s) and location(s) of the administration of the selection procedures and collection of criterion data, and the time between collection of data on selection procedures and criterion measures should be provided (Essential). If the study was conducted at several locations, the address of each location, including city and State, should be shown.

SECTION 15B (2)
PROBLEM AND
SETTING

(2) *Problem and setting.* An explicit definition of the purpose(s) of the study and the circumstances in which the study was conducted should be provided. A description of existing selection procedures and cutoff scores, if any, should be provided.

186

15A (3) (c). Completeness

PROFESSIONAL ANALYSIS

The subsection indicates that "validation reports completed after the effective date of these Guidelines are expected to contain the information set forth below." The provision that users may be given the opportunity to explain the absence of "essential" information is appropriate and suggests that enforcement may be somewhat more flexible than the rigidity of the "essential" requirements in Section 15 might indicate. See comments at Section 15A, above.

15B. Criterion-Related Validity Studies

PROFESSIONAL ANALYSIS

This section creates two pressing overall problems. First, there are 32 items considered "essential". It is unlikely that any validation report can be complete with respect to all of these items and the agencies claim that they may deem the report unacceptable if information on even one item is missing. But see comments at Section 15A (3) (c), above.

The second overall problem is that previously unmentioned substantive requirements are included as "documentation" standards. For example, there is a requirement in Section 15B (8) for data on every group which is a factor in the labor market, not merely the groups which were included in the study and of sufficient size to report on. More importantly, in Section 15 B (10)—and, for content validation, in Section 15C—there is a requirement for reporting utility as well as validity. If such a major undertaking as determining utility is required, it should be in the substantive sections of the Guidelines in order to be referenced at all in the documentation section. This particular requirement places a substantial burden on the user and it was for that reason that a utility requirement was deleted from early drafts of Section 14 of the Guidelines. It will create controversy, partly because there are no generally accepted standards for determining how "useful" a selection procedure must be to support its operational use. One can easily envision employers and compliance officials arguing about "how useful is useful?". Most other problems in this section are documentation problems reflecting improper substantive requirements in Section 14, as discussed above.

15B (1). User(s), Location(s) and Date(s) of Study

PROFESSIONAL ANALYSIS

This subsection contains a requirement that the "date(s) and location(s) of the job analysis or review of job information" be provided. This stems in part from the *Albemarle* case, where the consultant employed did not perform a detailed study of the jobs, although he had spent many years working in the industry. What is required here, however, is unrealistic, in that it ignores the fact that professionals derive a knowledge of job requirements from a wide variety of sources over time. Much of this information cannot possibly be categorized by "date(s) and location(s) of the job analysis or review of job information". This is obvious, for example, where it is recognized that often a widely distributed questionnaire may be used to obtain information about the job. It also should be noted that consortium studies may involve hundreds of locations, the listing of which adds little, if anything, to determinations of study adequacy.

15B (2). Problem and Setting

PROFESSIONAL ANALYSIS

This "requirement" is appropriate and will encourage rational explanation in narrative form of the purpose of a particular study. Employers can develop here the complete rationale of why it is important to have selection on the basis of qualifications or merit.

SECTION 15B (3)
JOB ANALYSIS

(3) *Job anlysis or review of job information.* A description of the procedure used to analyze the job or group of jobs, or to review the job information should be provided (Essential). Where a review of job information results in criteria which may be used without a full job analysis (see section 14B(3)), the basis for the selection of these criteria should be reported (Essential). Where a job analysis is required a complete description of the work behavior(s) or work outcome(s), and measures of their criticality or importance should be provided (Essential). The report should describe the basis on which the behavior(s) or outcome(s) were determined to be critical or important, such as the proportion of time spent on the respective behaviors, their level of difficulty, their frequency of performance, the consequences of error, or other appropriate factors (Essential). Where two or more jobs are grouped for a validity study, the information called for in this subsection should be provided for each of the jobs, and the justification for the grouping (see section 14B(1)) should be provided (Essential).

SECTION 15B (4)
JOB TITLES

(4) *Job titles and codes.* It is desirable to provide the user's job title(s) for the job(s) in question and the corresponding job title(s) and code(s) from U.S. Employment Service's Dictionary of Occupational Titles.

SECTION 15B (5)
CRITERION MEASURES

(5) *Criterion measures.* The bases for the selection of the criterion measures should be provided, together with references to the evidence considered in making the selection of criterion measures (essential). A full description of all criteria on which data were collected and means by which they were observed, recorded, evaluated, and quantified, should be provided (essential). If rating techniques are used as criterion measures, the appraisal form(s) and instructions to the rater(s) should be included as part of the validation evidence, or should be explicitly described and available (essential). All steps taken to insure that criterion measures are free from factors which would unfairly alter the scores of members of any group should be described (essential).

79. Q. What is required to show the content validity of a test of a job knowledge?

A. There must be a defined, well recognized body of information, and knowledge of the information must be prerequisite to performance of the required work behaviors. The work behavior(s) to which each knowledge is related should be identified on an item by item basis. The test should fairly sample the information that is actually used by the employee on the job, so that the level of difficulty of the test items should correspond to the level of difficulty of the knowledge as used in the work behavior. See Section 14C(1) and (4).

77. Q. Is a task analysis necessary to support a selection procedure based on content validity?

A. A description of all tasks is not required by the Guidelines. However, the job analysis should describe all important work behaviors and their relative importance and their level of difficulty. Sections 14C(2) and 15C(3). The job analysis should focus on observable work behaviors and, to the extent appropriate, observable work products, and the tasks associated with the important observable work behaviors and/or work products. The job analysis should identify how the critical or important work behaviors are used in the job, and should support the content of the selection procedure.

15B (3). Job Analysis or Review of Job Information

PROFESSIONAL ANALYSIS

Subsection 14A provides that "Any method of job analysis may be used if it provides the information required for the specific validation strategy used." Reference to the Definitions portion of the Guidelines, however, clearly suggests that only a "work behavior" oriented task checklist will meet the requirements of 15 B (3), even though this is expressly denied in Q & A 77. Moreover, this subsection appears to presume that there is a standard handbook of job analysis techniques. This is not the case and the 1980 version of the Division 14 *Principles* refrains from endorsing any particular method or methods. A professionally performed and acceptable job analysis may not meet the specifications delineated in this subsection. Again, users are being called upon to justify such criteria as turnover, when their critical nature is self-evident.

Finally, the answer to Question 79 repeats the error of requiring that *all* behaviors be included in the analysis and adds to this a further inappropriate requirement that "level of difficulty" and "relative importance" of all elements be specified. This is far in excess of professional standards and is virtually impossible to achieve.

15B (4). Job Titles and Codes

PROFESSIONAL ANALYSIS

Under many circumstances there would be no real problem with this section. The data asked for could contribute minimally to the quality of the validation study. However, when a study is performed on a job family which includes a great many specific job titles, such a listing and DOT comparison would be onerous. For example, a large employer may well have hundreds of clerical job titles which are grouped into four or five job families for selection purposes. Listing all the titles could be burdensome and would serve little purpose under such circumstances.

15B (5). Criterion Measures

PROFESSIONAL ANALYSIS

The first part of this subsection deals with the rationale behind the choice of criterion measures. This may overlap material provided in Section 15B (2), but some narrative justification is an appropriate requirement. The second part deals with the mechanics of collecting the criterion information and raises no problem.

The third part is devoted to rating techniques and requires that appraisal form(s) and instructions to rater(s) be included as part of the evidence, or that they be "fully described" and made available. It is difficult to see how this contributes to an evaluation of a validity study and yet it is labeled "essential". Articles on criterion validation in professional journals do not include copies of forms nor do they include instructions to raters unless they are unusual. They *do* require attention to the psychometric properties of the rating results.

The last part asks for a listing of all steps taken to ensure freedom from bias. Most researchers would feel that their normal attempts to maximize rating standardization, reliability and validity would suffice.

SECTION 15B (6)
SAMPLE
DESCRIPTION

(6) *Sample description.* A description of how the research sample was identified and selected should be included (essential). The race, sex, and ethnic composition of the sample, including those groups set forth in section 4A above, should be described (essential). This description should include the size of each subgroup (essential). A description of how the research sample compares with the relevant labor market or work force, the method by which the relevant labor market or work force was defined, and a discussion of the likely effects on validity of differences between the sample and the relevant labor market or work force, are also desirable. Descriptions of educational levels, length of service, and age are also desirable.

SECTION 15B (7)
SELECTION
PROCEDURES

(7) *Description of selection procedures.* Any measure, combination of measures, or procedure studied should be completely and explicitly described or attached (essential). If commercially available selection procedures are studied, they should be described by title, form, and publisher (essential). Reports of reliability estimates and how they were established are desirable.

SECTION 15B (8)
TECHNIQUES AND
RESULTS

(8) *Techniques and results.* Methods used in analyzing data should be described (essential). Measures of central tendency (e.g., means) and measures of dispersion (e.g., standard deviations and ranges) for all selection procedures and all criteria should be reported for each race, sex, and ethnic group which constitutes a significant factor in the relevant labor market (essential). The magnitude and direction of all relationships between selection procedures and criterion measures investigated should be reported for each relevant race, sex, and ethnic group and for the total group (essential). Where groups are too small to obtain reliable evidence of the magnitude of the relationship, need not be reported separately. Statements regarding the statistical significance of results should be made (essential). Any statistical adjustments, such as for less then perfect reliability or for restriction of score range in the selection procedure or criterion should be described and explained; and uncorrected correlation coefficients should also be shown (essential). Where the statistical technique categorizes continuous data, such as biserial correlation and the phi coefficient, the categories and the bases on which they were determined should be described and explained (essential). Studies of test fairness should be included where called for by the requirements of section 14B(8) (essential). These studies should include the rationale by which a selection procedure was determined to be fair to the group(s) in question. Where test fairness or unfairness has been demonstrated on the basis of other studies, a bibliography of the relevant studies should be included (essential). If the bibliography includes unpublished studies, copies of these studies, or adequate abstracts or summaries, should be attached (essential). Where revisions have been made in a selection procedure to assure compatability between successful job performance and the probability of being selected, the studies underlying such revisions should be included (essential). All statistical results should be organized and presented by relevant race, sex, and ethnic group (essential).

SECTION 15B (9)
ALTERNATIVE
PROCEDURES

(9) *Alternative procedures investigated.* The selection procedures investigated and available evidence of their impact should be identified (essential). The scope, method, and findings of the investigation, and the conclusions reached in light of the findings, should be fully described (essential).

15B (6). Sample Description

PROFESSIONAL ANALYSIS

A description of the research sample is an essential element of any validation study, but comparing the research sample with the labor market and extrapolating speculations on the effect of differences on validity, particularly in terms of race, sex, and ethnic groups, reflects the agencies' continued adherence to differential validity concepts no longer subscribed to by the profession. See Section 14B (8).

15B (7). Description of Selection Procedures

PROFESSIONAL ANALYSIS

There is no problem with this section, except that proprietary materials may not be adequately protected if they are attached. Commercially available and copyrighted materials certainly should not be attached or given to any agency representative without the permission of their publisher. Employers also should be mindful of the agencies' own lack of discretion or ability to protect much sensitive data because of the broad scope of the Freedom of Information Act. It is too little recognized that once a test is released and becomes available to potential examinees, it may become useless to the employer because test items cannot be reused and validation studies become impossible. See, *Detroit Edison Co. v. NLRB,* 440 U.S. 301 (1979). On the other hand, it is reasonable to require an "explicit description" of the tests.

15B (8). Techniques and Results

PROFESSIONAL ANALYSIS

Section 15B (8) incorrectly requires measures of central tendency and measures of dispersion to be reported for each race, sex and ethnic group which constitutes a "significant factor" in the relevant labor market. The standard for such reporting should be for each race, sex and ethnic group of sufficient size in the study sample to make such reporting reliable. Just as it is inappropriate to conduct a criterion-related study because of inadequate small samples, it is likewise inappropriate to report any data on any group in the study sample which is too small to make such reporting reliable.

The inclusion of "fairness" requirements further complicates the matter. See Section 14B (8) for a more extensive discussion of differential validity and "fairness".

15B (9). Alternative Procedures Investigated

LEGAL ANALYSIS

For legal objections to the required investigation of alternative procedures, see Part II, "Overview", Point V, "Validation: Consideration of Alternatives" and Sections 3B and 6A, above.

The language of this section is perhaps somewhat ambiguous as to what constitutes the burden of "investigation". It is unrealistic to imagine that employers can be required to empirically investigate the impact or validity of alternative procedures—it should be clear that the requirement goes no further than requiring a survey, which should include inquiries directed to the agencies themselves, to determine what evidence of this nature is readily available.

PROFESSIONAL ANALYSIS

It should be noted with regard to available evidence of the impact of alternative procedures that such evidence often is lacking and, when available, is likely to be uninterpretable. Impact is a function of use. Employer A may precede the administration of a test by an interview which screens out a proportion of the candidates. Employer B may use the same test as the initial screening device. The impact data on the test involved in the two situations will differ, since one employer had a pre-screen procedure and the second employer did not. On the other hand, it is sound professional practice to survey the literature prior to designing a validity study and select those procedures having the greatest potential for predicting job performance. In the same sense it is good professional practice in many situations to determine whether alternatives are available and to learn as much about them as is reasonable.

SECTION 15B (10) USES AND APPLICATIONS

(10) *Uses and applications.* The methods considered for use of the selection procedure (e.g., as a screening device with a cutoff score, for grouping or ranking, or combined with other procedures in a battery) and available evidence of their impact should be described (essential). This description should include the rationale for choosing the method for operational use, and the evidence of the validity and utility of the procedure as it is to be used (essential). The purpose for which the procedure is to be used (e.g., hiring, transfer, promotion) should be described (essential). If weights are assigned to different parts of the selection procedure, these weights and the validity of the weighted composite should be reported (essential). If the selection procedure is used with a cutoff score, the user should describe the way in which normal expectations of proficiency within the work force were determined and the way in which the cutoff score was determined (essential).

LEGAL ANALYSIS

The inclusion of a "normal expectation of proficiency" standard in this section appears to contradict the principle underlying Title VII and stressed by the Supreme Court in a line of cases going back to *Griggs* that employers may hire and promote according to relative qualifications. For fuller discussion of this issue, see Part II, "Analysis of Comments", Point 4, "Establishment of Cut-Off Scores and Rank Ordering" and also Sections 3B, 5G, 5H, 11, 14B (6), 14C (9) and 14D (1) in Part III.

PROFESSIONAL ANALYSIS

Any validity study should end with a recommendation on how the studied procedure is to be used. Further, the research undertaken should support the method recommended. The Guidelines add a requirement, however, that different methods of use be investigated to determine possible adverse impact and it should be noted that the net result of any use from these manipulations on the basis of impact will typically be inconsistent with the validity findings and will *lower* the utility of the technique involved.

Evidence of the impact of a validated procedure often will not be available for newly adopted procedures at the time studies are completed and reports are prepared.

Further, users should be required only to report the way in which cut-off scores were determined. They should not be required in addition to describe the way in which "normal" expectations of proficiency within the workforce were determined. "Normal" is a qualitative and a relative word. Users engaging in validity research generally have, as one objective of the research, an improvement in what was considered "normal" before the research was conducted—to enhance productivity a user will typically wish to set the cutoff score higher than the existing expectation of "normal" productivity in the workforce.

Finally, the tone of this section implies that use of a selection procedure is rigid when, in practice, use is almost always a function of availability. In a tight labor market where proportionately larger numbers of applicants are hired (high selection ratio), an employer may be less selective out of necessity. Alternately, in a time of relatively high unemployment when larger numbers of qualified applicants are available, an employer will typically hire proportionately fewer of the applicants (low selection ratio) and in so doing will tend to select the "best" candidates. Between these two extremes in labor market conditions, an employer's use of cutoff scores in practice falls and rises as a function of these external conditions.

SECTION 15B (11)
SOURCE DATA

(11) *Source data.* Each user should maintain records showing all pertinent information about individual sample members and raters where they are used, in studies involving the validation of selection procedures. These records should be made available upon request of a compliance agency. In the case of individual sample members these data should include scores on the selection procedure(s), scores on criterion measures, age, sex, race, or ethnic group status, and experience on the specific job on which the validation study was conducted, and may also include such things as education, training, and prior job experience, but should not include names and social security numbers. Records should be maintained which show the ratings given to each sample member by each rater.

SECTION 15B (12)
CONTACT PERSON

(12) *Contact person.* The name, mailing address, and telephone number of the person who may be contacted for further information about the validity study should be provided (essential).

SECTION 15B (13)
ACCURACY

(13) *Accuracy and completeness.* The report should describe the steps taken to assure the accuracy and completeness of the collection, analysis, and report of data and results.

SECTION 15C (1)
USER, LOCATION
AND DATE

C. *Content validity studies.* Reports of content validity for a selection procedure should include the following information:

(i) *User(s), location(s) and date(s) of study.* Dates and location(s) of the job analysis should be shown (essential).

90. Q. Although the records called for under "Source Data", Section 15B(11) and section 15D(11), are not listed as "Essential", the Guidelines state that each user should maintain such records, and have them available upon request of a compliance agency. Are these records necessary? Does the absence of complete records preclude the further use of research data compiled prior to the issuance of the Guidelines?

A. The Guidelines require the maintenance of these records in some form "as a necessary part of the study." Section 15A(3)(c). However, such records need not be compiled or maintained in any specific format. The term "Essential" as used in the Guidelines refers to information considered essential to the validity report. Section 15A(3)(b). The Source Data records need not be included with reports of validation or other formal reports until and unless they are specifically requested by a compliance agency. The absence of complete records does not preclude use of research data based on those records that are available. Validation studies submitted to comply with the requirements of the Guidelines may be considered inadequate to the extent that important data are missing or there is evidence that the collected data are inaccurate.

15B (11). Source Data

PROFESSIONAL ANALYSIS

The requirement that records be maintained which show the ratings given to each sample member by each rater may pose some difficulties, although researchers should record pertinent data on sample members. In many instances, such data on individual ratings cannot be obtained, e.g., when historical performance appraisal records are used as criteria or where the final rating is the product of several supervisors. Even where this is not so, it is not clear what use could be made of these data, other than developing inappropriate implications of rater bias because on the average one class of raters gives higher or lower ratings. The question in evaluating criteria is their relevance, not whether everyone is rated the same. Moreover, many study designs include guarantees of confidentiality to raters so as to increase their candor. Quite apart from the problem of preserving such guarantees, the knowledge that their ratings are subject to release could seriously affect rating quality.

Researchers should record pertinent data on individual sample members for a reasonable period of time. In a typical validation study, this will include score(s) on the selection procedure(s) and score(s) on the criterion measure(s). Whether the data roster includes information on any other variable will depend on the extent to which the researcher considered the variable worthy of investigation as a possible additional element to the validity, a source of contamination, or as an aid in explaining the results.

15B (12). Contact Person

PROFESSIONAL ANALYSIS

This is an appropriate requirement.

15B (13). Accuracy and Completeness

PROFESSIONAL ANALYSIS

Attention to these matters is certainly important, but precedent for handling this requirement is sparse and results will vary among researchers. There is no way, even with repeated verifications, to "assure" accuracy and completeness.

15C. Content Validity Studies

15C (1). User(s), Location(s) and Date(s) of Study

PROFESSIONAL ANALYSIS

The problems in this Section parallel those in the corresponding Section governing criterion-related validation. See Section 15B. There are 19 items required as "essential". If a report is incomplete with respect to even one of these, it is theoretically unacceptable to the enforcement agencies.

Like the section on criterion-related documentation, this section introduces substantive requirements not mentioned in the substantive sections of the Guidelines. In addition to utility studies, one such requirement is the justification of time limits. This requirement is particularly important in training, where the length of a training course is a major cost element and extensive cost analysis is needed to determine the appropriate length of a training course.

The suggestion that content valid procedures may be compared fails to recognize that there is no feasible method of comparing the validity of one work sample with another or of comparing the validity of a content-based procedure with that of a criterion-related procedure.

Other documentation problems stem primarily from the Guidelines' substantive requirements for content validity. Content validity is almost impossible to defend if the Guidelines are rigidly construed and applied.

SECTION 15C (2)
PROBLEM AND SETTING

(2) *Problem and setting.* An explicit definition of the purpose(s) of the study and the circumstances in which the study was conducted should be provided. A description of existing selection procedures and cutoff scores, if any, should be provided.

SECTION 15C (3)
JOB ANALYSIS

(3) *Job analysis—Content of the job.* A description of the method used to analyze the job should be provided (essential). The work behavior(s), the associated tasks, and, if the behavior results in a work product, the work products should be completely described (essential). Measures of criticality and/or importance of the work behavior(s) and the method of determining these measures should be provided (essential). Where the job analysis also identified the knowledges, skills, and abilities used in work behavior(s), an operational definition for each knowledge in terms of a body of learned information and for each skill and ability in terms of observable behaviors and outcomes, and the relationship between each knowledge, skill, or ability and each work behavior, as well as the method used to determine this relationship, should be provided (essential). The work situation should be described, including the setting in which work behavior(s) are performed, and where appropriate, the manner in which knowledges, skills, or abilities are used, and the complexity and difficulty of the knowledge, skill, or ability as used in the work behavior(s).

77. Q. Is a task analysis necessary to support a selection procedure based on content validity?

A. A description of all tasks is not required by the Guidelines. However, the job analysis should describe all important work behaviors and their relative importance and their level of difficulty. Sections 14C(2) and 15C(3). The job analysis should focus on observable work behaviors and, to the extent appropriate, observable work products, and the tasks associated with the important observable work behaviors and/or work products. The job analysis should identify how the critical or important work behaviors are used in the job, and should support the content of the selection procedure.

SECTION 15C (4)
SELECTION PROCEDURE

(4) *Selection procedure and its content.* Selection procedures, including those constructed by or for the user, specific training requirements, composites of selection procedures, and any other procedure supported by content validity, should be completely and explicitly described or attached (essential). If commercially available selection procedures are used, they should be described by title, form, and publisher (essential). The behaviors measured or sampled by the selection procedure should be explicitly described (essential). Where the selection procedure purports to measure a knowledge, skill, or ability, evidence that the selection procedure measures and is a representative sample of the knowledge, skill, or ability should be provided (essential).

196

15C (2). Problem and Setting

PROFESSIONAL ANALYSIS

There may be some confusion about the meaning of "circumstances"—it should be understood that the only relevant "circumstances" are those relating to the work requirements.

15C (3). Job Analysis

PROFESSIONAL ANALYSIS

Complete description of work behaviors and associated tasks as an "essential" requirement sounds as though a full task analysis is required, although Q & A 77 denies this. Moreover, even a full task analysis would not require a complete description of the work product.

Some of the requirements for job analysis in this section are excessive. Some methods of job analysis will not show "the relationship between each knowledge, skill or ability and each work behavior", yet this is labeled "essential". For certain common jobs, the requirements of this section are beyond reach and reason, particularly for smaller employers. For example, a detailed study of any kind in connection with a typing test is obviously excessive for jobs known to require typing skill. Some lesser requirements should be set where job relevance is manifest.

15C (4). Selection Procedure and Its Content

PROFESSIONAL ANALYSIS

The comments at Section 15B (7) regarding test security for criterion-related studies apply here.

Moreover, the stress on the "representativeness" of the knowledge, skill, or ability sample is misplaced. The stress should be on the appropriateness of the material sampled for measuring an important aspect of the job. As indicated earlier, the Guidelines' excessive focus on specifics leaves the measurement of general principles generally impossible to define using a content strategy. See *Guardians Association v. Civil Service Commission*.

197

SECTION 15C (5)
RELATIONSHIP

(5) *Relationship between the selection procedure and the job.* The evidence demonstrating that the selection procedure is a representative work sample, a representative sample of the work behavior(s), or a representative sample of a knowledge, skill, or ability as used as a part of a work behavior and necessary for that behavior should be provided (essential). The user should identify the work behavior(s) which each item or part of the selection procedure is intended to sample or measure (essential). Where the selection procedure purports to sample a work behavior or to provide a sample of a work product, a comparison should be provided of the manner, setting, and the level of complexity of the selection procedure with those of the work situation (essential). If any steps were taken to reduce adverse impact on a race, sex, or ethnic group in the content of the procedure or in its administration, these steps should be described. Establishment of time limits, if any, and how these limits are related to the speed with which duties must be performed on the job, should be explained. Measures of central tend- ency (e.g., means) and measures of dispersion (e.g., standard deviations) and estimates of realibility should be reported for all selection procedures if available. Such reports should be made for relevant race, sex, and ethnic subgroups, at least on a statistically reliable sample basis.

SECTION 15C (6)
ALTERNATIVE
PROCEDURES

(6) *Alternative procedures investigated.* The alternative selection procedures investigated and available evidence of their impact should be identified (essential). The scope, method, and findings of the investigation, and the conclusions reached in light of the findings, should be fully described (essential).

SECTION 15C (7)
USES AND
APPLICATIONS

(7) *Uses and applications.* The methods considered for use of the selection procedure (e.g., as a screening device with a cutoff score, for grouping or ranking, or combined with other procedures in a battery) and available evidence of their impact should be described (essential). This description should include the rationale for choosing the method for operational use, and the evidence of the validity and utility of the procedure as it is to be used (essential). The purpose for which the procedure is to be used (e.g., hiring, transfer, promotion) should be described (essential). If the selection procedure is used with a cutoff score, the user should describe the way in which normal expectations of proficiency within the work force were determined and the way in which the cutoff score was determined (essential). In addition, if the selection procedure is to be used for ranking, the user should specify the evidence showing that a higher score on the selection procedure is likely to result in better job performance.

15C (5). Relationship Between the Selection Procedure and the Job

PROFESSIONAL ANALYSIS

Measurement of job complexity is typically established through job evaluation in pricing jobs and determining salary structures. There is no professionally agreed-upon way to measure the complexity of job duties. The stress on job complexity far exceeds any professional standards for content-oriented test development.

Similarly, identification of work behaviors related to each item in the selection procedure is unduly restrictive. The desired reporting of measures of central tendency for relevant race, sex and ethnic subgroups should not be *required* under content validation, even though it may often be useful or appropriate in the judgment of the researcher. Establishing content validity is shown by the adequacy of sampling the job regardless of who is performing in it. Again, this requirement is an outgrowth of the differential validity theory. See discussion at Section 14B (8), Part III.

15C (6). Alternative Procedures Investigated

PROFESSIONAL ANALYSIS

The requirement to investigate alternative selection procedures as a requirement of content validity reflects a misunderstanding of what content validity represents. Content-oriented test development strives to replicate the knowledge, skills and abilities of one or more content domains of the job itself. For the Guidelines to require a search for alternatives virtually requires a search for an alternative way of doing the job.

15C (7). Uses and Applications

PROFESSIONAL ANALYSIS

The requirement that the user specify the evidence showing that a higher score on a content-valid selection procedure is more likely to result in better job performance in effect requires criterion-related validity evidence. As such, this requirement does not reflect professional opinion and subverts the Guidelines' purported recognition of the equal acceptability of content, criterion-related and construct validity. See discussion of Section 14A, Part III. The 1980 Division 14 *Principles* (p. 18) recognize that there typically is a linear relationship between a content-valid selection procedure and job performance, an opinion which is supported by a substantial body of professional research literature.

The requirement for utility evidence introduces a new and unnecessary substantive requirement. The utility of content-valid procedures is virtually self-evident and statistical "utility" evidence would in effect require considerable additional research and development, including a criterion-related study. Determination of "normal" expectations of proficiency in the workforce is likewise excessive. See Section 15B (10), above.

SECTION 15C (8)
CONTACT PERSON

(8) *Contact person.* The name, mailing address, and telephone number of the person who may be contacted for further information about the validity study should be provided (essential).

SECTION 15C (9)
ACCURACY

(9) *Accuracy and completeness.* The report should describe the steps taken to assure the accuracy and completeness of the collection, analysis, and report of data and results.

SECTION 15D (1)
USE, LOCATION
AND DATE

D. *Construct validity studies.* Reports of construct validity for a selection procedure should include the following information:

(1) *User(s), location(s), and date(s) of study.* Date(s) and location(s) of the job analysis and the gathering of other evidence called for by these guidelines should be provided (essential).

SECTION 15D (2)
PROBLEM AND
SETTING

(2) *Problem and setting.* An explicit definition of the purpose(s) of the study and the circumstances in which the study was conducted should be provided. A description of existing selection procedures and cutoff scores, if any, should be provided.

SECTION 15D (3)
CONSTRUCT
DEFINITION

(3) *Construct definition.* A clear definition of the construct(s) which are believed to underlie successful performance of the critical or important work behavior(s) should be provided (essential). This definition should include the levels of construct performance relevant to the job(s) for which the selection procedure is to be used (essential). There should be a summary of the position of the construct in the psychological literature, or in the absence of such a position, a description of the way in which the definition and measurement of the construct was developed and the psychological theory underlying it (essential). Any quantitative data which identify or define the job constructs, such as factor analyses, should be provided (essential).

15C (8). Contact Person

PROFESSIONAL ANALYSIS

This is an appropriate requirement.

15C (9). Accuracy and Completeness

Professional standards call for accuracy and completeness. However, see the discussion at 15(C) (1) for reasons why the "essential" requirements noted here are excessive.

15D. Construct Validity Studies

15D (1). User(s), Location(s) and Date(s) of Study

PROFESSIONAL ANALYSIS

There are 26 "essential" requirements here. Again, a report may be deemed unacceptable by one of the agencies if even one of these requirements is not met.

As with the other documentation sections, this Section introduces requirements not found in the substantive sections of the Guidelines. For example, although the applicable wording is vague, the section discussing factor analysis may lead compliance officials to demand factor analytic information in every instance where construct validity is claimed.

Other documentation requirements are problematic because they follow inappropriate substantive requirements in the body of the Guidelines. Indeed, there is perceptible effort to treat construct validity as being nearly identical to criterion-related validity. This is professionally inappropriate.

Since construct-oriented approaches to validation usually include an examination of earlier studies not conducted by the current user, detailed data regarding dates and locations of those studies are often not available. Users can provide dates and locations of their *own* job analysis subject to the limitations discussed earlier, but they cannot realistically be required to submit that data for studies conducted by others. The professional published research should be sufficient to meet the requirements of this Section.

15D (2). Problem and Setting

PROFESSIONAL ANALYSIS

It is not clear if the "study" described in this Section refers to user examinations of evidence supporting construct validity (which may or may not include a criterion-oriented study of their own) or to the outside studies on which the evidence for validity is based.

15D (3). Construct Definition

PROFESSIONAL ANALYSIS

Since construct definitions very often will not include "levels of construct performance", it often would be impossible for users to relate those levels to their own jobs as required by this Section. The requirement for quantitative data also may be misleading—what is wanted would be the *results* of a factor analysis, not the analysis itself. It should be made clear also that methods other than factor analysis are acceptable for defining job constructs.

SECTION 15D (4)
JOB ANALYSIS

(4) *Job analysis.* A description of the method used to analyze the job should be provided (essential). A complete description of the work behavior(s) and, to the extent appropriate, work outcomes and measures of their criticality and/or importance should be provided (essential). The report should also describe the basis on which the behavior(s) or outcomes were determined to be important, such as their level of difficulty, their frequency of performance, the consequences of error or other appropriate factors (essential). Where jobs are grouped or compared for the purposes of generalizing validity evidence, the work behavior(s) and work product(s) for each of the jobs should be described, and conclusions concerning the similarity of the jobs in terms of observable work behaviors or work products should be made (essential).

SECTION 15D (5)
JOB TITLES
AND CODES

(5) *Job titles and codes.* It is desirable to provide the selection procedure user's job title(s) for the job(s) in question and the corresponding job title(s) and code(s) from the United States Employment Service's dictionary of occupational titles.

SECTION 15D (6)
SELECTION
PROCEDURES

(6) *Selection procedure.* The selection procedure used as a measure of the construct should be completely and explicitly described or attached (essential). If commercially available selection procedures are used, they should be identified by title, form and publisher (essential). The research evidence of the relationship between the selection procedure and the construct, such as factor structure, should be included (essential). Measures of central tendency, variability and reliability of the selection procedure should be provided (essential). Whenever feasible, these measures should be provided separately for each relevant race, sex and ethnic group.

SECTION 15D (7)
RELATIONSHIPS

(7) *Relationship to job performance.* The criterion-related study(ies) and other empirical evidence of the relationship between the construct measured by the selection procedure and the related work behavior(s) for the job or jobs in question should be provided (essential). Documentation of the criterion-related study(ies) should satisfy the provisions of section 15B above or section 15E(1) below, except for studies conducted prior to the effective date of these guidelines (essential). Where a study pertains to a group of jobs, and, on the basis of the study, validity is asserted for a job in the group, the observed work behaviors and the observed work products for each of the jobs should be described (essential). Any other evidence used in determining whether the work behavior(s) in each of the jobs is the same should be fully described (essential).

SECTION 15D (8)
ALTERNATIVE
PROCEDURES

(8) *Alternative procedures investigated.* The alternative selection procedures investigated and available evidence of their impact should be identified (essential). The scope, method, and findings of the investigation, and the conclusions reached in light of the findings should be fully described (essential).

15D (4). Job Analysis

PROFESSIONAL ANALYSIS

This Section permits grouping of jobs for validity generalization purposes on the basis of observable work behaviors and/or products. This focus on observable behaviors rather than the more generalizable underlying abilities common both within and across job families fails to recognize that differences between jobs based on different duties may be of little if any consequence when viewed in the larger perspective of abilities common across jobs. The profession traditionally has viewed constructs in terms of traits, abilities and personal characteristics. This necessarily implies a metric dependent to some degree on inferences as part of the job analysis. To preclude less readily observed aspects of jobs from the study of construct validity is a distortion of professional standards.

15D (5). Job Titles and Codes

PROFESSIONAL ANALYSIS

The same concerns for listing large numbers of titles apply here as in the criterion-validity section.

15D (6). Selection Procedure

PROFESSIONAL ANALYSIS

Concerns for test security preclude attaching copies of tests to actual reports (see similar comments on Section 15B (7)). In addition, the desired reporting of measures for each relevant race, sex and ethnic group is an irrelevant holdover from test fairness concerns and should not be included here.

15D (7). Relationship to Job Performance

PROFESSIONAL ANALYSIS

Since any requirement that all studies used in support of construct validity meet the requirements of the Guidelines would eliminate almost all efforts to use this approach, it is essential that all studies, including those which preceded even the 1966 Guidelines, be given weight. What is important to the establishment of construct validity is the weight of the total body of research evidence *not* the specific items in any one study.

See comments at Section 15D (4).

15D (8). Alternative Procedures Investigated

PROFESSIONAL ANALYSIS

Identification of constructs and the proper measurement of them is a difficult process in itself. Any alternatives found as measures of the construct would be used if they were useful and discarded if they were not. Investigation of alternatives is particularly meaningless in this approach.

See comments at Section 15B (8).

SECTION 15D (9)
USES AND
APPLICATIONS

(9) *Uses and applications.* The methods considered for use of the selection procedure (e.g., as a screening device with a cutoff score, for grouping or ranking, or combined with other procedures in a battery) and available evidence of their impact should be described (essential). This description should include the rationale for choosing the method for operational use, and the evidence of the validity and utility of the procedure as it is to be used (essential). The purpose for which the procedure is to be used (e.g., hiring, transfer, promotion) should be described (essential). If weights are assigned to different parts of the selection procedure, these weights and the validity of the weighted composite should be reported (essential). If the selection procedure is used with a cutoff score, the user should describe the way in which normal expectations of proficiency within the work force were determined and the way in which the cutoff score was determined (essential).

SECTION 15D (10)
ACCURACY

(10) *Accuracy and completeness.* The report should describe the steps taken to assure the accuracy and completeness of the collection, analysis, and report of data and results.

SECTION 15D (11)
SOURCE DATA

(11) *Source data.* Each user should maintain records showing all pertinent information relating to its study of construct validity.

SECTION 15D (12)
CONTACT PERSON

(12) *Contact person.* The name, mailing address, and telephone number of the individual who may be contacted for further information about the validity study should be provided (essential).

SECTION 15E
EVIDENCE/
OTHER STUDIES

E. *Evidence of validity from other studies.* When validity of a selection procedure is supported by studies not done by the user, the evidence from the original study or studies should be compiled in a manner similar to that required in the appropriate section of this section 15 above. In addition, the following evidence should be supplied:

SECTION 15E (1)
FROM CRITERION-
RELATED STUDIES

(1) *Evidence from criterion-related validity studies.—a. Job information.* A description of the important job behavior(s) of the user's job and the basis on which the behaviors were determined to be important should be provided (essential). A full description of the basis for determining that these important work behaviors are the same as those of the job in the original study (or studies) should be provided (essential).

90. Q. Although the records called for under "Source Data", Section 15B(11) and section 15D(11), are not listed as "Essential" the Guidelines state that each user should maintain such records, and have them available upon request of a compliance agency. Are these records necessary? Does the absence of complete records preclude the further use of research data compiled prior to the issuance of the Guidelines?

A. The Guidelines require the maintenance of these records in some form "as a necessary part of the study." Section 15A(3)(c). However, such records need not be compiled or maintained in any specific format. The term "Essential" as used in the Guidelines refers to information considered essential to the validity report. Section 15A(3)(b). The Source Data records need not be included with reports of validation or other formal reports until and unless they are specifically requested by a compliance agency. The absence of complete records does not preclude use of research data based on those records that are available. Validation studies submitted to comply with the requirements of the Guidelines may be considered inadequate to the extent that important data are missing or there is evidence that the collected data are inaccurate.

15D (9). Uses and Applications

PROFESSIONAL ANALYSIS

The same comments regarding utility and cutoff scores made in the content and criterion sections apply to construct studies as well.

See comments at Section 15B (10).

15D (10). Accuracy and Completeness

PROFESSIONAL ANALYSIS

See 15A (3) (c) and 15B (13).

15D (11). Source Data

PROFESSIONAL ANALYSIS

Since construct evidence often relies on studies not conducted by the user, source data often will not be available. See comments at Section 15D (1).

15D (12). Contact Person

PROFESSIONAL ANALYSIS

This is an appropriate requirement.

15E. Evidence of Validity from Other Studies

PROFESSIONAL ANALYSIS

As written, this Section only permits use of other studies having documentation "similar to" the requirements set forth in these Guidelines. This is too restrictive as the persuasiveness of the validity evidence rather than its form would be the appropriate professional measure.

15E (1). Evidence from Criterion-Related Validity Studies

PROFESSIONAL ANALYSIS

While it is appropriate to require an employer to provide evidence that external studies are relevant, the requirements stated here are excessive. For example, a full description of job behaviors is irrelevant if the test in question is designed to predict success in a critical element of the job. Employers should be required to show that their jobs are *similar* to the jobs studied in the aspects measured by the test. They should *not,* however, be required to show that they are identical. Section 15E (1) requires a job analysis based on job behaviors restrictively defined. Since some methods of job analysis look at knowledge, skills and abilities used and others work from job outcomes, any type of approach should be permitted. Similarly, requiring a "full description" of the basis for criterion similarity may be excessive depending on the definition of "full description".

The requirements of Section 15E (1) (c) are also inappropriate. What is important is job and criterion similarity, *not* labor market or applicant pool characteristics, which are irrelevant. Research evidence to date

SECTION 15E (1)
FROM CRITERION-
RELATED STUDIES

(1) *Evidence from criterion-related validity studies.*—a. *Job information.* A description of the important job behavior(s) of the user's job and the basis on which the behaviors were determined to be important should be provided (essential). A full description of the basis for determining that these important work behaviors are the same as those of the job in the original study (or studies) should be provided (essential).

b. *Relevance of criteria.* A full description of the basis on which the criteria used in the original studies are determined to be relevant for the user should be provided (essential).

c. *Other variables.* The similarity of important applicant pool or sample characteristics reported in the original studies to those of the user should be described (essential). A description of the comparison between the race, sex and ethnic composition of the user's relevant labor market and the sample in the original validity studies should be provided (essential).

d. *Use of the selection procedure.* A full description should be provided showing that the use to be made of the selection procedure is consistent with the findings of the original validity studies (essential).

e. *Bibliography.* A bibliography of reports of validity of the selection procedure for the job or jobs in question should be provided (essential). Where any of the studies included an investigation of test fairness, the results of this investigation should be provided (essential). Copies of reports published in journals that are not commonly available should be described in detail or attached (essential). Where a user is relying upon unpublished studies, a reasonable effort should be made to obtain these studies. If these unpublished studies are the sole source of validity evidence they should be described in detail or attached (essential). If these studies are not available, the name and address of the source, an adequate abstract or summary of the validity study and data, and a contact person in the source organization should be provided (essential).

SECTION 15E (2)
EVIDENCE/
CONTENT VALIDITY

(2) *Evidence from content validity studies.* See section 14C(3) and section 15C above.

SECTION 15E (3)
EVIDENCE/
CONSTRUCT
VALIDITY

(3) *Evidence from construct validity studies.* See sections 14D(2) and 15D above.

SECTION 15F
COOPERATIVE
STUDIES

F. *Evidence of validity from cooperative studies.* Where a selection procedure has been validated through a cooperative study, evidence that the study satisfies the requirements of sections 7, 8 and 15E should be provided (essential).

indicates that among persons who typically apply for a given job, wide disparities in group characteristics appear to have little effect upon validity. A bibliography is desirable but not essential. Only the studies actually relied upon need be reported. This Section appropriately requires that the borrower show that the selection procedure is being used consistently with the findings of the original study.

The net effect of these subsections is to make it very difficult, if not impossible, for employers to rely on evidence of validity from other studies. It cannot be over-emphasized that virtually no professionally published study now in existence meets all the requirements of the Guidelines, and that the majority of employers have no choice but to rely on transported validity or consortium efforts. See the discussion of Section 7, above.

15E (2). Evidence from Content Validity ───────────────────── Studies

PROFESSIONAL ANALYSIS

See comments at Sections 14C (3) and 15C.

15E (3). Evidence from Construct Validity ───────────────── Studies

PROFESSIONAL ANALYSIS

See comments at Section 15E (1).

15F. Evidence of Validity from Cooperative ───────────────── Studies

PROFESSIONAL ANALYSIS

Requiring that the provisions of Section 15E be satisfied here adds confusion. If a user's employees or applicants have been part of a validation study, the user should not have to invoke, in defense, the provisions for borrowing someone else's study. Compliance with the provisions of Section 8 should be sufficient, since additional reporting requirements will only discourage cooperative studies, which is contrary to the purpose of Section 8.

SECTION 15G
SELECTION

G. *Selection for higher level job.* If a selection procedure is used to evaluate candidates for jobs at a higher level than those for which they will initially be employed, the validity evidence should satisfy the documentation provisions of this section 15 for the higher level job or jobs, and in addition, the user should provide: (1) a description of the job progression structure, formal or informal; (2) the data showing how many employees progress to the higher level job and the length of time needed to make this progression; and (3) an identification of any anticipated changes in the higher level job. In addition, if the test measures a knowledge, skill or ability, the user should provide evidence that the knowledge, skill or ability is required for the higher level job and the basis for the conclusion that the knowledge, skill or ability is not expected to develop from the training or experience on the job.

SECTION 15H
INTERIM USE

H. *Interim use of selection procedures.* If a selection procedure is being used on an interim basis because the procedure is not fully supported by the required evidence of validity, the user should maintain and have available (1) substantial evidence of validity for the procedure, and (2) a report showing the date on which the study to gather the additional evidence commenced, the estimated completion date of the study, and a description of the data to be collected (essential).

60. Q. What are the potential consequences to a user when a selection procedure is used on an interm basis?

A. The fact that the Guidelines permit interim use of a selection procedure under some conditions does not immunize the user from liability for back pay, attorney fees and the like, should use of the selection procedure later be found to be in violation of the Guidelines. Section 5J. For this reason, users should take steps to come into full compliance with the Guidelines as soon as possible. It is also appropriate for users to consider ways of minimizing adverse impact during the period of interim use.

15G. Selection for Higher Level Jobs

PROFESSIONAL ANALYSIS

Use of a selection procedure which evaluates candidates for skills needed for jobs at a higher level than those in which they will be initially employed is discouraged by both substantive and documentation requirements. For discussion of the substantive requirements see Section 5I, above.

The initial documentation requirement is that there be validity evidence satisfying the documentation provisions of Section 15 for the selection procedure as it relates to the higher level job or jobs for which the employer is selecting personnel. However, the Guidelines also require some description of the job progression structure which employees encounter, whether this structure is formal or informal, as well as actuarial data demonstrating the likelihood that a person will progress. The Section apparently assumes that most employers have a definite program of progression which virtually all employees experience. In fact, many employers use a flexible approach to employee progress and cross-training and provisions for varied career paths make the concept of "job progression" far more complex than is implied here.

The employer also is required to identify any anticipated changes in the higher level job, when all that is of interest is whether the job will change sufficiently to warrant concern about study currency.

Finally, the employer is required to prove a negative, i.e., that the knowledges, skills or abilities which are required for the higher level job and are measured by the selection procedure are not expected to develop from training or experience in the lower level positions. The employer would need to *prove* that subsequent learning on skills tested did *not* occur after the person was hired . . . an obvious impossibility. This also suggests that an employer that has a development program or training program accompanying the entry level positions must somehow prove that a person who as an applicant has skills or abilities relevant to higher level positions is preferable to an individual who would require training before being suitable for advancement. This limits the employer's ability to prefer individuals who learn quickly or are already qualified for higher level positions and especially injures employers having "promote from within" programs.

Subject to the discussion provided under Section 5I, a validation study of a selection procedure for a higher level job should include: (1) a general description of the job progression structure; (2) the underlying rationale for selection of the higher level job studied (i.e., the proportion of persons progressing to the job); (3) the length of time for progression; and (4) anticipated changes in the job which are likely to affect study currency.

15H. Interim Use of Selection Procedures

LEGAL ANALYSIS

The problem with interim use is found in Question and Answer 60 where it is suggested: "It is also appropriate for users to consider ways of minimizing adverse impact during the period of interim use." The suggestion that adverse impact be minimized during interim use is the exception that could swallow the rule and is related to the Guidelines' general encouragement to eliminate adverse impact rather than to validate selection procedures. As such, this section is based on the inappropriate premise that the only way an employer can justify adverse impact is to have done separate studies for each and every affected class.

This Section also must be read in connection with 14 B (8) (f) requiring the conduct of a "fairness" study when it becomes technically feasible to do so. A user conducting a criterion-related validity study who is unable to do a fairness study because of technical infeasibility is arguably only in interim compliance until such a separate fairness study is conducted.

See also the comments provided under Sections 5J, 6A and 6B.

SECTION 16A-E DEFINITIONS

DEFINITIONS

SEC. 16. *Definitions.* The following definitions shall apply throughout these guidelines:

A. *Ability.* A present competence to perform an observable behavior or a behavior which results in an observable product.

B. *Adverse impact.* A substantially different rate of selection in hiring, promotion, or other employment decision which works to the disadvantage of members of a race, sex, or ethnic group. See section 4 of these guidelines.

C. *Compliance with these guidelines.* Use of a selection procedure is in compliance with these guidelines if such use has been validated in accord with these guidelines (as defined below), or if such use does not result in adverse impact on any race, sex, or ethnic group (see section 4, above), or, in unusual circumstances, if use of the procedure is otherwise justified in accord with Federal law. See section 6B, above.

D. *Content validity.* Demonstrated by data showing that the content of a selection procedure is representative of important aspects of performance on the job. See section 5B and section 14C.

E. *Construct validity.* Demonstrated by data showing that the selection procedure measures the degree to which candidates have identifiable characteristics which have been determined to be important for successful job performance. See section 5B and section 14D.

---

10. Q. What is adverse impact?

A. Under the Guidelines adverse impact is a substantially different rate of selection in hiring, promotion or other employment decision which works to the disadvantage of members of a race, sex or ethnic group. Sections 4D and 16B. See Questions 11 and 12.

11. Q. What is a substantially different rate of selection?

A. The agencies have adopted a rule of thumb under which they will generally consider a selection rate for any race, sex, or ethnic group which is less than four-fifths (4/5ths) or eighty percent (80%) of the selection rate for the group with the highest selection rate as a substantially different rate of selection. See Section 4D. This "4/5ths" or "80%" rule of thumb is not intended as a legal definition, but is a practical means of keeping the attention of the enforcement agencies on serious discrepancies in rates of hiring, promotion and other selection decisions.

For example, if the hiring rate for whites other than Hispanics is 60%, for American Indians 45%, for Hispanics 48%, and for Blacks 51%, and each of these groups constitutes more than 2% of the labor force in the relevant labor area (see Question 16), a comparison should be made of the selection rate for each group with that of the highest group (whites). These comparisons show the following impact ratios: American Indians 45/60 or 75%; Hispanics 48/60 or 80%; and Blacks 51/60 or 85%. Applying the 4/5ths or 80% rule of thumb, on the basis of the above information alone, adverse impact is indicated for American Indians but not for Hispanics or Blacks.

12. Q. How is adverse impact determined?

A. Adverse impact is determined by a four step process.

(1) calculate the rate of selection for each group (divide the number of persons selected from a group by the number of applicants from that group).

(2) observe which group has the highest selection rate.

(3) calculate the impact ratios, by comparing the selection rate for each group with that of the highest group (divide the selection rate for a group by the selection rate for the highest group).

(4) observe whether the selection rate for any group is substantially less (i.e., usually less than 4/5ths or 80%) than the selection rate for the highest group. If it is, adverse impact is indicated in most circumstances. See Section 4D.

For example:

Applicants	Hires	Selection rate Percent hired
80 White	48	48/80 or 60%
40 Black	12	12/40 or 30%

A comparison of the black selection rate (30%) with the white selection rate (60%) shows that the black rate is 30/60, or one-half (or 50%) of the white rate. Since the one-half (50%) is less than 4/5ths (80%) adverse impact is usually indicated.

The determination of adverse impact is not purely arithmetic however; and other factors may be relevant. See, Section 4D.

16. Q. Should adverse impact determinations be made for all groups regardless of their size?

A. No. Section 15A(2) calls for annual adverse impact determinations to be made for each group which constitutes either 2% or more of the total labor force in the relevant labor area, or 2% or more of the applicable workforce. Thus, impact determinations should be made for any employment decision for each group which constitutes 2% or more of the labor force in the relevant labor area. For hiring, such determination should also be made for groups which constitute more than 2% of the applicants; and for promotions, determinations should also be made for those groups which constitute at least 2% of the user's workforce. There are record keeping obligations for all groups, even those which are less than 2%. See Question 86.

Definitions

Section 16. Definitions

16A. Ability

LEGAL ANALYSIS

The court in *Guardians Association v. Civil Service Commission* was very critical of the narrowness of the Guidelines' definition of ability and refused to apply it. The court preferred a definition that recognizes that "abilities" are in the nature of constructs.

PROFESSIONAL ANALYSIS

The definitions of "ability" and "skill" are vague and untried. They overlap significantly, and also impinge upon the definition of "knowledge". See Section 14C.

16B. Adverse Impact

LEGAL ANALYSIS

The use of the word "substantially" is appropriate, although the agencies' refusal to apply a test of statistical significance is open to criticism. See Section 4.

16C. Compliance With These Guidelines

LEGAL ANALYSIS

Procedures have often been found by courts to be job-related without formal validation. It is legally incorrect to say that this occurs only in "unusual circumstances". See Part II, Point IV and Sections 3A and 6B.

16D. Content Validity

PROFESSIONAL ANALYSIS

To adequately reflect professional standards, the definition should stipulate that a selection procedure may be related to one or more important aspects of the job, not all of them. See Sections 5B, 14C and 15C.

16E. Construct Validity

PROFESSIONAL ANALYSIS

See Sections 14D and 15D.

SECTION 16F-L DEFINITIONS

F. *Criterion-related validity.* Demonstrated by empirical data showing that the selection procedure is predictive of or significantly correlated with important elements of work behavior. See sections 5B and 14B.

G. *Employer.* Any employer subject to the provisions of the Civil Rights Act of 1964, as amended, including State or local governments and any Federal agency subject to the provisions of section 717 of the Civil Rights Act of 1964, as amended, and any Federal contractor or subcontractor or federally assisted construction contractor or subcontractor covered by Executive Order 11246, as amended.

H. *Employment agency.* Any employment agency subject to the provisions of the Civil Rights Act of 1964, as amended.

I. *Enforcement action.* For the purposes of section 4 a proceeding by a Federal enforcement agency such as a lawsuit or an administrative proceeding leading to debarment from or withholding, suspension, or termination of Federal Government contracts or the suspension or withholding of Federal Government funds; but not a finding of reasonable cause or a conciliation process or the issuance of right to sue letters under title VII or under Executive Order 11246 where such finding, conciliation, or issuance of notice of right to sue is based upon an individual complaint.

J. *Enforcement agency.* Any agency of the executive branch of the Federal Government which adopts these guidelines for purposes of the enforcement of the equal employment opportunity laws or which has responsibility for securing compliance with them.

K. *Job analysis.* A detailed statement of work behaviors and other information relevant to the job.

L. *Job description.* A general statement of job duties and responsibilities.

---

2. Q. What is the basic principle of the Guidelines?

A. A selection process which has an adverse impact on the employment opportunities of members of a race, color, religion, sex, or national origin group (referred to as "race, sex, and ethnic group," as defined in Section 16P) and thus disproportionately screens them out is unlawfully discriminatory unless the process or its component procedures have been validated in accord with the Guidelines, or the user otherwise justifies them in accord with Federal law. See Sections 3 and 6.[1] This principle was adopted by the Supreme Court unanimously in *Griggs* v. *Duke Power Co.*, 401 U.S. 424, and was ratified and endorsed by the Congress when it passed the Equal Employment Opportunity Act of 1972, which amended Title VII of the Civil Rights Act of 1964.

26. Q. Does the bottom line concept of Section 4C apply to the administrative processing of charges of discrimination filed with an issuing agency, alleging that a specific selection procedure is discriminatory?

A. No. The bottom line concept applies only to enforcement actions as defined in Section 16 of the Guidelines. Enforcement actions include only court enforcement actions and other similar proceedings as defined in Section 16I. The EEOC administrative processing of charges of discrimination (investigation, finding of reasonable cause/no cause, and conciliation) required by Section 706(b) of Title VII are specifically exempted from the bottom line concept by the definition of an enforcement action. The bottom line concept is a result of a decision by the various enforcement agencies that, as a matter of prosecutorial discretion, they will devote their limited enforcement resources to the most serious offenders of equal employment opportunity laws. Since the concept is not a rule of law, it does not affect the discharge by the EEOC of its statutory responsibilities to investigate charges of discrimination, render an administrative finding on its investigation, and engage in voluntary conciliation efforts. Similarly, with respect to the other issuing agencies, the bottom line concept applies not to the processing of individual charges, but to the initiation of enforcement action.

16F. Criterion-Related Validity

PROFESSIONAL ANALYSIS

This definition is professionally acceptable so long as it is clear that "work behavior" encompasses more than task performance. See Sections 14B and 15B.

16G. Employer

LEGAL ANALYSIS

None.

16H. Employment Agency

LEGAL ANALYSIS

None.

16I. Enforcement Action

LEGAL ANALYSIS

The exclusion of reasonable cause findings and conciliation efforts in individual cases from the definition of enforcement action is unwarranted in the context of these Guidelines. If there is a clear bottom line, that is the end of the matter from a statistical point of view. There is no reason for any agency to study the impact of a selection procedure or a component merely because an individual has brought a complaint. The individual might show disparate treatment, but that is outside the scope of the Guidelines.

The failure to include reasonable cause findings may also force an employer to make an injudicious allocation of limited professional resources. If there is a clear bottom line, the employer should have no validation responsibilities and should not be subject to investigation or conciliation on that point.

16J. Enforcement Agency

LEGAL ANALYSIS

None.

16K. Job Analysis

PROFESSIONAL ANALYSIS

The definition should refer to "work behaviors *or* other information" which describe important or critical aspects of the job. See Sections 14A, 14B (2) and 14C (2).

16L. Job Description

PROFESSIONAL ANALYSIS

Job descriptions may also include the underlying abilities necessary to successfully perform the job duties.

SECTION 16M-S DEFINITIONS

M. *Knowledge.* A body of information applied directly to the performance of a function.

N. *Labor organization.* Any labor organization subject to the provisions of the Civil Rights Act of 1964, as amended, and any committee subject thereto controlling apprenticeship or other training.

O. *Observable.* Able to be seen, heard, or otherwise perceived by a person other than the person performing the action.

P. *Race, sex, or ethnic group.* Any group of persons identifiable on the grounds of race, color, religion, sex, or national origin.

Q. *Selection procedure.* Any measure, combination of measures, or procedure used as a basis for any employment decision. Selection procedures include the full range of assessment techniques from traditional paper and pencil tests, performance tests, training programs, or probationary periods and physical, educational, and work experience requirements through informal or casual interviews and unscored application forms.

R. *Selection rate.* The proportion of applicants or candidates who are hired, promoted, or otherwise selected.

S. *Should.* The term "should" as used in these guidelines is intended to connote action which is necessary to achieve compliance with the guidelines, while recognizing that there are circumstances where alternative courses of action are open to users.

---

28. Q. The Uniform Guidelines apply to the requirements of Federal law prohibiting employment practices which discriminate on the grounds of race, color, religion, sex or national origin. However, records are required to be kept only by sex and by specified race and ethnic groups. How can adverse impact be determined for religious groups and for national origin groups other than those specified in Section 4B of the Guidelines?

A. The groups for which records are required to be maintained are the groups for which there is extensive evidence of continuing discriminatory practices. This limitation is designed in part to minimize the burden on employers for recordkeeping which may not be needed.

For groups for which records are not required, the person(s) complaining may obtain information from the employer or others (voluntarily or through legal process) to show that adverse impact has taken place. When that has been done, the various provisions of the Uniform Guidelines are fully applicable.

Whether or not there is adverse impact, Federal equal employment opportunity law prohibits any deliberate discrimination or disparate treatment on grounds of religion or national origin, as well as on grounds of sex, color, or race.

Whenever "ethnic" is used in the Guidelines or in these Questions and Answers, it is intended to include national origin and religion, as set forth in the statutes, executive orders, and regulations prohibiting discrimination. See Section 16P.

5. Q. Do the Guidelines apply only to written tests?

A. No. They apply to all selection procedures used to make employment decisions, including interviews, review of experience or education from application forms, work samples, physical requirements, and evaluations of performance. Sections 2B and 16Q, and see Question 6.

6. Q. What practices are covered by the Guidelines?

A. The Guidelines apply to employee selection procedures which are used in making employment decisions, such as hiring, retention, promotion, transfer, demotion, dismissal or referral. Section 2B. Employee selection procedures include job requirements (physical, education, experience), and evaluation of applicants or candidates on the basis of application forms, interviews, performance tests, paper and pencil tests, performance in training programs or probationary periods, and any other procedures used to make an employment decision whether administered by the employer or by an employment agency. See Section 2B.

67. Q. What does "unfairness of a selection procedure" mean?

A. When a specific score on a selection procedure has a different meaning in terms of expected job performance for members of one race, sex or ethnic group than the same score does for members of another group, the use of that selection procedure may be unfair for members of one of the groups. See section 16V. For example, if members of one group have an average score of 40 on the selection procedure, but perform on the job as well as another group which has an average score of 50, then some uses of the selection procedure would be unfair to the members of the lower scoring group. See Question 70.

16M. Knowledge

LEGAL ANALYSIS

See comments at "ability"

16N. Labor Organization

LEGAL ANALYSIS

None.

16O. Observable

PROFESSIONAL ANALYSIS

See comments on the Guidelines' overemphasis on the observable at Sections 14A, 14B (2) and 14C (2).

16P. Race, Sex or Ethnic Group

LEGAL ANALYSIS

The inclusion of "religion" in this list is inappropriate, as explained above in Section II.

Moreover, the groups should be limited to those used in preparing EEO-1, EEO-4 and other reports.

16Q. Selection Procedure

LEGAL ANALYSIS

To include every "employment decision" is too broad. "Selection" (for something) should be an important element of the definition.

16R. Selection Rate

PROFESSIONAL ANALYSIS

In the case of hiring, the employer should not be held responsible for persons who decline an offer of employment. Similarly, persons who decline promotions or who fail to bid on promotions should not be counted in determining impact or progression rates. See Sections 3A and 4C.

16S. Should

LEGAL ANALYSIS

The distinction between "should" and "must" is not apparent from this definition.

T. *Skill.* A present, observable competence to perform a learned psychomotor act.

U. *Technical feasibility.* The existence of conditions permitting the conduct of meaningful criterion-related validity studies. These conditions include: (1) An adequate sample of persons available for the study to achieve findings of statistical significance; (2) having or being able to obtain a sufficient range of scores on the selection procedure and job performance measures to produce validity results which can be expected to be representative of the results if the ranges normally expected were utilized; and (3) having or being able to devise unbiased, reliable and relevant measures of job performance or other criteria of employee adequacy. See section 14B(2). With respect to investigation of possible unfairness, the same considerations are applicable to each group for which the study is made. See section 14B(8).

V. *Unfairness of selection procedure.* A condition in which members of one race, sex, or ethnic group characteristically obtain lower scores on a selection procedure than members of another group, and the differences are not reflected in differences in measures of job performance. See section 14B(7).

W. *User.* Any employer, labor organization, employment agency, or licensing or certification board, to the extent it may be covered by Federal equal employment opportunity law, which uses a selection procedure as a basis for any employment decision. Whenever an employer, labor organization, or employment agency is required by law to restrict recruitment for any occupation to those applicants who have met licensing or certification requirements, the licensing or certifying authority to the extent it may be covered by Federal equal employment opportunity law will be considered the user with respect to those licensing or certification requirements. Whenever a State employment agency or service does no more than administer or monitor a procedure as permitted by Department of Labor regulations, and does so without making referrals or taking any other action on the basis of the results, the State employment agency will not be deemed to be a user.

X. *Validated in accord with these guidelines or properly validated.* A demonstration that one or more validity study or studies meeting the standards of these guidelines has been conducted, including investigation and, where appropriate, use of suitable alternative selection procedures as contemplated by section 3B, and has produced evidence of validity sufficient to warrant use of the procedure for the intended purpose under the standards of these guidelines.

Y. *Work behavior.* An activity performed to achieve the objectives of the job. Work behaviors involve observable (physical) components and unobservable (mental) components. A work behavior consists of the performance of one or more tasks. Knowledges, skills, and abilities are not behaviors, although they may be applied in work behaviors.

4. Q. Are college placement officers and similar organizations considered to be users subject to the Guidelines?

A. Placement offices may or may not be subject to the Guidelines depending on what services they offer. If a placement office uses a selection procedure as a basis for any employment decision, it is covered under the definition of "user". Section 16. For example, if a placement office selects some students for referral to an employer but rejects others, it is covered. However, if the placement office refers all interested students to an employer, it is not covered, even though it may offer office space and provision for informing the students of job openings. The Guidelines are intended to cover all users of employee selection procedures, including employment agencies, who are subject to Federal equal employment opportunity law.

70. Q. What should be done if a selection procedure is unfair for one or more groups in the relevant labor market?

A. The Guidelines discuss three options. See Section 14B(8)(d). First, the selection instrument may be replaced by another validated instrument which is fair to all groups. Second, the selection instrument may be revised to eliminate the sources of unfairness. For example, certain items may be found to be the only ones which cause the unfairness to a particular group, and these items may be deleted or replaced by others. Finally, revisions may be made in the method of use of the selection procedure to ensure that the probability of being selected is compatible with the probability of successful job performance.

The Federal enforcement agencies recognize that there is serious debate in the psychological profession on the question of test fairness, and that information on that concept is developing. Accordingly, the enforcement agencies will consider developments in this field in evaluating actions occasioned by a finding of test unfairness.

71. Q. How is test unfairness related to differential validity and to differential prediction?

A. Test unfairness refers to use of selection procedures based on scores when members of one group characteristically obtain lower scores than members of another group, and the differences are not reflected in measures of job performance. See Sections 16V and 14B(8)(a), and Question 67.

Differential validity and test unfairness are conceptually distinct. Differential validity is defined as a situation in which a given instrument has significantly different validity coefficients for different race, sex or ethnic groups. Use of a test may be unfair to some groups even when differential validity is not found.

Differential prediction is a central concept for one definition of test unfairness. Differential prediction occurs when the use of the same set of scores systematically overpredicts or underpredicts job performance for members of one group as compared to members of another group.

Other definitions of test unfairness which do not relate to differential prediction may, however, also be appropriately applied to employment decisions. Thus these Guidelines are not intended to choose between fairness models as long as the model selected is appropriate to the manner in which the selection procedure is used.

16T. Skill

PROFESSIONAL ANALYSIS

See comments at "ability".

16U. Technical Feasibility

PROFESSIONAL ANALYSIS

See Section 14B (8).

16V. Unfairness of Selection Procedure

PROFESSIONAL ANALYSIS

See Section 14B (8).

16W. User

LEGAL ANALYSIS

None.

16X. Validated in Accord With These Guidelines or Properly Validated

PROFESSIONAL ANALYSIS

It is unlikely that any study will meet all of the substantive and documentation sections of these Guidelines. See 16C and comments throughout the text of Part III, especially Sections 14 and 15.

16Y. Work Behavior

PROFESSIONAL ANALYSIS

This definition is inappropriate in that more than a behavior may be used in completing a task. The recognition of "unobservable (mental)" components is appropriate, but this recognition is not consistently acknowledged in the Guidelines text.

Commentary

The agencies do not provide definitions for terms critical for employer compliance with the Guidelines. Such undefined terms include:

large sample
low correlation
"as job related as possible"
"substantially the same"

Many more omissions could be noted.

APPENDIX
SECTION 17 AFFIRMATIVE ACTION POLICY STATEMENT

APPENDIX

17. *Policy statement on affirmative action* (see section 13B). The Equal Employment Opportunity Coordinating Council was established by act of Congress in 1972, and charged with responsibility for developing and implementing agreements and policies designed, among other things, to eliminate conflict and inconsistency among the agencies of the Federal Government responsible for administering Federal law prohibiting discrimination on grounds of race, color, sex, religion, and national origin. This statement is issued as an initial response to the requests of a number of State and local officials for clarification of the Government's policies concerning the role of affirmative action in the overall equal employment opportunity program. While the Coordinating Council's adoption of this statement expresses only the views of the signatory agencies concerning this important subject, the principles set forth below should serve as policy guidance for other Federal agencies as well.

(1) Equal employment opportunity is the law of the land. In the public sector of our society this means that all persons, regardless of race, color, religion, sex, or national origin shall have equal access to positions in the public service limited only by their ability to do the job. There is ample evidence in all sectors of our society that such equal access frequently has been denied to members of certain groups because of their sex, racial, or ethnic characteristics. The remedy for such past and present discrimination is twofold.

On the one hand, vigorous enforcement of the laws against discrimination is essential. But equally, and perhaps even more important are affirmative, voluntary efforts on the part of public employers to assure that positions in the public service are genuinely and equally accessible to qualified persons, without regard to their sex, racial, or ethnic characteristics. Without such efforts equal employment opportunity is no more than a wish. The importance of voluntary affirmative action on the part of employers is underscored by title VII of the Civil Rights Act of 1964, Executive Order 11246, and related laws and regulations—all of which emphasize voluntary action to achieve equal employment opportunity.

As with most management objectives, a systematic plan based on sound organizational analysis and problem identification is crucial to the accomplishment of affirmative action objectives. For this reason, the Council urges all State and local governments to develop and implement results oriented affirmative action plans which deal with the problems so identified.

The following paragraphs are intended to assist State and local governments by illustrating the kinds of analyses and activities which may be appropriate for a public employer's voluntary affirmative action plan. This statement does not address remedies imposed after a finding of unlawful discrimination.

(2) Voluntary affirmative action to assure equal employment opportunity is appropriate at any stage of the employment process. The first step in the construction of any affirmative action plan should be an analysis of the employer's work force to determine whether percentages of sex, race, or ethnic groups in individual job classifications are substantially similar to the precentages of those groups available in the relevant job market who possess the basic job-related qualifications.

When substantial disparities are found through such analyses, each element of the overall selection process should be examined to determine which elements operate to exclude persons on the basis of sex, race, or ethnic group. Such elements include, but are not limited to, recruitment, testing, ranking certification, interview, recommendations for selection, hiring, promotion, etc. The examination of each element of the selection process should at a minimum include a determination of its validity in predicting job performance.

(3) When an employer has reason to believe that its selection procedures have the exclusionary effect described in paragraph 2 above, it should initiate affirmative steps to remedy the situation. Such steps, which in design and execution may be race, color, sex, or ethnic "conscious," include, but are not limited to, the following:

(a) The establishment of a long-term goal, and short-range, interim goals and timetables for the specific job classifications, all of which should take into account the availability of basically qualified persons in the relevant job market;

(b) A recruitment program designed to attract qualified members of the group in question;

(c) A systematic effort to organize work and redesign jobs in ways that provide opportunities for persons lacking "journeyman" level knowledge or skills to enter and, with appropriate training, to progress in a career field;

(d) Revamping selection instruments or procedures which have not yet been validated in order to reduce or eliminate exclusionary effects on particular groups in particular job classifications;

(e) The initiation of measures designed to assure that members of the affected group who are qualified to perform the job are included within the pool of persons from which the selecting official makes the selection;

(f) A systematic effort to provide career advancement training, both classroom and on-the-job, to employees locked into dead end jobs; and

(g) The establishment of a system for regularly monitoring the effectiveness of the particular affirmative action program, and procedures for making timely adjustments in this program where effectiveness is not demonstrated.

(4) The goal of any affirmative action plan should be achievement of genuine equal employment opportunity for all qualified persons. Selection under such plans should be based upon the ability of the applicant(s) to do the work. Such plans should not require the selection of the unqualified, or the unneeded, nor should they require the selection of persons on the basis of race, color, sex, religion, or national origin. Moreover, while the Council believes that this statement should serve to assist State and local employers, as well as Federal agencies, it recognizes that affirmative action cannot be viewed as a standardized program which must be accomplished in the same way at all times in all places.

Accordingly, the Council has not attempted to set forth here either the minimum or maximum voluntary steps that employers may take to deal with their respective situations. Rather, the Council recognizes that under applicable authorities, State and local employers have flexibility to formulate affirmative action plans that are best suited to their particular situations. In this manner, the Council believes that affirmative action programs will best serve the goal of equal employment opportunity.

Respectfully submitted,

HAROLD R. TYLER, Jr.,
Deputy Attorney General and Chairman of the Equal Employment Coordinating Council.

MICHAEL H. MOSKOW.
Under Secretary of Labor.

ETHEL BENT WALSH,
Acting Chairman, Equal Employment Opportunity Commission.

ROBERT E. HAMPTON,
Chairman, Civil Service Commission.

ARTHUR E. FLEMMING.
Chairman, Commission on Civil Rights.

Because of its equal employment opportunity responsibilities under the State and Local Government Fiscal Assistance Act of 1972 (the revenue sharing act), the Department of Treasury was invited to participate in the formulation of this policy statement; and it concurs and joins in the adoption of this policy statement.

Done this 26th day of August 1976.

RICHARD ALBRECHT,
General Counsel, Department of the Treasury.

GUIDELINES
Appendix

Section 17. Policy Statement on Affirmative Action

LEGAL ANALYSIS

In general, affirmative action is a desirable undertaking for most employers and an effective affirmative action program can help establish the "general EEO posture" that the agencies will consider as an aspect of exercising prosecutorial discretion. See Section 4E. However, there is some concern as to whether a statement on affirmative action is appropriate in a document purporting to set forth minimum standards for compliance with Title VII. Aside from questions of its appropriateness, the "policy statement" also includes concepts that are legally unsound in light of present case law.

(1) Tying voluntary "affirmative action" to past discrimination is unnecessary and erroneous in light of *Regents of the University of California v. Bakke,* 438 U.S. 265 (1978), except where overt race preferences are used, in which case the criteria of *United Steelworkers v. Weber* may pose a problem. The concept of underutilization is not tied to any notion of discrimination in the legal sense. Tying it to Title VII is simply incorrect. Title VII emphasizes informal conciliation of discrimination complaints, not voluntary affirmative action to correct underutilization. It may be noted that not merely ability to do a job, but *relative* ability may limit access to employment.

(2) The use of the word "validity" in connection with a survey of job practices to correct underutilization is inappropriate, as it connotes formal validation as set forth in the Guidelines. If validity is established, however, the last sentence errs in stating that this is a "minimum" goal. Validity of components need only be examined when the component is responsible for adverse impact.

(3) (a) Establishment of goals based on availability should take into account those who are currently available and those who are already employed (e.g., in government jobs). Validation should be a listed alternative. This section, indeed, should be rewritten to reflect *Weber* standards.

(4) The emphasis on equality of "qualified" persons wholly ignores the *Griggs* protection for selection on the basis of *relative* qualifications. The emphasis on flexibility and the disclaimer of race, ethnic or sex-based decision-making is appropriate.

APPENDIX
SECTION 18
CITATIONS

Section 18. *Citations.* The official title of these guidelines is "Uniform Guidelines on Employee Selection Procedures (1978)". The Uniform Guidelines on Employee Selection Procedures (1978) are intended to establish a uniform Federal position in the area of prohibiting discrimination in employment practices on grounds of race, color, religion, sex, or national origin. These guidelines have been adopted by the Equal Employment Opportunity Commission, the Department of Labor, the Department of Justice, and the Civil Service Commission.

The official citation is:

"Section ——, Uniform Guidelines on Employee Selection Procedure (1978); 43 FR —— (August 25, 1978)."

The short form citation is:

"Section ——, U.G.E.S.P. (1978); 43 FR —— (August 25, 1978)."

When the guidelines are cited in connection with the activities of one of the issuing agencies, a specific citation to the regulations of that agency can be added at the end of the above citation. The specific additional citations are as follows:

Equal Employment Opportunity Commission
  29 CFR Part 1607
Department of Labor
Office of Federal Contract Compliance Programs
  41 CFR Part 60-3
Department of Justice
  28 CFR 50.14
Civil Service Commission
  5 CFR 300.103(c)

Normally when citing these guidelines, the section number immediately preceding the title of the guidelines will be from these guidelines series 1-18. If a section number from the codification for an individual agency is needed it can also be added at the end of the agency citation. For example, section 6A of these guidelines could be cited for EEOC as follows: "Section 6A, Uniform Guidelines on Employee Selection Procedures (1978); 43 FR ——, (August 25, 1978); 29 CFR Part 1607, section 6A."

ELEANOR HOLMES NORTON,
Chair, Equal Employment Opportunity Commission.

ALAN K. CAMPBELL,
Chairman, Civil Service Commission.

RAY MARSHALL,
Secretary of Labor.

GRIFFIN B. BELL,
Attorney General.

Appendix
References

American Psychological Association. *Technical recommendations for psychological tests and diagnostic techniques*. Washington, D.C.: Author, 1954.

American Psychological Association, American Educational Research Association, National Council on Measurement in Education. *Standards for educational and psychological tests* (Revised edition). Washington, D.C.: Author, 1975.

Anastasi, A. *Psychological testing* (3rd edition). New York: MacMillan Publishing Company, 1968.

Anastasi, A. *Psychological testing* (4th edition). New York: MacMillan Publishing Company, 1976.

Boehm, V.R. "Negro-white differences in validity of employment and training selection procedures", *Journal of Applied Psychology*, 1972, *56*, 33–39.

Boehm, V.R. "Differential prediction: A methodological artifact?", *Journal of Applied Psychology*, 1977, *62* (2), 146–154.

Bray, D.W., Campbell, R.J., and Grant, D. L. *Formative years in business: A long-term AT&T study of managerial lives*. New York: John Wiley and Sons, 1974.

Bray, D. W. and Moses, J. L. "Personnel Selection", *Annual Review of Psychology*, 1972, *23*, 545–576.

Brown, S. H. "Long-term validity of a personal history item scoring procedure", *Journal of Applied Psychology*, 1978, *63* (6), 673–676.

Campbell, D. T. "Recommendations for APA test standards regarding construct, trait, and discriminant validity", *American Psychologist*, 1960, *15*, 546–553.

Campbell, J. T., Crooks, L. A., Mahoney, M. H., and Rock, D. A. *An investigation of sources of bias in the prediction of job performance: A six-year study*. Final project Report No. PR-73-37. Princeton, N. J.: Educational Testing Service, 1973.

Cascio, W. F. "Turnover, biographical data, and fair employment practice", *Journal of Applied Psychology*, 1976, *61* (5), 576–580.

Cleary, T. A. "Test bias: Prediction of grades of negro and white students in integrated colleges", *Journal of Educational Measurement*, 1968, *5*, 115–124.

Comments of the ad hoc group. *Proposed uniform guidelines on employee selection procedures: As published in the Federal Register—December 30, 1977*. Washington, D. C.: The ad hoc group, February 17, 1978.

Committee on Psychological Tests and Assessment, American Psychological Association. Correspondence to Preston David, Executive Director of EEOC. February 11, 1980.

Committee on Psychological Tests and Assessment, American Psychological Association. Correspondence to Preston David, A. Diane Graham, OPM, David L. Rose, Justice, Weldon Rougeau, OFCCP. May 27, 1980.

Committee on Psychological Tests and Assessment, American Psychological Association. *Statement on the uniform guidelines on employee selection procedures*. Washington, D. C.: Author, February 17, 1978.

Cronbach, L. J. and Glesser, G. C. *Psychological tests and personnel decisions* (2nd edition). Urbana, Illinois: University of Illinois Press, 1965.

Cronbach, L. J. and Meehl, P. E. "Construct validity in psychological tests", *Psychological Bulletin*, 1955, *52*, 281–302.

Division of Industrial-Organizational Psychology, American Psychological Association. *Principles for the validation and use of personnel selection procedures*. Washington, D. C.: Author, 1975.

Division of Industrial-Organizational Psychology, American Psychological Association. *Principles for the validation and use of personnel selection procedures: Second edition*. Berkeley, California: Author, 1980.

Dunnette, M. D. *Personnel selection and placement*. Belmont, California: Wadsworth, 1966.

Dunnette, M. D. (Editor). *Handbook of industrial and organizational psychology*. Chicago: Rand McNally, 1976.

Equal Employment Opportunity Commission. "Employee selection procedures: Republication of guidelines", *Federal Register*, 1976, *41* (228), 51984–51986.

Equal Employment Opportunity Commission. "Guidelines on employee selection procedures", *Federal Register*, 1970, *35* (149), 12333–12336.

Equal Employment Opportunity Commission. "Guidelines on employment testing procedures", *Federal Register*, May 1966.

Fincher, C. "Differential validity and test bias", *Personnel Psychology*, 1975, *28* (4), 481–500.

Finkle, R. B. "Managerial assessment centers", in M. D. Dunnette, (Ed.), *Handbook of industrial and organizational psychology*. Chicago: Rand McNally, 1976.

Fox, H. and Lefkowitz, J. "Differential validity: Ethnic group as a moderator in predicting job performance", *Personnel Psychology*, 1974, *27*, 209–223.

Gael, S., Grant, D. L., and Ritchie, R. J. "Employment test validation for minority and nonminority clerks with work sample criteria", *Journal of Applied Psychology, 1975, 60,* 420–426. (a)

Gael, S., Grant, D. L., and Ritchie, R. J. "Employment test validation for minority and nonminority telephone operators", *Journal of Applied Psychology, 1975, 60,* 411–419. (b)

Gross, A. L. and Su, W. H. "Defining a fair or unbiased selection model: A question of utilities", *Journal of Applied Psychology, 1975, 60,* 345–351.

Guion, R. M. "Open a new window: Validities and values in psychological measurement", *American Psychologist, 1974, 29,* 287–296.

Guion, R. M. "Recruiting, selection and job placement", in M. D. Dunnette (Ed.), *Handbook of industrial and organizational psychology.* Chicago: Rand McNally, 1976.

Guion, R. M. "Scoring of content domain samples: The problem of fairness", *Journal of Applied Psychology, 1978, 63* (4), 499–506.

Huck, J. R. "The research base", in J. L. Moses and W. C. Byham (Eds.), *Applying the assessment center method.* New York: Pergamon Press, 1977.

Huck, J. R. and Bray, D. W. "Management assessment center evaluations and subsequent job performance of white and black females", *Personnel Psychology, 1976, 29,* 13–30.

Hunter, J. E. and Schmidt, F. L. "A critical analysis of the statistical and ethical implications of five definitions of test fairness", *Psychological Bulletin, 1976, 83* (6), 1053–1071.

International Personnel Management Association. *Special report: Progress and problems with the uniform guidelines on employee selection procedures. Agency Issues,* August 25, 1978.

Katzell, R. A. and Dyer, F. J. "Differential validity revived", *Journal of Applied Psychology, 1977, 62,* 137–145.

Katzell, R. A. and Dyer, F. J. "On differential validity and bias", *Journal of Applied Psychology, 1978, 63* (1), 19–21.

Lawshe, C. H. "A quantitative approach to content validity", *Personnel Psychology, 1975, 28,* 563–575.

Linn, R. L. "Fair test use in selection", *Review of Educational Research, 1973, 43,* 139–161.

Linn, R. L. "Single-group validity, differential validity and differential prediction", *Journal of Applied Psychology,* 1978, *63* (4), 507–512.

Office of Personnel Management. "Standards for a merit system of personnel administration", *Federal Register,* 1979, *44* (34), 10238–10264.

Reilly, R. R. and Chao, G. T. "Validity and fairness of alternative employee selection procedures", Unpublished report, Morristown, N. J.: American Telephone and Telegraph, 1980.

Ruch, W. W. "A re-analysis of published differential validity studies", Paper presented at the meeting of the American Psychological Association, Honolulu, September 1972.

Schmidt, F. L., Berner, J. G. and Hunter, J. E. "Racial differences in validity of employment tests: Reality or illusion?", *Journal of Applied Psychology,* 1973, *58,* 5–9.

Schmidt, F. L., Hunter, J. E. and Caplan, J. R. *Test of a new model of validity generalization: Results for two occupations in the petroleum industry.* Washington, D. C.: American Petroleum Institute, 1980.

Schmidt, F. L., Hunter, J. E., Pearlman, K., and Shane, G. S. "Further tests of the Schmidt-Hunter Bayesian validity generalization procedure", *Personnel Psychology,* 1979, *32* (2), 257–281.

Taylor, H. C. and Russell, J. T. "The relationship of validity coefficients to the practical validity of tests in selection: Discussion and tables", *Journal of Applied Psychology,* 1939, *23,* 565–578.

Tenopyr, M. L. "Content-construct confusion", *Personnel Psychology,* 1977, *30* (1), 47–54.

U. S. Department of Labor, Manpower Administration. *Dictionary of occupational titles.* Washington, D. C.: Author, 1977.

U. S. Department of Justice, U. S. Department of Labor, and the U. S. Civil Service Commission. "Federal executive agency guidelines on employee selection procedures", *Federal Register,* 1976, *41* (227), 51734 et seq.

U. S. Department of Labor. *Federal contract compliance manual.* Washington, D. C.: U. S. Government Printing Office, 1979.

Wallace, S. R. "Sources of bias in the prediction of job performance: Implications for future research", in L. A. Crooks (Ed.), *An investigation of sources of bias in the prediction of job performance: A six-year study (Proceedings of Invitational Conference).* Princeton, N. J.: Educational Testing Service, 1972.

Table of Cases

Members of the Ad Hoc Group

Allen-Bradley Company
American Telephone and Telegraph Company
Armco, Inc.
Atlantic Richfield Company
Bethlehem Steel Corporation
Caterpillar Tractor Company
Chrysler Corporation
Citibank, N. A.
Deere & Company
Dow Chemical U. S. A.
E. I. duPont de Nemours & Company, Inc.
Eastman Kodak Company
Exxon Company, U. S. A.
Ford Motor Company
General Electric Company
General Motors Corporation
General Telephone and Electronics Corporation
Honeywell, Inc.
Inland Steel Company
International Business Machines Corporation
Minnesota Mining & Manufacturing Company
Mobil Oil Corporation
Montgomery Ward
Nationwide Mutual Insurance Company
Peoples Gas Company
The Procter & Gamble Company

Reynolds Metals Company
Sears Roebuck & Company
Shell Oil Company
Standard Oil Company (OHIO)
Sun Company
Sun Chemical Corporation
Sundstrand Corporation
The Travelers Insurance Companies
United Airlines
United Parcel Service
Wells Fargo
West Point Pepperell
Weyerhaeuser Company
American Iron & Steel Institute
American Paper Institute
American Petroleum Institute
American Society for Personnel Administration
Business Roundtable
Chamber of Commerce of the United States
Edison Electric Institute
Equal Employment Advisory Council
International Personnel Management Association
International Association for Personnel Women
Master Printers of America
National Association of Manufacturers